DICTIONARY

THE IMPORTANT TERMS
USED IN MUSIC WITH
THEIR PRONUNCIATION
AND DEFINITION,
TOGETHER WITH THE
ELEMENTS OF NOTATION AND
A BIOGRAPHICAL LIST OF
OVER SEVEN HUNDRED
NOTED NAMES IN MUSIC.

By

LOUIS C. ELSON

Former Professor of Theory of Music in the
New England Conservatory of Music

© 1909 by
OLIVER DITSON COMPANY

PREFACE.

IN this book will be found all the important terms used in music with their pronunciation and concise definition. Where clear explanation could not be given in a few words, necessary space has been taken.

The Italian terminology is given preference to a large extent, for it has most general use. (See Elson's Music Dictionary, note on page 302.) In this connection it may be stated that some Italian words are quite similar to their English equivalents and can be easily translated: for instance, *abbandono* " with abandon," *affabile*, " affable," *carezzando*, " caressingly," etc. There are many terminal variants in Italian words, such as *dolore, dolente, dolorosamente, dolentemente*, etc. In a condensed work, such as this, only the root-forms are given, but as many as possible of these.

Where compound terms are not given look up the words separately.

For practical and immediate use in the class-room, I believe that the little volume will be found sufficient to the needs of the teacher.

LOUIS C. ELSON.

THE ELEMENTS OF NOTATION.

THE STAFF.

The **Staff** upon which music is written consists of five horizontal, parallel lines and the four intervening spaces. **Ledger lines** are added to extend the Staff above or below as needed.

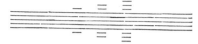

THE CLEFS.

Clefs are placed on the Staff to locate the position of one note, from which the positions of the other notes are determined. The following clefs all show the position of **Middle C**. (See *Clef* in body of the book.)

THE NOTES AND RESTS. — **Note-heads** are placed upon the Staff to represent the **notes** proper, giving the *pitch* of the note by their position, and the *time-value* or duration of the note according to their shape. Characters called **Rests,** with corresponding time-value to notes, are used to indicate periods of silence, through which the pulse of the music, however, proceeds. The **Double Whole-Note** or **Rest** is rarely seen in modern music, and has been principally confined to church music.

| Eighth-Note | Eighth-Rest | Sixteenth-Note | Sixteenth Rest |
| Thirty-second-Note | Thirty-second-Rest | Sixty-fourth-Note | Sixty-fourth-Rest |

THE SCALE.

The **Scale** (or ladder) is a direct succession of notes or tones. The difference between these consecutive notes is measured by **Steps** and **Half-steps**. Scales are classified as **Major, Minor, Chromatic** or **Wholetone** according to their content of Steps and Half-steps. There are two forms of the Minor Scale in common use, called **Harmonic** and **Melodic**; in the latter, the notes chromatically raised in ascent are restored to their original pitch in descent.

In the following examples, the Half-steps occurring in the **Natural Scale** (C) and its relative minor (A) are indicated by ties ($\smile$) between the notes. Observe the **Augmented Second** between the 6th and 7th degrees of the Minor (Harmonic) Scale, indicated by an asterisk (*).

SCALE FORMULAS.

Diatonic.
Major

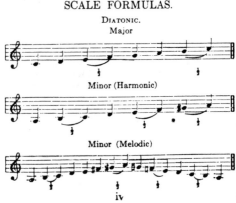

Minor (Harmonic)

Minor (Melodic)

CHROMATIC.

WHOLE TONE.

The Chromatic Scale is composed exclusively of Half-steps. In the ascending scale, the Half-step succession is brought about by the use of sharps to raise certain natural notes; in the descending scale, flats are used to lower certain natural notes.

The Whole-tone scale is only used in ultra modern music. It is so called through its succession of Whole-steps and entire lack of Half-steps. The octave is divided into six parts, in two divisions, three from C to F♯. and three from G♭ (Enharmonic equivalent of F♯) to C above.

SCALES IN ALL KEYS.

The **Scale Formulas** given above are all in the **Natural Scale** (key of C); but they apply to scales built on any Key-note. Enforcing the formula as to succession of steps and half-steps results in the addition of **sharps** or **flats** to the natural notes. These necessary sharps or flats instead of being applied to the notes as they occur, are placed at the beginning of the staff after the clef, and constitute the **Key-signature.**

INTERVALS.

An **Interval** is the measurement of distance between any two notes, counted by degrees on the staff. They are always reckoned by counting the lowest note one. *e. g.*, from c to d is the interval of a *second*, from c to f, a *fourth*, etc. Apart from their numerical name, Intervals are in addition classified as **Major, Minor, Perfect, Augmented** and **Diminished,** according to their *notation* and *content* The following table of Intervals while based on C, establishes a measurement for corresponding intervals in any position or key.

INTERVALS.

Intervals may be either Perfect, Major, Minor, Augmented or Diminished, *e.g.* —

Primes — Per. Unison, Aug. or Prime

Seconds — Maj. Min. Aug.

Thirds — Maj. Min. Dim.

Fourths — Per. Dim. Aug.

Fifths — Per. Dim. Aug.

Sixths — Maj. Min. Aug.

Sevenths — Maj. Min. Dim.

Octaves — Per. Dim. Aug.

Ninths — Maj. Min. Aug.

CHORDS.

A **Chord** is a combination of three or more notes sounded simultaneously. Chords may be formed on any note of the scale, and variously classified, as follows:

MAJOR MODE.

Primary Triads with their Inversions.

Tonic Major   Dominant Major   Sub-Dominant Major

1st Inv. 2nd Inv.   1st Inv. 2nd Inv.   1st Inv. 2nd Inv.

Secondary Triads (Inversions as above).

Super-Tonic Minor   Mediant Minor   Super-Dominant Minor   Leading-Note Diminished

MINOR MODE.

Primary Triads with their Inversions.

Tonic
Minor

Dominant
Major

Sub-Dominant
Minor

Secondary Triads (Inversions as before).

Super-
Tonic
Diminished

Mediant
Augmented

Super-
Dominant
Major

Leading-
Note
Diminished

NOTE: The Triad on the sixth degree (Super-Dominant) is often called Sub-Mediant.

DOMINANT SEVENTH CHORD WITH INVERSIONS.

Major

Minor

1st Inv. 2nd Inv. 3rd Inv.   1st Inv. 2nd Inv. 3rd Inv.

The **Dominant Seventh Chord** is the *Principal*, but **Secondary Seventh Chords** may be formed on all other degrees of the Major and Minor Modes. Among the Secondary Seventh Chords of importance may be mentioned the **Diminished Seventh Chord,** formed on the Leading-Note in the Minor Mode:

CHORDS OF THE NINTH.

Chords of the Ninth are formed by adding the third above to a Seventh Chord, that is, the **Ninth** from the **Root.** The **Dominant Ninth Chord** is in most common use:

Major Minor

KEY-SIGNATURES WITH THE TONIC TRIADS.

TIME-SIGNATURES.

SIMPLE.

SIMPLE.

COMPOUND.

The lower figure shows the *character* of the *unit* of which the measure is composed. The upper figure denotes the *number* of said *units* into which the measure is divided.

FUNDAMENTAL TEMPO MARKS.

FROM THE SLOWEST TO THE FASTEST.

The term *Moderato* may be considered the neutral or medium point between the slowest and fastest movements.

Lerghissimo — The superlative of *Largo*. Extremely slow and the slowest tempo used.

Largo — Very slow and stately.

Largamente — Quite slow. Broadly.

Larghetto — Somewhat faster than *Largo*, of which term it is the diminutive.

Grave — Seriously, solemnly. Slower than *Adagio*.

Lento — Slowly, often used temporarily.

Adagissimo — The superlative of *Adagio*. Slower than *Adagio*.

Adagio — Slowly with great expression.

Adagietto — Slightly faster than *Adagio*, of which term it is the diminutive.

Andantino — Rather slower than *Andante*, but generally interpreted as slightly faster.

Andante — In tranquil or quiet time, but moving (literally "going").

Moderato — Moderately.

Allegretto — With some animation, but less than *Allegro*, of which term it is the diminutive.

Allegro — Lively, animated in movement.

Vivace — Vivaciously, with more rapid movement than *Allegro*.

Presto — With great rapidity.

Prestissimo — With extreme rapidity, the superlative of *Presto*, and the fastest tempo used.

These terms are relative and do not indicate an *absolute* rate of speed. They must therefore be interpreted only in a general way. Exact speed can be indicated only by metronome marks.

ACCELERATIONS.

Accelerando — With gradual, though definite, increase in speed.

Affrettando — Hurriedly, a spasmodic, or temporary, increase in movement.

Doppio movimento — Double movement. Twice as fast as the previous movement.

Incalzando — With growing warmth and fervor.

Piu mosso } With more speed of movement immediately, but
Piu moto } steadily when assumed.

Veloce — A greatly increased speed of movement.

Velocissimo — With the utmost velocity.

Più means more, *poco a poco*, little by little.

RETARDATIONS.

Allargando — Retarding and broadening, gradually or suddenly.

Calando — Gradually slower and more subdued.

Mancando — Decreasing the time and volume of sound.

Meno mosso } With less speed of movement immediately,
Meno moto } but steadily when assumed.

Molto meno mosso — Much slower than the previous movement. The opposite of *Doppio Movimento*.

Morendo — Dying away by degrees, gradually slower and softer.

Rallentando } Slower by degrees, without decrease of volume.
Ritardando

Ritenuto — Detained, generally for a short period.

Slargando } Relaxing the vigor or spirit of the movement.
Slentando

Smorzando — Literally "smothering." Rapidly diminishing the time and volume.

Strascinando — Dragging the movement.

Tardando — Lingeringly.

Trattenuto — Holding back.

Meno means less.

Accelerations of tempo often presuppose, and generally incite, an increase in *volume of sound*. Retardations, on the contrary, often tend toward *diminishing* the volume, but judgment must be used in either case, according to the term used, and the musical context.

ABBREVIATIONS IN GENERAL USE

A. see p. 1
accel.......accelerando
accomp ....accompaniment
Adg° or **Ad°**..Adagio
ad lib........ad libitum
affett°......affettuoso
affrett°......affrettando
ag° or **ag:t**......agitato
All°.........Allegro
Allgett°......Allegretto
all' ott......all' ottava
al seq .....al segno
And°°......Andantino
And¹ᵉ ......Andante
Anim°......animato
arc.........arcato, or coll'
                         arco
arp°.........arpeggio
B. see p. 16
B. C. or **Bass**
   Con......basso continuo
Bl..........Bläser
Br..........Bratsche
Brill.........brillante
C. see p. 25
cad.......cadenza
cal.........calando
calm........calmato
cantab.....cantabile
C. B......contra basso or
                         col basso
Cb.........Contrabässe
c. f.........canto fermo
'cello.......violoncello
Ch.........choir organ
Clar........clarinet
Clar°.......clarino
coll' ott. or **c.8ᵛᵃ**.coll' ottava
con espr....con espressione
Cor........corno
cresc.......crescendo
Cᵗᵒ.........concerto
c. voc.......colla voce
D. see p. 45
d............destra, droite
D. C........da capo
D. C. S. R..da capo senza
                         replica, or senza
                         ripetizione
Dec.......decani
decresc.....decrescendo
Diap........diapason
dim........diminuendo
div.........divisi
dol.........dolce
dolciss......dolcissimo
dopp. ped...doppio pedale
D. S........dal segno
E. see p. 55
esp. or **espres.** espressivo

Energ ......energico
F. see p. 61
f............forte
Fag.........fagotto
ff...........fortissimo
fff..........fortississimo
Fl...........flauto
F. O........full organ
fp..........forte piano
fz. or **fortz.**......forzato or for-
                         zando
G. see p. 76
G. O........great organ
Grand......grandioso
Graz° ... grazioso
H. see p. 77
Haut.......hautboy
Hlzbl......Holzbläser
Hr. or **Hrn**....Hörner
I. see p. 82
Incalz......incalzando
Intro.......Introduction
L. see p. 92
leg.........legato
legg........leggiero
l. h.........left hand, linke
                         Hand
lusing .....lusingando
M. see p. 96
Magg......Maggiore
manc.......mancando
marc.......marcato
m. d.......mano destra, or
                         main droite
men........meno
mez.......mezzo
mf.........mezzo forte
m. g.......main gauche
M. M......Maelzel's Met-
                         ronome
mod. or **modto** moderato
mor........morendo
mp.........mezzo piano
MS.........manuscript
m. s........mano sinistra
Mus. Bac. or **Mus. B.**
                         Bachelor of
                         Music
Mus. Doc. or **Mus. D.**
                         Doctor of Music
m. v........mezza voce
O. see p. 107
Ob.........oboe
Obb........obbligato
Op.........Opus
Opp........Oppure
Org........organ
Ott., **Oᵛᵃ**, or **8ᵛᵃ**. ottava
P. see p. 112
p...........piano

p. a. p	poco a poco
Ped	pedal
Perd	Perdendosi
Pes	Pesante
P. F	Più forte
Piang	Piangendo
Pianiss	Pianissimo
Pizz	Pizzicato
PP	Pianissimo
PPP	Pianississimo
I^{ma}	Prima (volta)
I^{mo}	Primo
Q^{tte}	{ Quartet / { Quintet
R. see p. 122	
Rall	Rallentando
Recit., or Rec.	Recitative
Rf., rfz., or rinf.	Rinforzando
R. H.	Right Hand / Rechte Hand
Ritar	Ritardando
Riten. or Rit.	Ritenuto
S. see p. 126	
Salic	Salicional
S:	A Sign from which to repeat
Scherz	Scherzando
2da	Seconda (volta)
2do	Secondo
Seg	Segue
Sem. or Semp.	Sempre
7^{tt}	Septet
6^{tt}	Sextet
Sfz	Sforzando
Sinf	Sinfonia
Smorz	Smorzando
S. R	Senza ripetizione

S.S. or S. sord	Senza sordini
Sos or Sos^t	Sostenuto
Spir	Spiritoso
Stacc	Staccato
Stent	Stentando
St. Diap	Stopped Diapason
String	Stringendo
Sw	Swell Organ
Sym	Symphony
T. see p. 142	
T. C	Tre corde
Tem	Tempo
Tem. 1°.	Tempo primo
Ten	Tenuto
Timp	Timpani
Tr	Trillo
Tratt	Trattenuto
Trem	Tremolando
Tromb	Trombi Tromboni
T. S	Tasto solo
U	Una
U. C	Una corda
Unis	Unisoni
V. see p. 155	
Va	Viola
Var	Variation
Vc, VcL	Violoncello
Viv	Vivace
Vo / Vno / Viol°	} Violino
V. S	Volti subito
Vⁿⁱ	Violini
	See also, *Trill*, *Signs*, *Rests*, and *Repeats*.

VOWEL SOUNDS AND THEIR MARKINGS AS USED TO INDICATE PRONUNCIATION IN THIS DICTIONARY.

ä as in *ah;* ā as in *hate;* ă as in *at;* ē as in *tree,* ĕ as in *eh;* ī as in *pine;* ĭ as in *pin;* ō as in *tone;* ô as in *dove;* ŏ as in *not;* ŭ as in *up;* ü the French sound of *u.*

ELSON'S POCKET MUSIC DICTIONARY

A. 1. The sixth tone of the diatonic major scale of C; in France and Italy called *La*.

2. The first note of the natural minor scale (the relative of C major), which, as the older scale, begins on the first letter of the alphabet. See *C*.

3. The note from which the orchestra is tuned, usually sounded by the oboe.

A. (It.) (äh.) By, for, to, at, in, etc.

Ab (Ger.) (äb.) Off. Used in organ music.

A balláta (It.) (ä bäl-*lä*-tä.) In the style of a ballad.

Abandon (Fr.) (ä-bänh-dônh.) Without restraint.

A battúta (It.) (ä bĭ *-too*-tä.) As beaten; strictly in time.

Abbandonataménte (It.) (äb-bän-dō-nä-tä-*men*-tĕ.) Vehemently; violently.

Abbandóno (It.) (äb-bän-dō-nō.) With passionate expression; with abandon.

Abbellire (It.) (äb-bĕl-*lēe*-rĕ.) To embellish with ornaments.

Abbreviation marks. For abbreviations in notation see *Elson's Music Dictionary*.

Abellimento (It.) (ä-bĕl-lē-*men*-tō.) A decoration, ornament, or embellishment.

Abendmusik (Ger.) (ä-bĕnd-moo-*zïk*.) Evening or night music; serenade.

Abgestossen (Ger.) (*äb*-ghĕ-stōs-s'n.) Detached, struck off, staccato.

Abkürzung (Ger.) (*äb*-kiert-soong.) Abridgment, abbreviation.

Abnehmend (Ger.) (*äb*-nay-mend.) Diminishing.

Abrégé (Fr.) (ah-bray-zhay.) Abridgment; also the trackers in an organ.

Abstossen (Ger.) (*äb*-stos-s'n.) Similar in manner of performance to staccato.

Abwechselnd (Ger.) (*äb*-veck-s'lnd.) Alternating, changing. In organ playing, alternately; in choir singing, antiphonally; in dance music, change of movements.

A cappélla (It.) (ä käp-*pel*-lä). In the church or chapel style, that is, vocal music, unaccompanied.

A capríccio (It.) (ä käp-*preet*-shō.) In a capricious style; according to the taste of the performer.

1

Accarezzévole (It.) (äk-kä-rĕt-*zeh*-vō-le.) Blandishing; in a persuasive and caressing manner.

Accelerándo (It.) (ät-chay-lay-*rän*-dō.) Accelerating the time; gradually increasing the velocity of the movement.

Acceleráto (It.) (ät-chay-lay-*räh*-to.) Accelerated; increased rapidity.

Accent. A stress or emphasis upon a certain note or passage to mark its position in the measure, or its relative importance in regard to the composition.

Accénto (It.) (ät-*tshen*-tō.) Accent or emphasis laid upon certain notes.

Accentuáre (It.) (ät-tshĕn-too-ä-rĕ.) To accentuate; to mark with an accent.

Accessory notes. Those notes situated one degree above, and one degree below the principal note of a turn. The upper note of a trill is also called the accessory or auxiliary note.

Acciaccáto (It.) (ät-tshäk-*kä*-tō.) Brusquely, forcibly.

Acciaccatúra (It.) (ät-tshäh-kä-*too*-rä.) A very short grace note; an accessory note placed before the principal note, which latter takes the accent.

Written.   Played.

The acciaccatúra is distinguished by a light diagonal line through note hook. See *Appoggiatura.*

Accidentals. Sharps, flats, naturals, introduced apart from the signature. See *Chromatic Signs.*

Accidental chords. Chords containing one or more notes foreign to their proper harmony.

Accompaniment. The secondary parts or voices that accompany the principal parts or voices in any form of composition. Most accompaniments are necessary to the general effect, but some are *ad lib.* and can be omitted.

Accompaniments, Additional, are parts added to a composition by an editor, generally to supply the place of an obsolete instrument.

Accopiáto (It.) (äk-kō-pē-ä-tō.) Bound, tied, joined together.

Accord (Fr.) (äk-kŏr.) A chord; a concord; consonance.

Accordamento (It.) (äk-kŏr-dä-*men*-tō.) Consonance, unison, harmony of parts.

Accordatúra (It.) (äk-kŏr-dä-*too*-rä.) Concord, harmony. Also, the set of notes to which the open strings of an instrument are tuned.

Accordeon. An instrument consisting of two oblong sound boxes enclosing metal reeds; the flexible connection between the two boxes forming a bellows. The key-board for right-hand giving a diatonic scale, that of left giving a few fundamental basses and chords.

Accrescéndo (It.) (äk-krĕ-*shen*-dō.) Increasing; augmenting in tone and power.

Acoustics (Ger. *Akustik;* It. *Acustica;* Fr. *Acoustique.*) The science of sound; the science treating of the laws of sound.

Action. The mechanism attached to the keys of a piano or organ; also, the mechanism attached to the pedals of a harp, which changes the pitch of the strings by shortening them.

Acuta (Lat.) (ah-*koot*-a.) A mixture stop in the organ.

Acute. High, in reference to pitch.

Adagietto (It.) (ah-dah-*jiet*-to.) 1. A short *adagio.* 2. A movement somewhat less slow than *adagio.*

Adagio (It.) (ah-*dah*-jio.) Slow, but quicker than *largo* and slower than *andante.*

Adagio assái (It.) (äs-*sä*-ē.)   } Very slow.
Adagio di mólto (It.)   }

Addolorato (It.) (ah-doh-lo-*rah*-toh.) Sorrowful.

A demi jeu (Fr.) (ad-mee-zhŭ.) With half the power of the instrument.

A demi voix (Fr.) (ad-mee voo-wah.) At half voice; whispered.

A deux (Fr.) (ä-*düh*.) For two instruments or voices.

A deux mains (Fr.) (ä-düh mänh.) For two hands.

Adirataménte (It.) (ä-di-rä-tä-*men*-tĕ.)   }
Adiráto (It.) (äd-*i*-rä-tō.)   } Angrily, sternly.

Adjunct notes. Unaccented auxiliary notes.

Ad libitum (Lat.) (äd-*lĭb*-i-tŭm.) At will; at pleasure; changing the time of a particular passage at the discretion of the performer; also a part that may be omitted if desired.

3

A dúe, or A 2 (It.) (ä *doo-ĕ.*) For two voices or instruments; a duet. Also used to indicate that two instruments playing from the same part or score are to play in unison, after *divisi* or a solo passage for one of the instruments.

A dúe córde (It.) (ä-*doo-ĕ kŏr*-dĕ.) Upon two strings; the soft pedal of a grand piano pressed half way down.

A dur (Ger.) (ä dōer.) The key of A major.

Æolian Harp. A simple contrivance of sound-box and strings so constructed that a current of air sets the strings in vibration.

Affábile (It.) (äf-*fä*-bē-lĕ.) In an affable and pleasing manner.

Affabilita (It.) (äf-fä-*bē*-lē-tä.) With ease and elegance; with affability; in a pleasing and agreeable manner.

Affannáto (It.) (äf-fä-*nä*-tō.) Sad, distressed.

Affannóso (It.) (äf-fä-*nō*-zō.) With anxious expression.

Affettivo (It.) (äf-fĕt-*tē*-vō.) Affecting; pathetic.

Affétto (It.) (äf-*fet*-tō.) Feeling; tenderness; pathos.

Affettuosaménte (It.) (äf-fĕt-too-ō-zä-*men*-tĕ.) With tenderness and feeling.

Affettuóso (It.) (äf-fĕt-too-ō-zō.) With tender and passionate expression.

Afflítto (äf-fleet-tō.)
(It.)
Afflizióne (äf-flee-tsé-ō-nĕ.) } Sorrowfully; with mournful expression.

Affrettándo (äf-frĕt-*tän*-dō.)
(It.)
Affrettáte (äf-frĕt-*tä*-tĕ.) } Hurrying; quickening; accelerating the time.

After-note. A small note occurring on an unaccented part of the measure, and taking its time from the note preceding it.

Written. Performed.

Agévole (It.) (ä-*jeh*-vŏ-lĕ.)
Agevolménte (It.) (ä-jeh-vōl-*men*-tĕ.) } Lightly; easily; with agility.

Agevolézza (It.) (ä-jay-vō-*lay*-tsä.) Lightness, ease, agility.

Agilità (It.) (ä-*jeel*-ē-tä.) Lightness, agility.

Agilità, con. (It.) With agility; with lightness; with rapidity.

Agitamento (It.) (ä-jē-tä-*men*-tō.) Agitation, restlessness, motion.

4

Agitáto (It.) (äj-i-*tä*-tō.) Agitated, hurried, restless.

Agité (Fr.) (ä-zhee-*tay*.) Agitated.

Agnus Dei (Lat.) (*äg*-nŭs *dä*-ē.) Lamb of God; one of the movements in a Mass.

Agraffe. A metallic support of the string in a pianoforte, between the pin and the bridge, serving to check vibration at that part.

Agréments (Fr. pl.) (ă-grāy-mänh.) Embellishments applied in Harpsichord or Spinet music.

Ai (It.) (äē-.) To the; in the style of.

Aigrement (Fr.) (āgr-mănh.) Sharply, harshly.

Aigu (Fr.) (ā-gü.) Acute, high, sharp, shrill.

Air. A short song, melody, or tune, with or without words. The upper voice in a harmonized composition.

Air à boire (Fr.) (âr-ä-boo-war.) A drinking song.

Air varié (Fr.) (âr-vä-rĭ-āy.) Air with variations; an air embellished and ornamented.

Ais (Ger.) (ah-*iss*.) The note A sharp.

Aisément (Fr.) (āy-zä-mänh.) Easily, freely.

Ajoutez (Fr.) (äh-zhoo-tay.) Add. Used in organ-music.

Alberti Bass. A species of bass, the chords of which are taken in arpeggios of a particular kind; broken chords.

Album leaf. A short and simple piece.

Alcuna licenza, con. (It.) (äl-*koo*-nä lē-*tschěn*-tsä, kŏn.) With a little license.

Al fíne (It.) (äl *fēe*-ně.) To the end.

Al fíne, e pói la códa (äl *fēe*-ně ā pō-ē lä *kō*-dä.) After playing to where the Fine is marked, go on to the coda.

Al (It.) (äl.)
All. (It.) (äl.)
Alla (It.) (äl-lä.)
Alle (It.) (äl-lě.) To the; in the style or manner of.
Agli (It.) (äl-yēe.)
Allo (It.) (äl-lō.)

Alla Bréve (It.) (äl-lä *brä*-vě.) This was originally ½ rhythm, so called from the fact that one *breve*, or double-whole-note, filled each measure. To-day the term is more generally applied to ⅖ rhythm, marked ₵.

Alla cáccia (It.) (*äl*-lä *kät*-tsha.) In the style of hunting music.

Alla cámera (It.) (*äl*-lä kä-mě-rä.) In the style of chamber music.

5

Alla Cappélla (It.) (*äl*-lä käp-*pel*-lä.) In the church or sacred style; derived from Alla Breve style, the measure being sub-divided, also unaccompanied vocal music. See *Alla Breve*.

Allargando (It.) (äh-lahr-*gän*-doh.) Growing broader, *i.e.*, louder and slower.

Alle (Ger.) (*äl*-lĕ.) All: *alle Instrumente*, all the instruments; the whole orchestra.

Allegraménte (It.) (äl-lĕ-grä-*men*-tĕ.) Gaily, joyfully, quickly.

Allegrétto (It.) (äl-lĕ-*gret*-tō.) Rather light and cheerful but not as quick as Allegro.

Allegríssimo (It.) (äl-lä-*gris*-si-mō.) Extremely quick and lively; the superlative of Allegro.

Allégro (Fr. and It.) (äl-*lāy*-grō.) Quick, lively; a rapid, vivacious movement, frequently modified by the addition of other words that change its expression: as,

Allégro assái (It.) (äl-*lay*-grō äs-sä-ē.) Very quick.

Allégro di bravúra (It.) (äl-*lä*-grō dē brä-*voo*-rä.) Quick, with brilliant and spirited execution.

Allégro di molto (It.) (äl-*lä*-grō di *mōl*-tō.) Exceedingly quick and animated.

Allégro giústo (It.) (äl-*lä*-grō *joos*-tō.) Quick, with exactness; in steady and precise time.

Allégro moderáto (It.) (äl-*lä*-grō mō-dĕ-*rä*-tō.) Moderately quick. For various other modifications of *Allegro* look for the secondary words.

Aliéluia (Fr.) (äl-lĕ-loo-yä.) Praise the Lord; Hallelujah.

Allemande (Fr.) (ăll-mänhd.) A lively German dance in ²/₄ and also in ³/₄ rhythm; also a slow dance or melody in ⁴/₄ rhythm. The first dance movement in the old suite.

Alle Saiten (Ger.) (ălleh *zigh*-ten.) Tutte Corde. All the strings. Release the soft pedal.

All' Espagnuóla (It.) (älĕs-pän-yoo-ō-lä.) In the Spanish style.

All' Inglése (It.) (äl ēn-*glāy*-zĕ.) In the English style.

All' Italiána (It.) (äl ē-tä-lē-ä-nä.) In the Italian style.

Allmählich (Ger.) (äl-*mä*-llĭkh.) Little by little.

All' Ongarése (It.) (äl ōn-gä-*rāy*-zĕ.) In the Hungarian style.

Allonger (Fr.) (äl-lŏnh-zhāy.) To lengthen, prolong, delay.

Allonger l'archet (Fr.) (äl-lŏnh-zhāy lär-shay.) To lengthen or prolong the stroke of the bow in violin music.

Allontandosi (It.) (äl-ōn-*tän*-dō-zē.) Gradually disappearing in the distance; further and further away.

Al rigóre di tempo (It.) (äl ri-*gō*-rĕ di *tĕm*-po.) In very vigorous and strict time.

A la Russe (Fr.) (ä lä *rüss*.) In the Russian style.

Al Segno (It.) (äl *sen*-yō.) See *Dal Segno*.

Alt (It.) (ält.) High. This term is applied to the notes which lie between F on the fifth line of treble staff and G on the fourth added line above.

Al Tedésco (It.) (äl tĕ-*des*-kō.) In the German style.

Alternativo (It.) (äl-tĕr-nä-*lēe*-vō.) Alternating one movement with another.

Altgeige (Ger.) (*ält*-ghi-ghĕ.) The viola.

Altieraménte (It.) (äl-te-ĕr-ä-*men*-tĕ.) With grandeur; haughtily.

Altísono (It.) (äl-*lē*-sō-nō.) Sonorous.

Altissimo (It.) (äl-*tees*-sē-mō.) The highest; extremely high as to pitch. It is applied to notes above the staff.

Alto (It.) (*äl*-tō.) High. In olden days an artificial or head voice (counter-tenor) was cultivated in men, and this voice singing the highest part was called *Alto;* in modern vocal terminology the word applies to the lowest female voice or unchanged (young boy's) voice, which is of about the same range and pitch. The *Viola* is sometimes called the *Alto. Alto* is also the name given to a brass instrument of the Sax-horn group, standing in Eb, a fifth below the Bb Cornet, and with about the same written compass.

Alto clef. The C clef on the third line of the staff.

Alt' ottáva (It.) (ält ōt-*tä*-vä.) The same notes an octave higher.

Altra (It.) (*äl*-trä.) ⎱ Other, another.
Altro (It.) (*äl*-trō.) ⎰

Alzaménto (It.) (äl-tsä-*men*-tō.) An elevating of the voice; lifting up.

7

Alzándo (It.) (äl-*tsän*-dō.) Raising; lifting up.

Amábile (It.) (ä-*mä*-bē-lĕ.) Amiable, gentle, graceful.

Amabilitá (It.) (ä-mä-bē-lē-*tä*.) Tenderness, amiability.

Amabilménte (It.) (ä-mä-beel-*men*-tĕ.) Amiably, gently.

Amáro (It.) (ä-*mä*-rō.) Grief, bitterness, affliction.

Ambrosian Chant. A series of sacred melodies or chants collected and introduced into the church by St. Ambrose. It was purely diatonic.

Amen (Heb.) (ä-mĕn.) So be it. A word used as a termination to psalms, hymns, and other sacred music.

American fingering. See *Fingering*.

A moll (Ger.) (ä mŏll.) The key of A minor.

Amóre (It.) (ä-*mō*-rĕ.) Tenderness, affection, love.

Amóre, con. (It.) With tenderness and affection.

Amorévole (It.) (ä-mō-*rä*-vō-lĕ.) Tenderly, gently, lovingly.

Amorévolménte (It.) (ä-mō-rä-vŏl-*men*-tĕ.) With extreme tenderness.

A morésco (It.) (ä mō-*res*-kō.) In the Moorish style; in the style of a Moorish dance.

Amorosaménte (It.) (ä-mō-rō-zä-*men*-tĕ.) In a tender and affectionate style.

Amoróso (It.) (ä-mō-*rō*-zō.) See *Amorosaménte*.

Amphibrach (Gr.) (*ăm*-fĭ-brăk.) A musical foot, comprising one short, one long and one short note or syllable, accented and marked thus, ◡ — ◡.

An (*Ger*.) (ähn.) On; to; in organ music, draw, or add.

Anapest (Gr.) (ăn-ä-pĕst.) A musical foot, containing two short notes or syllables, and a long one, accented and marked thus, ◡ ◡ —.

Anche (Fr.) (änhsh.) The reed of the oboe, bassoon, clarinet etc.; also the various reed stops in an organ.

Ancóra (It.) (än-*kō*-rä.) Once more; repeat again; also, yet, still, etc.

Andacht (Ger.) (*än*-däkht.) Devotion.

Andante (It.) (än-*dän*-tĕ.) A movement in moderate time but flowing easily, gracefully. **An-**

8

dante literally means "going." For various qualifications of *Andante* see secondary words.

Andantíno (It.) (än-dän-*tēe*-nō.) A little slower than Andante is the literal meaning of Andantino, but it has become a doubtful term, and is generally used as meaning *quicker* than Andante.

Andare (It.) (ähn-*dâh*-rĕ.) To go; go on.

Anfang (Ger.) (*än*-fäng.) Beginning, commencement.

Angemessen (Ger.) (*än*-ghĕ-*mĕs*-s'n.) Comfortable, suitable, fit.

Angenehm (Ger.) (*än*-ghĕn-āym.) Agreeable, pleasing. sweet.

Anglaise (Fr.) (änh-*glāz*.) } In the English style;
Anglico (It.) (*än*-glee-kō.) } a tune adapted for an English air or country dance. It has been used by Bach in his French Suites. It somewhat resembles the Hornpipe.

Angóscia (It.) (än-*gōs*-shä.) } Anxiety, anguish, grief.
Angosciaménte (It.) (än-gōs-shä-*men*-tĕ.) }

Ängstlich (Ger.) (*engst*-lĭkh.) Uneasy, timid, anxious.

Anhang (Ger.) (*än*-häng.) A coda; a postscript; an appendix.

Anima, con. (It.) (*ah*-nee-mah.) With life and animation. It can also be applied as meaning "soulful"; thus Chopin uses *Lento e con anima*, as "slow and with soul."

Animáto (It.) (än-ē-*mä*-to.) Animated; with life and spirit.

Animé (Fr.) (änh-ē-may.) Animated, lively, spirited.

Animóso (It.) (än-ē-*mō*-zō.) In an animated manner; lively, energetic.

Anlage (Ger.) (*än*-lä-ghĕ.) The plan or outline of a composition.

Anlaufen (Ger.) (*än*-lou-f'n.) To increase in sound; to swell.

Anleitung (Ger.) (*än*-lī-toong.) An introduction; a preface, guidance, instruction.

Anmuthig (Ger.) (*än*-moo-tĭg.) Agreeable, sweet, pleasant.

Ansatz (Ger.) (*än*-säts.) The embouchure of a wind instrument; the setting of the lips of a wind instrument player; the attack of a vocal phrase.

Anschlag (Ger.) (*än*-shläg.) A stroke; the percussion of a chord; the striking of a chord or key; the touch in piano playing; a double grace note.

Anstimmen (Ger.) (*än*-stĭm-mĕn.) To strike up; to begin to sing; to tune.

Anstimmung (Ger.) (*än*-stĭm-moong.) Intonation, tuning.

Answer (Lat. *Comés;* Ger. *Gefährte;* Fr. *Response;* It. *Riposta.*) The response to the subject of a fugue, given by the second voice, either above or below.

Antecedent (ăn-tĕ-sē-dĕnt.) The subject of a fugue or of a canon; the first phrase of a musical period.

Anthem. A vocal composition, the words of which are usually selected from the Bible, used in church either with or without organ accompaniment.

Antibacchius (ăn-ti-*băk*-kĭ-ŭs.) A musical foot of three syllables, the first two long or accented and the last short or unaccented, thus, — — ⌣.

Anticipation. One or more harmonic voices or parts moving to their particular position in a new chord, m advance of the other parts, or the accent.

Antíco (It.) (än-*tē*-kō.) Ancient.

Antiphon. See *Antiphone.*

Antiphone (Gr.) (ăn-tĕ-fō-ne.) The response made by one part of the choir to another, or by the congregation to the priest in the Roman Catholic service; also, alternate singing.

Antithesis. In fugues this term is applied to the *answer.*

Antwort (Ger.) (*ahnt*-vohrt.) Answer.

Anwachsend (Ger.) (*än*-väkh-sĕnd Swelling, increasing.

Apérto (It.) (ä-*pair*-tō.) Open; in pianoforte music it signifies that the damper or open pedal is to be pressed down; clear, distinct; (organ) open pipe.

Aphony (*af*-ō-ny.) Dumbness; loss of voice.

A piacere (It.) (ä pē-ä-*tshair*-rĕ.) At pleasure.

Aplomb (Fr.) (ä-plŏnh.) Firm, in exact time steadiness, coolness.

A póco (It.) (ä *pō*-kō.) By degrees; gradually.

A póco a póco (It.) (ä *pō*-kō ä *pō*-kō.) By little and little.

Apollo. In ancient mythology, the god of music, and said to be the inventor of the lyre.

Appassionataménte (It.) (äp-päs-sē-ō-nä-tä-*men*-tĕ.) ⎱
Appassionataménto (It.) (äp-päs-sē-ō-nä-tä-*men*-tō.) ⎬ Passionately; with intense emotion and feeling.
Appassionáto (It.) (äp-päs-sē-ō-*nä*-tō.) ⎰

Appenáto (It.) (äp-pĕ-*nä*-tō.) Grieved, distressed; an expression of suffering and melancholy.

Appoggiáto (It.) (äp-pōd-jē-*ä*-tō.) Leaning upon; dwelt upon; drawn out.

Appoggiatura (It.) (äp-pŏd-jē-ä-*too*-rä.) Leaning note; grace note; note of embellishment. Observe that in contradistinction to the *Acciaccatura*, there is no diagonal line through the stem and hook.

The word "Appoggiare," to lean against, accurately describes the character of this long grace-note. It is one of the most charming embellishments of song and of instrumental music. The character of the appoggiatura is almost always yearning, sorrowful or tender. The cause of writing so long and accented a note as a grace note lies in the fact that the appoggiatura is almost always extraneous to the melody and to the harmony. It has become customary, in recent days, to write the appoggiatura out in full notation. Before an even note the appoggiatura generally receives its face value, *i.e.*, one-half the value of the note which follows. Before a dotted note it receives more than its face value, *i.e.*, it should be given two-thirds of the value of the following note.

If the next note is of the same pitch as the principal note of the appoggiatura, the grace note receives the entire value of its principal note, but is carried to the next note with a strong portamento. This occurs chiefly in vocal music.

Apprestáre (It.) (äp-prĕs-*tä*-rĕ.) To prepare, or put in a condition to be played.

Âpre (Fr.) (äpr.) Harsh.

A púnta d'arco (It.) (ä *poon*-tä *d'*är-kō.) With the point of the bow.

À quatre mains (Fr.) (ä kätr-mänh.) For four hands.

Arabesque or **Arabesk.** An ornament, or an embellished work. From the Moorish architecture which was much ornamented.

Arbítrio, al (It.) (är-*bē*-trē-ō.) At the will or pleasure of the performer.

Arcáto (It.) (är-*kä*-tö.) Bowed; played with the bow.

Archet (Fr.) (är-shāy.) } A violin bow.
Arco (It.) (*är*-kō.) }

Ardénte (It.) (är-*den*-tĕ.) With fire; glowing, vehement.

Ardeneménte (It.) (är-dĕn-tĕ-*men*-tĕ.) Ardently, vehemently.

Ardíto (It.) (är-*dē*-to.) Bold; with energy.

Ardóre (It.) (ahr-*dō*-rĕh.) *Con Ardore;* with ardor and warmth.

Aretinian syllables. See *Solfaing.*

Aria (It.) (*ä*-rē-ä.) An air; a song; a tune; sung by a single voice either with or without an accompaniment. Generally composed of two contrasting movements or divisions (I and II), ending with a literal or elaborated repeat of Div. I. The aria first developed into shape in the early operas.

Aria búffa (It.) (*ä*-rē-ä *boof*-fä.) A comic or humorous air.

Aria cantábile (It.) (*ä*-rē-ä-kän-*tä*-bē-lĕ.) An air in a graceful and melodious style.

Aria concertáta (It.) (*ä*-rē-ä kŏn-tshĕr-*tä*-tä.) An air with orchestral accompaniment in a Concertánte style; a concerted air.

Aria di bravúra (It.) (*ä*-rē-ä dē brä-*voo*-rä.) A

12

florid air in bold, marked style and permitting great freedom of execution.

Aria fugáta (It.) (ä-rē-ä foo-*gä*-tä.) An air accompanied in the fugue style.

Aria parlánte (It.) (ä-rē-ä pär-*län*-tĕ.) An air in the declamatory style; a recitative *a tempo*.

Arie (It. pl.) (ä-rē-ĕ.)
Arien (Ger. pl.) (ä-rĭ-ĕn.) } Airs or songs.

Ariétta (It.) (ä-rē-*et*-tä.)
Ariette (Fr.) (ä-rē-ĕt.) } A short air or melody.
Ariettina (It.) (ä-rē-ĕt-*te*-nä.)

A rigore del tempo (It.) (ä rē-*gō*-rĕ dĕl *tĕm*-pō.) In strict time.

Ariosa (It.) (ä-rē-*ō*-zä.) In the movement of an aria or tune.

Arióso (It.) (ä-rē-ō-zō.) Melodious, graceful; a short piece in the style of an aria, but less symmetrical in construction.

Armoneggiáre (It.) (är-mŏ-nĕd-jē-*ä*-rĕ.) To sound in harmony.

Armónica (It.) (är-*mō*-nē-kä.) The earliest form of the accordion; a collection of musical glasses, so arranged as to produce musical effects.

Armoniosaménte (It.) (är-mō-nē-ō-zä-*men*-tĕ.) Harmoniously.

Armonióso (It.) (är-mō-nē-ō-zō.) Concordant, harmonious.

Arpa (It.) (*är*-pä.) The harp.

Arpa dóppia (It.) (*är*-pä *dō*p-pē-ä.) The double action harp; it meant formerly a harp with two strings to each note.

Arpeggiándo (It.) (är-ped-jē-*än*-dō.)
Arpeggiáto (It.) (är-ped-jē-*ä*-tō.) } Music played arpeggio, in imitation of the harp.

Arpeggiáre (It.) (är-ped-jē-*ä*-rĕ.) To play upon the harp.

Arpéggio (It.) (är-*ped*-jē-o.) Playing the notes

of a chord consecutively (harp style). In piano music the rapid *arpeggio* is abbreviated in notation by drawing a wavy line before the chord. The *arpeggio* beginning on the accent, and with lowest note.

Arrangement. The selection and adaptation of a composition or parts of a composition to instruments for which it was not originally designed, or for some other use for which it was not at first written.

Arsis (Gr.) (är-sĬs.) The upstroke of the hand in beating time. The light accent of the measure. Not employed by musicians in the same sense that it is used in poetry. See *Accent.*

Articoláto (It.) (är-tē-kō-*lä*-tō.) Articulated; distinctly enunciated.

Artificial Harmonics. Tones produced on a string; the vibrating length of which has been temporarily fixed by *stopping*: See *Harmonics.*

As (Ger.) (äs.) The note A flat.

Asas, Ases (Ger.) (äs-äs, äs-äz.) The note A double flat.

As dur (Ger.) (äs doer.) The key of A flat major.

As moll (Ger.) (äs mōll.) The key of A flat minor.

Asperges me (Lat.) (äs-pĕr-gĕs mā.) The opening of the Mass in the Catholic service. Not a number of the musical Mass itself, but sung during the purification of the altar at the beginning of the service.

Asprézza (It.) (äs-*pred*-sä.) Roughness, dryness, harshness.

Assái (It.) (äs-*sä*-ē.) Very, extremely; in a high degree, as Allégro Assái, very quick.

Assai più (It.) (äs-*sä*-ē pēe-*oo*.) Much more.

Assez (Fr.) (äs-sāy.) Enough, sufficiently.

Assolúto (It.) (äs-sō-*loo*-tō.) Absolute, free, alone, one voice.

Assonanz (Ger.) (äs-sō-*nänts*.) } Similarity, or
Assonánza (It.) (äs-sō-*nän*-tsä.) } consonance of tone.

A témpo (It.) (ä *tĕm*-pō.) In time; a term used to denote that after some deviation or relaxation of the *tempo*, the performer must return to the regular *tempo*.

Athemlos (Ger.) (ā-tĕm-los.) Breathlessly.

Attácca (It.) (ät-*täk*-kä.) Go on. Begin the next.

Attácca súbito (It.) (ät-*täk*-kä soo-bē-tō.) Attack or commence the next movement immediately.

Attack. The method or clearness of beginning a phrase. The term is applied to solo or concerted music, either vocal or instrumental.

Attendant keys. Those scales having most sounds in common with the scale of any given key; the relative keys. In C major the attendant keys are: its relative minor A, the dominant G, and its relative minor E, the sub-dominant F, and its relative minor D.

Atto (It.) (*ät*-tō.) An act of an opera or play.

Aubade (Fr.) (ō-bäd.) Morning music; a morning concert in the open air.

Audáce (It.) (ä-oo-*dä*-tshĕ.) Bold, spirited, audacious.

Auf (Ger.) (ouf.) On, upon, in, at, etc.

Auf dem Oberwerk (Ger.) (ouf dĕm ō-bĕr-värk.) Upon the *upper-work* or highest row of keys in organ playing.

Aufführung (Ger.) (*ouf*-fear-roong.) Performance.

Aufgeregt (Ger.) (*ouf*-gĕ-raygt.) With agitation; excitedly.

Aufgeweckt (Ger.) (*ouf*-ghĕ-vĕkt.) Lively, sprightly, cheerful, wide awake.

Aufhalten (Ger.) (*ouf*-häl-t'n.) To stop; to retard; to keep back.

Aufstrich (Ger.) (*ouf*-streekh.) An upbow.

Auftakt (Ger.) (*ouf*-täkt.) The arsis; the up-beat.

Augmentation. Writing a theme or melody in notes of longer duration than the original presentation.

Augmented intervals. Those which are larger by a half-step than major or perfect intervals; as,

A úna córda (It.) (ä oo-nä *kōr*-dä.) The soft pedal, in piano playing; one string.

Aus (Ger.) (ous.) From; out of.

Ausdruck (Ger.) (*ous*-drook.) Expression.

Ausdrucksvoll (Ger.) (*ous*-drooks-fōll.) Expressive.

Ausgabe (Ger.) (*ous*-gä-bĕ.) Edition.

Ausgehalten (Ger.) (*ous*-ghĕ-häl-t'n.) Sustained.

Ausgelassen (Ger.) (*ous*-ghĕ-*läs*-s'n.) Wild, ungovernable, with abandon.

Aushalten (Ger.) (*ous*-häl-t'n.) To hold on; to sustain a note.

Authentic cadence. The old name for a perfect cadence; the harmony of the dominant followed by that of the tonic, or the progression of the dominant to the tonic. See *Cadence*.

Authentic mode. A church mode or scale in which the *final* or key-note was the lowest tone.

Auxiliary notes. Notes (generally *grace*) immediately above or below a principal or harmonic note.

Ave (Lat.) (*ä-vĕ.*) Hail.

Avec (Fr.) (*ä-vĕk.*) With.

Ave Maria (Lat.) (*ä-vĕ mä-ree-ä.*) Hail, Mary. A hymn or prayer to the Virgin Mary.

Ave Maris Stella. (*ä-vĕ mä-ris stel-lä.*) A hymn of the Catholic Church, the words meaning, "Hail, Star of the Sea."

Ave Regina (Lat.) (*ä-vĕ rĕ-gē-nä.*) Vesper hymn to the Virgin.

À volonté (Fr.) (*ä vō-lŏnh-tä.*) At will; at pleasure.

B

B. The seventh note in the scale of C. It is called *Si* in France and Italy, and *H* in Germany. The Germans use the letter B to designate B flat. As the flat came from the letter B the Germans still call flats "B's." See *Flat, Sharp, Natural*.

Babillage (Fr.) (*bä-biy-ähg.*) Playful chatter.

Bachelor of Music. The first musical degree taken at the universities.

Badinage (Fr.) (*bä-dĭ-näzh.*) Playfulness, sportiveness.

Bagatelle (Fr.) (*băg-ä-tĕl.*) A trifle; a toy; a short easy piece of music.

Bagpipe. An instrument of great antiquity. One or more reed pipes are attached to a wind bag or bellows. The most elaborate bagpipes are the Irish and Scotch, the latter having three or four *drone* or single note pipes and a "chanter," or fingered pipe, for the melody.

Baldaménte (It.) (*bäl-dä-men-tĕ.*) Boldly.

Ballábile (It.) (*bäl-lä-bēe-lĕ.*) In the style of a dance.

Ballad. A short, simple song of natural construction, usually in the narrative or descriptive form. It formerly had a wider signification and was applied to music set to a romance or historical poem, and also to a light kind of music used both in singing and dancing.

Ballade (Ger.) (*bäl-lä-dĕ.*)   } A dance; dancing;
Balláta (It.) (*bäl-lä-tä.*)   } also a Ballad.

Balleríno (It.) (bäl-lĕ-*rēe*-nō.) A dancing master; a male dancer.

Ballet (Fr.) (bă-lā.) ⎫ A theatrical represen-
Balléto (It.) (bäl-*lĕt*-tō.) ⎬ tation of some story
by means of dances or pantomimic action accompanied with music.

Bállo (It.) (*bäl*-lō.) A dance or dance tune.

Band. A number of instrumental performers playing together, generally wood-wind, brass and percussion instruments.

Band-master. The leader or conductor of a band, generally military.

Bandola (Spa.) (bän-*dō*-lä.) An instrument resembling a lute.

Bandurría (Spa.) (bän-door-*rē*-ä.) A species of Spanish guitar; a *Bandora*.

Banjo. The typical instrument of the American Negro; consisting of an elongated neck and fretted finger-board attached to a circular, parchment covered body, over which the five strings are vibrated.

Bar. Lines drawn perpendicularly across the staff to divide it into measures; the term is also applied to each of these measures by European usage, but strictly the bar is the line itself, not the measure it defines. The bar came into use in music after 1600.

Barcaróla (It.) (bär-kä-*rō*-lä.) ⎫ A song or air sung
Barcarolle (Fr.) (bär-kä-rōl.) ⎬ by the Venetian
gondoliêrs, or boatmen, while following their vocations; it is generally in $\frac{6}{8}$ time.

Bar, double. Heavy lines drawn across the staff to divide off different parts of the movement or show the end of the piece. Dots either side of the double bar show that the preceding or following measures are to be repeated.

Bariolage (Fr.) (bär-ee-ō-läzh.) A passage for the violin, etc., in which the open strings are more especially used; a group of notes on several strings played in the same position; a Cadenza; a Medley.

Bariton (Fr.) (bä-rĭ-*tonh*.) ⎫ A male voice in-
Baritono (It.) (bä-rē-*lō*-nō.) ⎬ termediate (in
Baritone. ⎭ respect to pitch)
between the bass and tenor, the compass usually extending from:

Also a brass instrument in Sax-horn group, standing an octave below B♭ Cornet, and with similar compass.

Barócco (It.) (bä-*rōk*-kō.) } A term applied to
Baroque (Fr.) (bä-*rōk*.) } music in which the harmony is confused and abounding in unnatural modulations; eccentric; bizarre.

Barré (Fr.) (băr-rā.) In guitar playing, a temporary nut formed by placing the forefinger of the left hand across some of the strings.

Barrel organ. An organ, the tones of which are produced by the revolution of a cylinder. See *Orchestrion.*

Baryton (Fr.) (bä-ri-*tönh*.) See Baritone.

Base. } The lowest or deepest male voice; the
Bass. } lowest part in a musical composition. See *Voice.* Also the deepest Sax-horn.

Bássa (It.) (*bäs*-sä.) Low, deep; 8va bássa; play the notes an octave lower.

Bass bar. A strip of wood on the inside of a violin, etc., running under the lower string.

Bass clef. The base or F clef, placed upon the fourth line. See *Clefs.*

Bass, double. The double bass viol; the contra bass.

Basset horn. (It. *Corno di Bassetto.*) An obsolete instrument of the clarinet family similar in shape, tonal quality and compass to the modern Bass clarinet.

Bass, fundamental. The bass which contains the roots of the chords only.

Bass, given. A bass to which harmony is to be added above.

Bass, ground. A bass consisting of a few notes or measures containing a subject of its own repeated throughout the movement, and each time accompanied by a new or varied melody.

Básso (It.) (*bäs*-sō.) The lowest male voice; the bass part; the contra-bass; an 8-foot organ stop.

Básso búffo (It.) (*bäs*-sō *boof*-fō.) A humorous bass; a musical comedian of bass register.

Básso cantánte (It.) (*bäs*-sō kän-*tän*-tĕ.) A bass voice of baritone quality; a lyric bass.

Básso concertánte (It.) (*bäs*-sō kŏn-tshĕr-*tän*-tĕ.) The principal bass; also, the lighter and more delicate parts performed by the violoncello or bassoon.

Básso contínuo (It.) (*bäs*-sō kŏn-*tē*-noo-ō.) The continued bass; a bass that is figured to indicate the harmony.

Básso ostináto (It.) (*bäs*-sō ōs-tē-*nä*-tō.) A ground bass; a single bass figure constantly repeated.

Rassoon (Ger. *Fagott*, It. *Faggotto*.) 1. A double reed wind-instrument of deep pitch, with a compass of about three octaves. The bassoon ordinarily forms the bass of wood wind-instruments, and is capable of excellent independent effects. It is often used for comical or grotesque effects. 2. A reed stop in the organ which imitates the tones of the bassoon.

Bass trombone. A trombone with a compass extending from C below the bass staff to the E above.

Bass tuba (Lat.) (bäss *too*-bä.) A brass wind instrument, the lowest in pitch of the Sax-horn family. The tone is powerful and impressive, the compass is as follows:

Bâton (Fr.) (Bah-tong.) A conductor's stick.

Batterie (Fr.)(bắt-tree.) The roll of the drum; also the percussion instruments of an orchestra collectively.

Battuta (It.) (Bä-*too*-täh.) A beat; a measure or bar; *A Battuta*, in strict time.

B dur (Ger.) (Bä doer.) The key of B flat major.

Bearbeitet (Ger.) (bĕ-*är*-bī-tĕt.) Arranged; adapted.

Beat. The rise or fall of the hand or *bâton* in marking the divisions of time in music; an important musical embellishment, consisting of the principal note and the note *below* it, resembling a short trill; a throbbing which is heard when two tones are slightly out of unison.

Bebung (Ger.) (*bāy*-boong.) A shaking; a vibration; a German organ stop.

Becken (Ger.) (bek'n.) Cymbals.

Be (Ger.) (bā.) Flat, b flat.

Begleiten (Ger.) (bĕ-*glī*-t'n.) To accompany.

Bel canto (It.) (bell-*kahn*-to.) Literally, " beautiful song." In one sense it can be applied to all good singing, but, practically, it means a

19

tender, pure, and sympathetic legato, the opposite of bravura singing.

Belieben (Ger.) (bĕ-lē-b'n.) Pleasure; at pleasure.

Bell. A hollow metal instrument, set in vibration by a clapper inside or a hammer outside. Tubular chimes have been substituted with some success for regular bells. The small scale or chime of bells used in the orchestra is called *Glockenspiel*. The flaring end of the tube of various wind instruments is called the *bell*.

Bellézza (It.) (bĕl-*let*-sä.) Beauty of tone and expression.

Bell gamba. A gamba stop in an organ; the top of each pipe spreading out like a bell.

Bellicosaménte (It.) (bĕl-lē-kō-zä-*men*-tĕ.) ⎱ In a
Bellicóso (It.) (bĕl-lē-*kō*-zō.) ⎰
martial and warlike style.

Bellows. A pneumatic appendage for supplying organ pipes with air.

Belly. The sound-board of an instrument; that part over which the strings are distended.

Bémol (Fr.) (bā-mōl.) ⎱ The mark called a *flat* (♭).
Bémolle (It.) (bā-mōl.) ⎰

Bén (It.) (bān.) ⎱ Well, good.
Béne (It.) (*bā*-nĕ.) ⎰

Benedictus (Lat.) (bĕ-nĕ-*dĭk*-tŭs.) One of the movements in a Mass.

Béne plácito (It.) (*be*-nĕ plä-tshē-tō.) At will; at pleasure.

Ben marcáto (It.) (bĕn mär-*kä*-tō.) ⎱ Well marked
Bene marcáto (It.) (*bā*-nĕ mär-*kä*-to.) ⎰
in a distinct and strongly accented manner.

Be quadro (It.) (bāy *quä*-drō.) ⎱ The mark called a
Béquarré (Fr.) (bāy-kär-rā.) ⎰ natural (♮).

Bequem (Ger.) (bĕ-*quaim*,) Convenient.

Berceuse (Fr.) (bāir-sāys.) A cradle song; a lullaby.

Bergamásca (It.) (bĕr-gä-*mäs*-kä.) ⎱ A kind of rustic
Bergomask. ⎰
dance. Used in Shakespeare's "Midsummer Night's Dream."

Bes (Ger.) (bĕs.) The note B double flat, B♭♭, also called *Doppel B*, or *bb*.

Bestimmt (Ger.) (bĕ-*steemt*.) With decision. **Distinct.**

Betónend (Ger.) (bĕ-tō-nĕnd.) ⎱ Accented.
Betont (Ger.) (bĕ-*tōnt*.) ⎰

Betrübt (Ger.) (bĕ-*trübt.*) Afflicted, grieved.

Bewegung (Ger.) (bĕ-*vā-*goong.) Motion, movement.

Bewegt (Ger.) (bĕ-*vāgt.*) Moved; rather fast.

Binary. Two-fold. Binary form, — a form of two divisions, periods, or sections.

Binary measure. Two beats to a measure.

Bis (Lat.) (bĭs.) Twice; indicating that the passage marked (a few measures only) is to be repeated. It may mean a subdivision of some section or number of a musical work, as 1 *bis*, 2 *bis*, etc.

Bizzarraménte (It.) (bĭt-sär-rä-*men*-tĕ.) Oddly; in a whimsical style.

Bizzarría (It.) (bĭt-sär-*rēe*-ä.) Written in a capricious, fantastic style; sudden, unexpected modulations.

Bizzáro (It.) (bit-*sär*-rō.) Whimsical, odd, fantastical.

Blas-musik (Ger.) (*bläs*-moo-*zēk.*) Music for wind instruments.

Blasen (Ger.) (*blä*-z'n.) To blow; to sound.

Blech-instrumente (Ger.) (blĕkh-in-stroo-*mĕn*-tĕ.) The brass instruments, as trumpets, trombones, etc.

Blockflöte (Ger.) (*blŏk*-flô-tĕ.) An organ stop composed of large scale-pipes, the tone of which is full and broad.

Bluette (Fr.) (blü-ĕt.) A short, brilliant piece. The word means a spark, or a flash.

B-mol (Fr.) (bāy-mŏl.) The character called a flat (♭). See *Bémol.*

B-moll (Ger.) (bāy-mŏl.) The key of B-flat minor.

Bóccá (It.) (*bōk*-kä.) The mouth-piece of a horn, trumpet, trombone, and similar instruments.

Bocca chiusa (It.) (*bōk*-kä kē-*oo*-zä.) With closed mouth. Humming.

Body. The resonance box of a string instrument. That part of a wind instrument which remains after the removal of mouth-piece, crooks, and bell. The tube of an organ-pipe above its mouth.

Boehm Flute. A flute with perfect system of sound holes, closed by pads; with a key mechanism that greatly facilitates execution. Invented by Theobald Boehm.

Bogen (Ger.) (bō-g'n.) The bow of a violin, etc.; a slur or tie.

Boléro (Spa.) (bō-lā-ro.) A lively Spanish dance, in ¾ time. It is much like the Andalusian cachucha. It is accompanied by castanets, and sometimes with singing.

Bombarde (Fr.) (bŏnh-bärd.) ⎱ A powerful reed
Bombárdo (It.) (bŏm-bär-dō.) ⎰ stop in an organ of 16-foot scale; also an old wind instrument of the oboe species.

Bombardon (Ger.) (bóm-bär-dōn.) A form of *Tuba*.

Bones. Strips of wood or bone slightly curved, a pair being held in each hand and clicked together in varied rhythm. Typical of negro minstrel music.

Boot. The foot of a reed pipe.

Bordóne (It.) (bŏr-dō-nĕ.) ⎱ An organ stop, the
Bourdon (Fr.) (boor-dŏnh.) ⎰ pipes of which are stopped or covered, and produce the 16-foot, and sometimes the 32-foot tone; also a drone bass.

Bouche fermée (Boosh fair-may.) With closed mouth; humming.

Bouchée (Fr.) (Boo-shay.) Applied to wind-instruments this means muted; applied to organ pipes means stopped.

Bourrée (Fr.) (boor-rā.) An old French dance said to have come from Auvergne, but others claim it to be a Spanish dance coming from Biscay, where it is still in use. It is very rapid and hearty, generally in ⅖ or in ⅖ time.

Bow. An instrument of wood and horsehair, employed to set the strings of the violin, etc., in vibration. The bow, originally curved, as its name implies, has been subject to many changes of shape from time to time, from a large curve to an almost flat form.

Bow hand. The right hand; the hand which holds the bow.

Bowing. The art of using the bow; playing with the bow. "The bowing" also refers to the marks used to guide the player, as ⊓ a downstroke, V an upstroke, etc.

Brace. A character curved or straight used to connect together the different staves; the leather slide which tightens or loosens the cords of a drum.

Branle (Fr.) (bränhl.) A lively old dance in $\frac{4}{4}$ time; a species of "follow my leader," in which all the motions of the leading couple were imitated.

Brass band. A number of performers whose instruments are exclusively brass.

Brass wind. The term applied to the horns, trumpets, trombones, and tuba of an orchestra.

Bratsche (Ger.) (*brä*-tshĕ.) The viola or tenor violin. See *Viola.*

Braut-lied (Ger.) (*brout*-lēd.) A bridal hymn; a wedding song.

Bravo (It. mas.) (*brä*-vō.) An exclamation of approval often used in theatres; excellent, very good, etc.

Bravíssima, etc. (It. fem.) (brä-*vēs*-sē-mä.) Exceedingly good; exceedingly well done.

Bravúra (It.) (brä-*voo*-rä.) Spirit; skill; requiring great dexterity and skill in execution.

Bravúra, con. (It.) (brä-*voo*-rä, kŏn.) With spirit and boldness of execution.

Brawl. See *Branle.*

Break. 1. The point of change in the quality of tenor, soprano, and alto voices. A genuine bass voice has no break. The lower range is called *voce di petto,* or chest voice; the upper, *voce di testa,* or head voice; and the place of junction is called the *break.* A properly cultivated voice should have the break so under control, that the change of the quality should be practically imperceptible. 2. In the clarinet the break in the tone of the instrument occurs between B flat and B natural.

3. An imperfectly-formed tone on horn, trumpet or clarinet.

Breit (Ger.) (brīt.) Broad.

Bréve (It.) (*brā*-vĕ.) 1. Short; in ancient times the Breve was the shortest note. The notes then used were the Large, the Long, and the Breve. The Breve is now the longest note; it is equal to two *semibreves* or whole notes. 2. A Double whole note (𝅜) or (𝅜).

Bridge. That part of a stringed instrument that supports the strings.

Brillánte (It.) (brĕl-*yän-te*.) Bright, sparkling,
Brillante (Fr.) (brē-yänht.) brilliant.

Brindisi (It.) (breen-*dee*-zee.) A drinking song.

Brío (It.) (*brēe*-ō.) Vigor, animation, spirit.

Bríoso (It.) (brēe-ō-zō.) Lively; vigorous; with spirit.

Brisé (Fr.) (brē-zāy.) Split; broken into an *ar-péggio*.

Broken chords. Chords whose notes are not taken simultaneously, but successively.

Broken octaves. Octaves in which the notes are played separately, as

Bruit (Fr.) (brü-ē.) Noise, rattle, clatter.

Brúmmen (Gr.) (*broom*-mĕn.) To hum; to growl.

Bruscaménte (It.) (broos-kä-*men*-tĕ.) Abruptly, coarsely.

Búffa (It.) (*boof*-fä.) Comic; humorous; in the
Búffo (It.) (*boof*-fō.) comic style; also a singer who takes comic parts in the opera.

Buffonescaménte (It.) (boof-fō-nĕs-kä-*men*-tĕ.) In a burlesque and comical manner.

Buffa, opera (It.) (*boof*-fä ō-pĕ-rä.) A comic opera; a burletta.

Bugle. 1. A hunting horn. 2. An instrument of copper or brass, similar to the cornet, but higher and more piercing in pitch. Formerly it was equipped with keys or valves, but now exists only in natural form and is used in military field music.

It gives the following open tones.

Burden. A regular return of a theme or phrase in a song, at the close of each verse; the drone of a bagpipe.

Burla (It.) (*boor*-lä.) Facetious, droll, com-
Burlándo (It.) (boor-*län*-dō.) ical; in a playful
Burléscó (It.) (boor-*lĕs*-kō.) manner.

Burlétta (It.) (boor-*lĕt*-tä.) A comic operetta; a light musical and dramatic piece, somewhat in the nature of the English farce.

C

C. The first note of the natural scale. The note *Ut* of the Guidonian System. (See *Solfaing.*) The note from which pianos and organs are tuned.

C is called *Ut* in France and *Do* in Italy. It is an error to suppose that the sign 𝄴 is C as an abbreviation for "Common Time." The sign came from a broken circle, used in the Middle Ages and called the *Imperfectum.* See *Time.*

Cabalétta (It.) (kä-bä-*lĕt*-tä.) A simple melody of a pleasing and attractive character; an operatic air like the rondo in form; a cavaletta.

Cachúcha (Spa.) (kä-*tchoo*-tchä.) A popular Spanish dance in triple time, very similar to the Bolero.

Cadence (Fr.) (kä-dänhs.) A shake or trill; also a close in harmony. (See *Cadenza.*)

Cadence. 1. A close in melody or harmony, dividing it into numbers or periods, or bringing it to a final termination. 2. An ornamental passage. See below and also *Cadenza.*

Cadence, authentic or perfect. A perfect or final cadence; the harmony of the dominant followed by that of the tonic or the progression of the dominant to the tonic.

Cadence, church. The plagal cadence.

Cadence, complete. A full cadence; when the final sound of a verse in a chant is on the keynote.

Cadence, deceptive. When the dominant chord resolves into another harmony instead of the tonic.

Cadence, half or imperfect. When the dominant harmony is preceded by the common chord of the tonic; a half cadence.

Cadence, plagal. When tonic harmony is preceded by subdominant.

Perfect Cadences.   Half

V   I   V   I   I

or Imperfect Cadences.

Interrupted, False or Deceptive Cadences.

Plagal Cadences.

Cadénza (It.) (kä-*den*-tsä.) A cadence; an ornamental passage introduced near the close of a song or solo, either by the composer or extemporaneously by the performer.

Caisse (Fr.) (käss.) A drum.

Caisse grosse (Fr.) (käss gross.) The bass drum.

Caisse roulante (Fr.) (käss roo-länht.) The side drum.

Caland (It.) (kä-*länd*.) } Gradually diminishing
Calándo (It.) (kä-*län*-dō.) } the tone and retarding the time; becoming softer and slower by degrees.

Calcándo (It.) (käl-*kän*-dō.) Pressing forward and hurrying the time.

Calcant (Ger.) (*käl*-känt.) The bellows treader, in old German organs.

Calliope (Kăl-*lēe*-ŏ-pĕ.) 1. In pagan mythology the muse that presided over eloquence and heroic

26

poetry. 2 A pipe (or whistle) organ of limited compass, the loud and coarse tone being produced by steam instead of air

Cálma (It.) (käl-mä.) |
Calmáte (It.) (käl-*mä*-tĕ.) | Calmness, tranquillity,
Calmáto (It.) (käl-mä-tō.) | repose.

Calóre (It.) (kä-*lō*-rĕ.) { Warmth, anima-
Caloróso (It.) (käl-ō-*rō*-zo) } tion.

Cámera (It) (*kä*-mĕ-rä.) Chamber; a term applied to music composed for private performance or small concerts.

Caminándo (It.) (kä-mi-*nän*-dō.) Flowing; with easy and gentle progression.

Campána (It.) (käm-*pä*-nä) A bell.

Campanélla (It) (käm-pä-*nĕl*-lä.) A little bell.

Canaries (Eng) (kă-*nā*-rĕs.) An old dance, in lively $\frac{4}{4}$ or $\frac{6}{8}$, and sometimes $\frac{12}{8}$ time, of two strains. It derives its name from the Canary Islands, whence it is supposed to have come.

Cancelling sign. A natural (♮), employed to remove the effect of a previous accidental.

Cancion (Spa.) (kän-thē-*ōn*.) A song; words set to music.

Cancrizans (It.) (kän-*krē*-tsäns.) } Retrograde
Cancrizante (It.) (kän-krē-*tsän*-tĕ.) }
movement; going backward; crab-like.

Canon. The strictest form of contrapuntal composition, in which each voice imitates exactly the melody sung or played by the first voice. See Richter, Chadwick, Jadassohn, Goetschius, works on Counterpoint or " Elson's Music Dictionary."

Cantábile (It.) (kän-*tä*-bi-lĕ.) Singing or playing in a melodious and graceful style, full of expression.

Cantando (It.) (kän-*tän*-dōh.) In a singing style; *cantabile.*

Cantáre (It.) (kän-*tä*-rĕ.) To sing; to celebrate; to praise.

Cantáta (It.) (kän-*tä*-tä.) } A poem set to mu-
Cantate (Fr.) (känh-tät.) } sic; a vocal com-
Cantate (Ger.) (kän-*tä*-tĕ.) } position of several
movements, comprising airs, recitatives and choruses.

Cántica (It.) (kän-*tē*-kä.) { Canticle; the ancient
Canticæ (Lat.) (*kăn*-tĭ-sē.) } *laudi*, or sacred
songs of the Roman Catholic Church.

Canticle. A sacred hymn or song. One of the non-metrical hymns of praise and jubilation in the Bible.

Cantiléna (It.) (kän-tǐ-*lāy*-nä.) The melody, air, or principal part in any composition; generally the highest vocal part; it is also applied to any light and simple song, or in instrumental music, a piece of song-like character. It sometimes indicates a smooth, *cantabile* style of playing.

Cánto (It.) (*kän*-tō.) 1. Song, air, melody; the highest vocal part in choral music. 2. A part or division of a poem.

Cánto férmo (It.) (*kän*-tō *fair*-mō.) 1. A chant or melody. 2. Choral singing in unison on a plain melody. 3. The subject or " fixed song " against which other melodic figures are set, " point against point," in contrapuntal writing; also, *Cantus firmus.*

Cantór (It.) (kän-*tór*.) A singer; a chanter.

Cantoris (Lat.) (kăn-*tō*-ris.) A term used in cathedral music to indicate the passages intended to be sung by those singers who are placed on that side of the choir where the *cantor* or *precentor* sits. This is usually on the left-hand side on entering the choir from the nave. See *Decani.*

Cantus (Lat.) (*kăn*-tŭs.) A song; a melody; also, the treble or soprano part. Canto.

Cantus firmus (Lat.) (*kăn*-tus *fĭr*-mŭs.) See *cánto férmo.*

Cantus Gregorianus (Lat.) (*kăn*-tŭs Grĕ-gō-rǐ-*ä*-nŭs.) See *Gregorian chant.*

Canzóna (It.) (kän-*tsō*-nä.) }
Canzóne (It.) (kän-*tsō*-nĕ.) } 1. Song; ballad; canzonet. 2 A graceful and somewhat elaborate air in two or three strains or divisions. 3. An air in two or three parts with passages of fugue and imitation, somewhat similar to the madrigal.

Canzonet A short song in one, two, or three parts.

Canzonétta (It.) (kän-tsō-*net*-tä.) A short *canzóne.* A little song.

Capell-meister. (Ger.) (kä-*pĕl*-mīs-ter.) The director, composer, or master of the music in a choir or orchestra.

Capo (It.) (kä-pō.) The head or beginning; the top.

Capotásto (It.) (kä-pō-täs-tō.) 1. The nut or upper part of the finger board of a violin, violoncello, etc. 2. A piece of wood or ivory with clamp, used by guitar players to form a temporary nut upon the finger board, to raise the pitch of all the strings simultaneously. Incorrectly written in English *Capo d'astro*.

Cappélla (It.) (käp-*pel*-lä.) 1. A chapel or church. 2. A band of musicians that sing or play in a church, or in private employ. 3. An orchestra.

Cappricciétto (It.) (kä-prēt-shē-ĕt-tō.) A short *capríccio*.

Capríccio (It.) (kä-*prēt*-shē-ō.) A fanciful and irregular species of composition; a species of *fantasia;* in a capricious and free style.

Capricciosaménte (It.) (kä-prēt-shē-ō-zä-*men*-tĕ.) Capriciously.

Capriccióso (It.) (kä-prēt-shē-ō-zō.) In a fanciful and capricious style.

Caprice (Fr.) (kä-prēs.) A caprice. See *Capríccio.*

Caráttere (It.) (kä-*rät*-tāi-rĕ.) Character, quality, degree.

Caressant (Fr.) (kä-rĕs-sänh.) Caressing, tenderly.

Carezzándo (It.) (kä-rĕt-*tsän*-dō.) } In a caressing
Carezzovole (It.) (kä-rĕt-sŏ-*vō*-lĕ.) } and tender manner.

Caricatura (It.) (kä-rē-kä-*too*-rä.) A caricature; an exaggerated representation.

Carillon (Fr.) (kä-rē-yŏnh.) Chime.

Carillons (Fr. pl.) (kä-rē-yŏnh.) 1. Chimes; a peal or set of bells, upon which tunes are played by the machinery of a clock, or by means of keys, like those of a pianoforte. 2. Short simple airs adapted to such bells. 3. A mixture stop in an organ, to imitate a peal of bells.

Caríta (It.) (kä-*rē*-tä.) Tenderness, feeling.

Caríta, con. (It.) (kä-*rē*-tä, kŏn.) With tenderness.

Carol. 1. A song. 2. A song of joy and exultation; a song of devotion. 3. Old ballads sung at Christmas and Easter.

Cássa (It.) (käs-sä.) A large drum.

Cássa grande (It.) (käs-sä *grän*-dĕ.) The bass drum in military music.

Castanets. Clappers used to accompany dancing; formed of small concave shells of ivory, or hard wood. Castanets are used by dancers in Spain and other southern countries to mark the rhythm of the *boléro*, cachucha, etc.

Castráto (It.) (käs-*trä*-tō.) A male singer with a soprano voice; a eunuch.

Catch. A humorous composition for three or four voices, supposed to be of English invention and dating back to the Tudors. The parts are so contrived that the singers catch up each other's words, thus giving them a different sense from that of the original reading. The oldest catches were rounds.

Catgut. A small string for violins and other instruments of a similar kind, made of the intestines of sheep, lambs, or goats.

Cavatína (It.) (kä-vä-*tēe*-nä.) An air of one strain only; generally of simple and expressive character.

C clef. It is called the C clef, because, on whatever line it is placed, it gives to the notes on that line the name and pitch of *middle* C. Is used for Tenor, Sop., and Alt. See *Clef*.

C dur (Ger.) (tsä doer.) The key of C major.

Cebell. The name of an old air in common time, characterized by a quick and sudden alternation of high and low notes.

Célere (It.) (*tshä*-lĕ-rĕ.) Quick; rapid; with velocity.

Celeritá (It.) (tshä-lā-*rē*-tä.) } Celerity, velocity,
Célérité (Fr.) (sä-lā-rē-tä.) } rapidity.

Celesta. An instrument invented by Mustel in Paris, in 1886. It consists of steel tuning forks set in sound boxes and struck with mallets through medium of a key-board.

Céleste (Fr.) (sä-lĕst.) Celestial, heavenly; *voix céleste*, a sweet-toned organ stop.

Celestína (It.) (tshä-lĕs-*tē*-nä.) An organ stop of small 4-foot scale, producing a very delicate and subdued tone.

'Céllo (It.) (*tshĕl*-lō.) An abbreviation of *violoncello*.

Cémbalo (It.) (*tshĕm*-bä-lō.) A harpsichord.

Ces (Ger.) (tsĕs.) The note C flat.

Ces dur (tsĕs doer.) The key of C flat major.

Chaconne (Fr.) (shä-konne.) A graceful, slow Spanish movement in ¾ time, and composed upon a ground bass. Also an instrumental form used by the old masters.

Chalmeau (Fr.) (shǎl-mō.)) The lowest regis-
Chalumeau (Fr.) (shäl-u-mō.)) ter of instruments of the clarinet family is called the *chalumeau*, from the obsolete instrument *shawm, shalmey*, precursor of the oboe and clarinet.

Chamade (Fr.) (shä-mäd.) Beat of drum declaring a surrender or parley.

Chamber band. A company of musicians whose performances are confined to chamber music.

Chamber music. In a broad sense "chamber music" is *any* music suited to a room, or small hall, as distinct from music for a large auditorium, as church, operatic, or symphonic music. Practically, the term is most frequently applied to concerted pieces of instrumental music in the sonata form, as string or wood-wind quartets, quintets, etc.

Changes. The various alternations and different passages produced by a peal of bells.

Changing notes. A term applied by some theorists to passing notes or discords, which occur on the *accented* parts of a measure.

Chanson (Fr.) (shänh-sǒnh.) A song.

Chant. 1. A short sacred song, generally harmonized in four part , to which lyrical portions of the Scriptures are set, part of the words being recited *ad libitum*, and part sung in strict time. A Gregorian chant consists of five parts: the intonation; the first reciting note or dominant; the mediation; the second reciting note or dominant; the cadence. The Gregorian chant is the one chiefly used in the Catholic and Anglican service. 2. To recite musically; to sing.

Chant (Fr.) (shänh.) The voice part; a song or melody; singing.

Chantant (Fr.) (shänh-tänh.) Adapted to singing; in a melodious and singing style.

Chantante (Fr.) (shänh-tänht.) Singing.

Chant, double. A chant extending through two verses of a psalm. It should have four reciting-notes and four cadences.

Chanter. The melody pipe in a bagpipe.

Chanterelle (Fr.) (shänht-rel.) Treble string; the

31

E string of the violin. The highest string of any instrument of the violin or lute family.

Chant, plain. A single chant, seldom extending beyond the limits of an octave, or through more than one verse of a psalm.

Chant, single. A simple harmonized melody, extending only through one verse of a psalm.

Charivari (Fr.) (shä-rī-vä-rē.) Noisy music made with tin dishes, horns, bells, etc.; clatter; a mock serenade.

Chasse (Fr.) (shäss.) Hunting; in the hunting style.

Che (It.) (kā.) Then, that, which.

Chef (Fr.) (shĕf.) Leader, chief.

Chef-d'œuvre (Fr.) (shā d'oovr.) A masterpiece; the principal or most important composition of an author.

Chef-d'orchestre (Fr.) (shā d'ŏr-kĕstr.) The conductor of an orchestra.

Chest tones. } The lowest register of the voice
Chest voice. }

Chest, wind. A reservoir in an organ for holding the air supplied by the bellows.

Chiamare (It.) (kē-ä-*mä*-rē.) To chime.

Chiaraménte (It.) (kē-ä-rä-*män*-tĕ.) Clearly, brightly, purely.

Chiarézza, con. (It.) (kē-ä-*ret*-sä.) Clearness, neatness, purity.

Chiésa (It.) (kē-ä-zä.) A church. Applied to various musical works.

Chime. A set of bells tuned to a musical scale; the sound of bells in harmony; a correspondence of sound.

Chitárra (It.) (kē-*tär*-rä.) A guitar; a cithara.

Chiuso (It.) (ki-*oo*-zo.) Close; hidden; *Bocca chiuso*, with closed mouth; humming.

Choir. 1. That part of a cathedral or church set apart for the singers. 2. The singers themselves taken collectively.

Choir, grand. In organ playing, the union of all the reed stops.

Choir organ. In a large organ, the lowest row of keys is generally the choir organ, which contains some of the softer and more delicate stops, and is used for accompanying solos, duets, etc.

Choral. Belonging to the choir; full, or for many voices.

Choral (Ger.) (kō-*räl.*)
Chorale (*pl.*) (kō-rä-lĕ.) } Hymn tunes of the early German Protestant church.

Chord. The union of two or more sounds heard at the same time. Chords are often indicated by figures attached to their bass notes. See *Thorough Bass.* Consult Stainer's " Harmony," or York's " Harmony Simplified."

Chord, accidental. A chord produced either by anticipation or suspension.

Chord, common. A chord consisting of a fundamental note together with its third and fifth.

Chord, dominant. 1. A chord that is found on the dominant of the key in which the music is written. 2. The *leading* or *characteristic* chord.

Chord, fundamental. A chord consisting of the fundamental tone with its third and fifth.

Chord, inverted. A chord, the notes of which are so dispersed that the *root* does not appear as the lowest note.

Chord.   Inversions.

Chorister. A leader of a choir; a singer.

Chorus. 1. A company of singers. 2. A composition intended to be sung by a number of voices. 3. A refrain.

Christe eleison (Gr.) (*krĭs*-tĕ-ā-*lī*-sŏn or a-*lay*-ee-sŏn.) " O Christ, have mercy"; a part of the Kyrie or first movement in a Mass.

Chromatic. 1. Proceeding by half-steps. 2. Any music or chord containing notes not belonging to the diatonic scale.

Chromatic keys. 1. The black keys of a pianoforte. 2. Every key in the scale of which one or more chromatic tones occur.

Chromatic scale. A scale which divides every whole step of the diatonic scale, and consists of twelve half-steps in an octave.

Chromatic signs. Accidentals; sharps, flats, and naturals. The chromatic signs used in modern music are the sharp (♯), the (♭), the natural (♮), the double sharp (✕), and the double flat (♭♭). See Elson's " Theory of Music," and "Elson's Music Dictionary."

Church Cadence. Another name for the *Plagal Cadence.*

Church modes. See *Gregorian modes.*

Ciaccóna (It.) (tshēe-ä-*kō*-nä.) ⎰ See *Chaconne.*
Ciaccónne (It.) (tshēe-ä-*kōn*-nĕ.) ⎱

C in alt. The fourth note of the *alt* octave.

See *Tablature.*

Cinelli (It.) (tschĭ-*nel*-lee.) Cymbals.

Ciphering (sĭ-fĕr-ĭng.) The sounding of the pipes of the organ when the keys are not touched.

Circle of fifths. A method of modulation, from dominant to dominant, which conveys us, round through all the scales, back to the point from which we started.

Cis (Ger.) (tsĭs.) The note C sharp.

Cis-cis (Ger.) (tsĭs-tsĭs.) The note C double sharp.

Civettería (It.) (tshē-vĕt-*tā*-rē-ä.) Coquetry; in a coquettish manner.

Clarabella (Lat.) (*klä*-rä-*bĕl*-lä.) An organ stop of eight-foot scale, with a soft fluty tone; the pipes are of wood and not stopped.

Clarinet (also Clarinette.) A rich full-toned wind instrument of wood, with a single reed mouth-piece. It is one of the most important wood wind-instruments. It is said to have been invented about 1700, by J. C. Denner, of Nuremburg. It consists of a cylindrical tube, with finger-holes and keys, which terminates in a bell, and has a beak-like mouth-piece. Its extreme compass is There are clarinets of different pitch; those commonly used in the orchestra are the clarinets in C, in B♭, and in A. The clarinets in E♭ or A♭ are rarely used except in military bands. All clarinets, the one in C excepted, are transposing instruments. See A. Elson's "Orchestral Instruments and their Use," and Prout's "The Orchestra."

Clarinet, bass. A clarinet whose tones are an octave deeper than those of the C or B-flat clarinet.

Clarinette (Fr.) (klär-i-nĕt.) ⎰ The clarinet; also an
Clarionet. ⎱ organ reed stop of 8-foot scale and soft quality of tone.

Claríno (It.) (klä-*rēe*-nô). } A small or octave trum-
Clarion. } pet; also the name of
a 4-foot organ reed stop tuned an octave above
the trumpet stop. The term is also used to indicate the trumpet parts in full score.

Classical music. Standard music; music of first
rank, written by composers of the highest order.
Music whose form and style has been accepted
as suitable for a model to composers.

Clavecin (Fr.) (kläv-ĕ-*sănh*.) The harpsichord, or
the spinet.

Clavichord. A small, keyed instrument, like the
spinet, and the forerunner of the pianoforte.
The tone of the clavichord was agreeable and
impressive, but very weak. Its mechanism
pushed a sharp edge, like the point of a chisel,
against the wire, and this point remained, pressing the wire while the key was held, forming
a bridge. See Weitzmann's " History of Pianoforte Music."

Clavier (Fr.) (klä-vee-ay.) } The keys or key-board
Clavier (Ger.) (klä-*fēer*.) } of pianoforte, organ,
etc. The German name for spinets, harp-
sichords and clavichords. At present the
Germans call the piano "Clavier" or "Klavier."

Clavier-auszug (Ger.) (klä-*fēer* *ous*-tsoog.) An
arrangement of a full score for the use of piano
players.

Clé (Fr.) (klā.) } A key; a character used to
Clef. } determine the name and pitch
of the notes on the staff to which it is prefixed.
The following are used in music to-day: — The G

clef, placing ḡ on the second line, thus ;

the bass, or F clef, placing f on the fourth line,

thus ; these two are now fixed, im-

movable clefs. The C clef, which fixes the position of middle c, or c̄, is a movable clef, and is
used to-day, as follows:

Alto clef

Tenor clef

and often in America

In Italy vocal tenor parts are written nowadays with a combined treble and tenor clef as follows:

See Elson's "Realm of Music," article on "The Rise of Notation."

Cloche (Fr.) (klōsh.) A bell.

Close. A cadence; the end of a piece or passage.

Close harmony. Harmony in which the notes or parts are kept as close together as possible.

C moll (Ger.) (tsā mōl.) The key of C minor.

Co (It.) (kō.) } With, with the.
Coi (It.) (kō-ēe.) }

Códa (It.) (kō-dä.) The *tail* or *end;* a few measures added to the end of a piece of music to make a more effective termination. From the Latin "Cauda" — a tail. The coda, originally a few added chords after the completion of the musical form, was developed into a great summing-up of the movement or composition; a climax of the entire work. The final episode of a fugue is called *Coda.*

Codétta (It.) (kō-*det*-tä.) A short coda or passage added to a piece; a connecting passage in a fugue.

Cogli (It.) (kōl-yēe.) } With the.
Col (It.) (kōl.) }

Colla párte (It.) (kŏl-lä pär-tĕ.) *With the part;* indicating that the time is to be accommodated to the solo singer or player.

Colla vóce (It.) (kŏl-lä vō-tshĕ.) *With the voice;* implying that the accompanist must accommodate and take the time from the s nger.

Coll' árco (It.) (kŏl-l'är-kō.) *With the bow;* the notes are to be played with the bow, and not *pizzicáto.*

Col' legno (It.) (kŏl-lān-yō.) *With the bow stick.*

Colophon (Fr.) (kŏl-ō-fŏnh.) Resin.

Coloratúra (It.) (kō-lō-rä-*too*-rä.) Ornamental passages, roulades, embellishments, etc., in vocal music.

Combination pedals. See *Composition Pedals.*

Cóme (It.) (*kō*-mĕ.) As, like, the same as.

Cóme prima (It.) (*kō*-mĕ *prē*-mä.) As before, as at first.

Cóme sópra (It.) (*kō*-mĕ *sō*-prä.) As above; as before, indicating the repetition of a previous or similar passage.

Cóme sta (It.) (*kō*-mĕ *stä*.) As it stands; perform exactly as written.

Cómma (It.) (*kŏm*-mä.) An extremely small differentiation in pitch barely recognizable by the ear, but which exists theoretically between so-called enharmonic notes like D♯ and E♭. In the science of musical sound a whole step or tone is divided into nine *commas*. The sign of a comma (,) is often used as a breathing mark in vocal music.

Common chord. A chord consisting of a root with its third and fifth.

Common hallelujah metre. A stanza of six lines of iambic measure, the syllables of each being in number and order as follows: 8, 6, 8, 6, 8, 8.

Common measure. That measure which has an even number of parts in a measure; $\frac{4}{4}$ rhythm, sometimes marked

Common metre. A verse or stanza of four lines in iambic measure, the syllables of each being in number and order, thus: 8, 6, 8, 6.

Common time. A term sometimes used to express that time which has an even number of parts in a measure; *common measure;* $\frac{4}{4}$ rhythm.

Comodaménte (It.) (kō-mō-dä-*men*-tĕ.) } Conveniently, quietly, easily, with composure.
Cómodo (It.) (*kō*-mō-dō.)

Compass. The range of notes or sounds of which any voice or instrument is capable.

Compiacévole (It.) (kŏm-pē-ä-*tshe*-vō-lĕ.) Agreeable, pleasing.

Compiacevolmente (It.) (kŏm-pē-ä-tshĕ-vōl-*men*-tĕ.) In a pleasant and agreeable style.

Complementary part. That part which is added to the subject and counter-subject of a fugue.

Complin (Lat.) (*kŏm*-plin.) The latest evening service of the Catholic church.

Composition. Any musical production; the art of inventing or composing music, according to the rules of harmony.

Composition pedals. Pedals connected with a system of mechanism for arranging the stops of an organ.

Compósso (It.) (kŏm-*pōs*-sō.) } Composed; set to
Compósto (It.) (kŏm-*pōs*-tō.) } music.

Compound harmony. Simple harmony with an octave added.

Compound intervals. Those which exceed the extent of an octave; as a ninth, tenth, etc.

Compound stops. Where three or more organ stops are arranged so that by pressing down one key a note from each stop is sounded.

Compound times. Those which include or exceed *six* parts in a measure, and contain *two*, or more, principal accents, as $\frac{6}{4}$, $\frac{6}{8}$, $\frac{9}{4}$, $\frac{9}{8}$, $\frac{12}{8}$. See *Rhythm*, and *Time*.

Con (It.) (kŏn.) With. For definition of various phrases beginning with *con* see other words.

Concénto (It.) (kŏn-*tshĕn*-to.) Concord; agreement; harmony of voices and instruments.

Concert. 1. A performance in public of practical musicians, either vocal or instrumental, or both. 2. Harmony, unison; (Ger.) a concerto. *Concert Spirituel* (Fr.) (con-sair spee-ree-tü-ell), a sacred concert.

Concertant (Fr.) (kŏhn-sair-tänh.) Performer in a concert; a musician.

Concertánte (It.) (kŏn-tshĕr-*tän*-tĕ.) 1. A piece in which each part is alternately principal and subordinate, as in a *dúo concertánte*. 2. A concerto for two or more instruments, with accompaniments for a full band. 3. A female concert performer.

Concertato (It.) (kŏn-tshĕr-*tä*-tō.) Concerted. See also *Concertánte*.

Concerted music. Music in which several voices or instruments are heard at the same time; in opposition to *sólo* music.

Concert-grand pianoforte. The largest grand pianoforte.

Concertina (It.) (kŏn-tshĕr-*tēe*-nä.) A small instrument, similar in principle to the accordion, the sound boxes being hexagonal in shape instead of oblong. The English concertina has a complete chromatic scale of four octaves The tone is clear and sweet, and much is possible in way of expression and harmonic effect.

Concert-meister (Ger.) (kŏn-*tsĕrt-mīs*-tĕr.) The chief violinist of the orchestra.

Concerto (It.) (kon-*tschair*-to); (Ger.) Konzert (kont-*sairt*.) Also pronounced as an English word — concerto. Originally the term was applied loosely to almost any kind of concerted music. The central idea of the modern concerto is the display of a solo instrument, or sometimes more than one. The accompaniment being generally orchestral, and the form that of *Sonata*.

Concert pitch. The pitch adopted by different manufacturers of musical instruments as best suited to display them. It is a dubious and vague standard, but almost always means a very high pitch. In America it has been displaced by the " International Pitch." See *Pitch*.

Concert-stück (Ger.) (kŏn-*tsĕrt* stük.) A concert-piece; a concerto.

Concord. A harmonious combination of sounds; the opposite to a *discord*.

Concords, perfect. The perfect fourth, fifth and eighth.

Con dólce maniéra (It.) (kŏn *dŏl*-tshĕ mä-nē-*ā*-rä.)

Conductor. A director or leader of an orchestra or chorus. See " Elson's Music Dictionary."

Conduttóre (It.) (kŏn-doot-*tō*-rĕ.) A conductor.

Conjoint tetrachords. Two tetrachords or fourths of which the highest note of one is the lowest of the other.

Conjunct degree. A degree in which two notes form the interval of a second.

Conjunct succession. Where a succession of tones proceed regularly upward or downward through several degrees.

Connecting note. A note held in common by two successive chords

Consecutive fifths. Two or more perfect fifths, immediately following one another in similar motion.

Consecutive intervals. Where two parallel parts or voices of a score proceed in succession by similar motion.

Consecutive octaves. Two parts moving in octaves with each other.

Consecutives covered. Passages in which consecutive fifths may be imagined, though they do not really exist; as, where a third or a sixth moves to a fifth.

Consequent (Lat.) (kŏn-sĕ-quĕnt.) } The *answer* in
Consequente (It.) (kŏn-sĕ-*quen*-tĕ.) } a fugue, or of a point of imitation. A musical phrase following a similar one. In musical periods the antecedent and consequent are two balancing divisions, like two rhyming lines, in a verse or couplet. See *Form*.

Conservatoire (Fr.) (kŏn-sĕr-vä-twär.) } A school
Conservatory. } or academy of music, in which every branch of musical art is taught.

Consolánte (It.) (kŏn-sō-*län*-tĕ.) In a cheering and consoling manner.

Consolataménte (It.) (kŏn-sō-lä-tä-*men*-tĕ.) Quietly, cheerfully.

Console. The keyboard, pedals, stops, of an organ, etc. Sometimes apart from the sounding portion and connected by electric cable.

Consonance. An accord of sounds agreeable and satisfactory to the ear; the opposite to a discord or dissonance.
> *Perfect consonances*, Fourths, Fifths and Octaves.
> *Imperfect*, Major and Minor Thirds and Sixths.

Consonant. Accordant, harmonious.

Consonáre (It.) (kŏn-sō-*nä*-rĕ.) To tune in unison with another.

Consoniren (Ger.) (kŏn-sō-*nē*-r'n.) To harmonize; to agree in sound.

Con sordíni (It. pl.) (kŏn sōr-*dē*-nĕ.) *With mutes*, in violin playing; in pianoforte music, *with dampers*, indicating that the dampers are not to be raised by the pedal; the damper pedal *not* to be used.

Contano (It.) (kŏn-*tä*-nō.) To count or rest; a term applied to certain parts having rests for the time being, while the other parts continue.

Continued harmony. A harmony that does not change, though the bass varies.

Continued rest. A long rest or period of silence for a certain voice or instrument while others proceed. A large figure with or without a block under it denotes the number of measures to be counted in silence.

Continuo (It.) (kŏn-tē-noo-ō.) Without cessation.

Contra (It.) (kŏn-trä.) Low, under.

Cóntra-bass (It.) (kŏn-trä-bäs.) The double bass; the deepest-toned stringed instrument of the viol species. The strings are usually tuned a fourth apart, to the following notes

The contra-bass sounds an octave lower than written. The ordinary compass begins on the e below staff and extends to

Contra-bassoon. The contra-bassoon, or double bassoon, is the deepest instrument of the bassoon family. Its tone is powerful and solemn. Its compass is as given: but it sounds an octave deeper. It is the deepest instrument that is ever used in the orchestra. It is found only in large scores and in great orchestras. See A. Elson's "Orchestral Instruments and Their Use" and Prout's "The Orchestra."

Contraction. When two parts in a fugue compress the subject, counter-subject, or an intervening subject.

Cóntra-fagótto (It.) (kŏn-trä-fä-gôt-tō.) The contra-bassoon; also, the name of an organ-stop of 16 or 32-foot scale.

Contrálto (It.) (kŏn-träl-tō.) The deepest species of female voice. It is often used as synonymous with alto. See *Alto*.

Contra-posaune (Ger.) (kŏn-trä-pō-zou-ně.) A 16 or 32-foot reed-stop in an organ.

Contrappúnto (It.) (kŏn-träp-poon-tō.) Counterpoint.

Contrappúnto dóppio (It.) (kŏn-träp-poon-tō dŭp-pē-ō.) Double counterpoint.

Contrapunkt (Ger.) (kŏn-trä-poonkt.) Counterpoint.

Contrary motion. Motion in an opposite direction to some other part; one rising as the other falls.

Contredance (Fr.) (kŏntr-dähns.) A country dance; a dance in which the parties engaged stand in two opposite ranks. See *Country Dance.*

Copérto (It.) (kŏ-*pār*-tō.) Covered, muffled.

Coppel-flöte (Ger.) (*kŏp*-p'l-*flō*-tĕ.) *Coupling* flute, an organ stop of the clarabella, or stopped diapason species, intended to be used in combination with some other stop.

Cópula (It.) (kō-poo-lä.) { A *coupler;* an arrange-
Copule (Fr.) (kŏ-*pül*.) } ment by which two rows of keys can be connected together, or the keys connected with the pedals; a codetta; a connecting phrase in a fugue.

Cor (Fr.) (kŏr.) A horn; commonly called the French horn.

Coróle (It.) (kō-*rä*-lĕ.) Choral; the plain chant.

Cor Anglais (Fr.) (kŏr änh-glāy.) *English horn;* the tenor oboe; also a reed stop in an organ. The compass of the English horn is written about the same as that of the oboe, but it sounds a fifth deeper than notated. Its music is written in the treble clef. The tone being veiled and mournful, it has been largely used in imitation of the shepherd's pipe, in modern scores. See A. Elson's "Orchestral Instruments," Prout's "Orchestra," etc.

Coránte (It.) (kō-*rän*-tĕ.) } A dance in ⅜ or ¼ time.
Coránto (It.) (kō-*rän*-to.) } See *Courante.*

Córda (It.) (kŏr-dä.) A string; *úna córda,* one string.

Cordatúra (It.) (kŏr-dä-*too*-rä.) The scale or series of notes to which the strings of any instrument are tuned.

Cornet. Formerly called *Cornet à pistons.* A small brass wind instrument with three valves and similar to the *trumpet,* but of slightly different model. The cornet most used in band and orchestra, stands in B♭ with a shank or special valve to lower the pitch to A. A cornet in E♭ (above) has been used in brass bands. The tone is mellow, but lacks the peculiar ringing quality of *trumpet.* The ordinary compass used in modern works is about

42

with all chromatics, sounding one tone deeper upon the B-flat cornet. See Prout's "Orchestra" or A. Elson's "Orchestral Instruments."

Echo Cornet, Dulciana Cornet are stops on the organ. The *Cornet* of Shakspeare's time was a *Serpent* in smaller form.

Cornet stop. An organ-stop, consisting of from three to five pipes to each note.

Córno (It.) (kŏr-nō.) A horn.

Córno di bassétto (It.) (kŏr-nō dē bäs-*set*-tō.) 1. The basset horn. 2. A delicate-toned organ-stop (reed) of 8-foot scale.

Córno Inglése (It.) (kŏr-nō In-*glä*-zĕ.) The English horn. See *Cor Anglais.*

Cornopean. An organ reed-stop of 8-foot scale; also, a crude cornet.

Córo (It.) (kō-rō.) A choir; a chorus; a piece for many voices.

Coróna (It.) (kō-rō-nä.) A pause or hold, ⌢

Corps (Fr.) (kŏr.) 1. The body of a musical instrument. 2. A band of musicians.

Corps de ballet (Fr.) (kŏr dŭh băl-lā.) A general name for the performers in a ballet.

Corrénte (It.) (kŏr-*ren*-tĕ.) See *Coránto.*

Cosaque (Fr.) (kō-săk.) A Cossack dance.

Cotillon (Fr.) (kō-tē-yŏnh.) A lively dance, similar to the "German"; a quadrille.

Coulé (Fr.) (koo-*lāy*.) A group of two notes, connected by a slur.

Counter. A name given to a part sung or played against another, as *counter tenor.*

Counterpoint. *Point against point.* The art of adding one or more parts to a given theme or subject. Before the invention of notes, the various sounds were expressed by *points.* Counterpoint is the support of melody by melody instead of by chords (harmony).

Counterpoint, double. A counterpart that admits of an inversion of two parts.

Counterpoint, quadruple. Counterpoint in four parts, all of which can invert above or below each other, in twenty-four different positions.

Counterpoint, single. Where the parts are not invertible.

Counterpoint, triple. A counterpoint in three parts, all of which can be inverted, making six possible positions.

Counter-subject. The second division in a fugue coming against the answer in the second voice.

Counter-tenor. High-tenor; the highest male voice. It is generally *a falsétto*.

Counter theme. See *Counter-subject*.

Country Dance. *Contre-danse* (Fr.); *Contradanza* (It.). A rustic dance, of English origin, in ⅔ or ¾ time, and sprightly movement. Two lines of dancers faced each other and performed various figures.

Coup d'Archet (Fr.) (koo där-shay.) A stroke of the bow.

Couper le sujet (Fr.) (koo-pā lŭh soo-zhă.)

Coupler. See *Cópula*.

Courante (Fr.) (koo-ränht.) *Running;* an old dance in triple time; the second number in the old Suites des Danses. It is in rapid *tempo*.

Cracovienne (Fr.) (kră-kō-vē-ĕnn.) A Polish dance in ⅔ (sometimes erroneously given as ¾) rhythm.

Credo (Lat.) (krāy-dō.) I *believe;* one of the principal movements of the Mass. The Creed.

Cremóna (It.) (krĕ-mō-nä.) An organ-stop; the name of a superior make of violins. See Stoeving's "The Violin."

Cremorn. A reed-stop organ of 8-foot scale.

Crescéndo (It.) (krĕ-shen-dō.) A word denoting an increasing power of tone; it is often indicated by the sign, ◁.

Crescendo-zug (Ger.) (krĕ-shĕn-dō-tsoog.) The swell-box in the organ.

Crescent. A Turkish instrument made of small bells hung on an inverted crescent.

Crotchet. Old name for the quarter note.

Crom-horn (Ger.) (krōm-hŏrn.) A reed-stop in an organ. Also *Krum-horn*.

Cromorna-stop. (krō-mōr-nä.) ⎱ A reed-stop in an
Cromorne (Fr.) (krō-mōrn.) ⎰ organ.

Crooks. Small curved tubes to be added to horns, trumpets, etc., to change their pitch, and adapt them to the key of the piece in which they are to be used.

Crucifixus (Lat.) (kru-sĭ-fĭx-ŭs.) Part of the *Credo* in a Mass.

Crwth (Welsh) (krŭth.) (En. *Crowd., Crowth.*) An old Welsh instrument, having six strings resembling the violin. By some the *Crwth* is held to be the progenitor of the violin.

Csardas (Hun.) (*tsär·däs.*) Hungarian dance.

Cue. Certain small notes giving a prominent phrase of the music to serve as guide for the entrance of the player or singer after a long rest.

Cum Sancto Spiritu (Lat.) (kŭm sănk-tō spĭr-ĭ-tū.) Part of the *Gloria* in a Mass.

Cupo (It.) (*koo-pō.*) Dark, obscure.

Cycle forms, or Cyclical forms. Such forms in music as are made up of several complete forms, movements, or compositions placed in contrast with each other. The Sonata, Symphony, Suite, String-Quartet, etc., are examples.

Cymbals. Circular brass plates used in band or orchestra. They originally came from Turkey.

Cymbale (Fr.) (sähm-bäl.) } A mixture organ-stop
Cymbel (Ger.) (*tsĭm*-b'l.) } of a very acute quality of tone.

Czardas. See *Csardas.*

D

D. The second note in the diatonic scale of C; the syllable *re* is applied to this note. The major scale with two sharps in its signature. Abbreviation for " Da " or " Dal," as *D. S.* — " Dal Segno"; *D. C.* — " Da Capo."

Da (It.) (dä.) By, from, for, through, etc.

Da cápo (It.) (dä kä-pō.) *From the beginning;* an expression placed at the end of a movement to indicate that the performer must return to the first strain. In such a case the repeats indicated by dots are generally not made after *D. C.*

Da cápo al fíne (It.) (dä *kä*-pō äl *fēe*-nĕ.) } Return
Da cápo, sin' al fíne (It.) (dä *kä*-pō sĕn) to the
äl *fēe*-nĕ.) beginning and conclude with the word *Fine.*

Da cápo e pói la códa (It.) (dä *kä*-pō ā *pō*-ē lä *kō*-dä.) Begin again and then play to the *Códa.*

Da capo sin' al ségno (It.) (dä *kä*-pō sĕn äl *sän*-yō) Return to the beginning and play to the sign ⊕, after which play the *coda.*

Dal (It) (däl.)
Dall' (It.) (däll')
Dalla (It) (*däl*-lä.) } From the; by the, of the; etc.
Dalle (It) (*däl*-lĕ.)
Dallo (It.) (*däl*-lō.)

Dal ségno (It.) (dăl *săn*-yō.) *From the sign* 𝄋 A mark directing a repetition from the sign

Damper pedal. That pedal in a pianoforte which raises the dampers from the strings and allows them to vibrate freely. Its use is indicated by the abbreviation *ped.* See *Pedal.*

Dampers. A portion of the movable mechanism of the pianoforte, covered with felt; ordinarily resting on the strings to prevent undue vibration after the note is struck. The mute of any brass instrument.

Dämpfen (Ger.) (dĕm-pfĕn.) To muffle, or deaden the tone of an instrument.

Danse (Fr.) (dänhs.) A dance tune.

Danseuse (Fr.) (dänh-surse.) A female dancer.

Dánza (It.) (dän-tsä.)
Danza (Spa.) (dän-thä.) } A dance.

Dauer (Ger.) (dou-ĕr.) The length or duration of tones.

Daum (Ger.) (doum.) The thumb.

D. C. The initials of *Da Capo.*

D dur (Ger.) (dā-doer.) D Major; the key of D major.

Débile (It.) (*day*-bee-lay.)
Débole (It.) (*day*-bō-lay.) } Weak, feeble, faint.

Début (Fr.) (dä-bü.) First appearance; the first public performance.

Débutant (Fr.) (dā-bü-tănh.) } A singer or per-
Débutante (Fr.) (dā-bü-tănht.) } former who appears for the first time before the public.

Decani (Lat. pl.) (dĕ-kä-nē.) In cathedral music this term implies that the passages thus marked must be taken by the singers on the side of the choir where the *Dean* usually sits.

Decastich. A poem consisting of ten lines.

Deceptive cadence. See *Cadence, deceptive.*

Decima (Lat.) (dĕs-ĭ-mä.) A *tenth;* an interval of ten degrees in the scale; also the name of an organ-stop sounding the tenth.

Decimole. A group of ten notes of artificial value, equal to eight of the natural notes of the same denomination. See *Note, Notation.*

Decisívo (It.) (dā-tshē-zē-vō.) } In a bold and de-
Decíso (It.) (dā-tshē-zō) } cided manner.

Decke (Ger.) (dĕk-ĕ.) The sound board of a violin, violoncello, etc.; also the cover or top in those organ-stops which are *covered* or *stopped.*

46

Declamándo (It.) (day-klä-*män*-dō.) With declamatory expression.

Decrescéndo (It.) (dā-krĕ-*shen*-dō.) Gradually diminishing in power of tone $\Longrightarrow$.

Deglí (It.) (dāl-yē.) Of the.

Degree. The step between two notes; also each line and space of the staff.

In the study of Harmony each note in the scale of each key has its specific name as a *degree;* beginning with the key-note as *first degree*, and counting upwards, line and space alternately to the octave.

In reckoning intervals, however, the lowest of the two notes under consideration, no matter what its position as a degree in any particular scale (Harmonic terminology) happens to be, is reckoned *one* and we count line and space alternately up to and inclusive of the upper note. Thus *c* to *a* or *e* to *c* would both be intervals of a sixth, each including six diatonic *degrees* on the staff.

Dehnen (Ger.) (*day*-nen.) To extend, or prolong.

Del (It.) (dĕl.) Of the.

Deliberataménte (It.) (dĕ-lē-bĕ-rä-tä-*men*-tĕ.) Deliberately.

Delicataménte (It.) (dĕl-ē-kä-tä-*men*-tĕ.) }
Delicato (dĕl-ē-*kä*-tō.) } Delicately, smoothly.

Delírio (It.) (dĕ-*lē*-rē-ō.) Frenzy, excitement.

Delivery. The act of controlling the respiration and using the vocal organs so as to produce a good tone.

Dell' (It.) (dĕll.) }
Della (It.) (*dĕl*-lä.) }
Delle (It.) (*dĕl*-lĕ.) } Of the, by the, etc.
Dello (It.) (*dĕl*-lō.) }

Dem (Ger.) (dĕm) To the.

Demi (Fr.) (dĕ-*mē*.) Half.

Demi-cadence (Fr.) (dĕ-*mē* kä-*dänhs*.) A half cadence, or cadence on the dominant.

Demi-semiquaver. A 32d note $\eighthnote$ or thus ξ.

De profundis (Lat.) (dĕ-prō-*fŭn*-dĭs.) One of the seven penitential psalms.

Derivative chords. Chords derived from others by inversion.

Des (Ger.) (dĕs.) The note D flat.

Descant, Discantus (Lat.) 1. The addition of a part or parts to a tenor or subject. This art, the forerunner of modern counterpoint and harmony, grew out of the still earlier art of diaphony or the organum. In the latter the parts ran in parallel motion, generally in consecutive fifths or fourths, but in descant, oblique and contrary motion of parts began to appear as early as the eleventh or twelfth century. 2. *Descant* or *discant* is the treble or soprano voice.

Des dur (Gr.) (dĕs-doer.) D flat major.

Des moll (Ger.) (dĕs mŏll.) The key of D flat minor.

Desterita (It.) (dās-tĕr-ē-*tä*.) Dexterity.

Désto (It.) (*des*-tō.) Brisk, sprightly.

Déstra (It.) (*des*-trä.) *Right; déstra máno*, the right hand.

Détaché (Fr.) (dā-tä-shāy.) Detached, staccato. Used in violin music.

Determináto (It.) (dā-tĕr-mē-*nä*-tō.) Determined, resolute.

Détto (It.) (*dāt*-tō.) The same.

Deux (Fr.) (dü.) Two.

Development. The elaboration of a theme by making new combinations of its figures and phrases. It forms a most important part in symphony and sonata. Ger. *Durchführung*.

Devóto (It.) (dā-*vō*-tō.) Devout, religious.

Devozióne, con. (It.) (dā-vō-tsē-ō-nĕ, kŏn.) Devotion; religious feeling.

Dextra (Lat.) (*dĕx*-trä.) The right; right hand.

Di (It.) (dē.) Of, with, for, from, to.

Dia (Gr.) (*dĭ*-ä.) Through, throughout.

Diapase (Gr.) (dē-ă-*pä*-sĕ.) Diapason.

Diapason (Lat.) (dē-ă-*pä*-sŏn.) } 1. *The whole octave.*
Diapason (Eng.) (dī-ă-*pä*-sŏn.) }
2. Among musical instrument makers, a rule or scale by which they adjust the pipes of organs, the holes of flutes, etc., in order to give the proper proportion for expressing the tones and semitones. 3. The two foundation stops in an organ (sometimes called *Principal*) — the open diapason and the stopped diapason. 4. Fixed pitch; *normal diapason;* a recognized standard of pitch. See *Pitch.*

Diatonic (Gr. origin) (dē-ä-*tŏn*-ĭk.) *Naturally;* proceeding in the order of the degrees of the natural

48

scale, including tones and semi-tones, as established in the *Key of C*, or in any Key according to its *Key-signature*.

Diatonic scale. The different gradations of tone of the scale arranged in proper order in conformity to some particular key.

Diatonic scale, major. Where the semi-tones fall between the third and fourth and seventh and eighth, both in ascending and descending.

Diatonic scale, minor. That in which the semitones occur between the second and third and seventh and eighth ascending, and between the fifth and sixth and second and third descending. See *Scale*.

Dièse (Fr.) (dee-ez.) A sharp (♯).

Dièse, double (Fr.) (dee-àz, doobl.) A double sharp (𝄪).

Dies iræ (Lat.) (dee-āzē-rā.) "The Day of Wrath," the Judgment-day. A principal movement in a requiem.

Diésis (Gr. and It.) (dē-*à*y-sĭs.) } In modern music
Diésis (Fr.) (dee-ez-sĭs.) } means a *sharp*.

Difficile (It.) (dĕf-*fē*-tshē-lĕ.) Difficult.

Dignitá (It.) (dēn-yē-*tā*.) Dignity, grandeur.

Dilettánte (It.) (dē-lĕt-*tänh*-tĕ.) A lover of art; an amateur.

Diligénza, con (It.) (dē-lē-*jen*-tsä, kŏn.) In a diligent and careful manner.

Diluéndo (It.) (dē-lōō-*en*-dō.) Diminishing; a gradual dying away of the tone until it is extinct.

Diminished. This word is applied to intervals, which are less than minor or perfect intervals.

Diminished chords. Chords that have a diminished interval between their highest and lowest notes.

Diminuéndo (It.) (dē-mē-nōō-*en*-dō.) Diminishing gradually the intensity or power of the tone.

Diminution. In counterpoint this means the imitation of a given subject or theme, in notes of shorter length or duration; in opposition to *augmentation*.

Di molto (It.) (dē mŏl-tō.) *Very much;* an expression which serves to augment the meaning of the word to which it is applied.

Direct. A mark sometimes placed at the end of

a staff; a phrase or figure to indicate the note next following ().

Direct motion. Similar or parallel motion; the parts rising or falling in the same direction.

Dirge. A musical composition, either vocal or instrumental, designed to be performed at a funeral, or in commemoration of the dead.

Dirítta (It.) (dē-*rēt*-tä.) Direct; straight on, in ascending or descending intervals.

Dis (Ger.) (dēs.) The note D♯.

Discant. See *Descant.*

Discantus (Lat.) (dís-*kăn*-tŭs.) Descant.

Disciólto (It.) (di-shē-*ōl*-tō.) Skilful, dexterous.

Discord. A dissonant or inharmonious combination of sounds. In strict harmony it requires to be resolved or proceed to a concord in order to satisfy the ear.

Discord, prepared. Where the discordant note has been held over from a previous concord.

Discréto (It.) (dis-*krä*-to.) Discreetly.

Dis-dis (Ger.) (diss-diss.) D ※ also called *disis.*

Disinvólto (It.) (diz-ēn-*vōl*-tō.) } Off-
Disinvolturáto (It.) (diz-ēn-vōl-too-*rä*-tō.) } hand; bold; not forced; naturally.

Disjunct succession. Progressing by skips.

Dis moll. (Ger.) (dís-moll.) The key of D♯ minor.

Di sopra (It.) (dē *sō*-prä.) Above.

Disperáto (It.) (dēz-pĕ-*rä*-tō.) With desperation.

Dispersed harmony. Harmony in which the notes forming the various chords are separated from each other by wide intervals.

Dissonance. See *Discord.*

Distinto (It.) (dēs-*tin*-tō.) Clear; distinct.

Divertiménto (It.) (dē-vĕr-tē-*men*-tō.) A short, light composition, written in a pleasing and familiar style; a series of airs and dances introduced between the acts or at the conclusion of an opera; also, an instrumental composition like the suite, of several short movements.

Divided accompaniment. A form of accompaniment in which the intervals are taken by both hands in pianoforte playing.

Divísi (It.) (di-*vē*-zē.) Divided, separated. In orchestral parts this word implies that one-half the performers must play the upper notes and the others the lower notes. The term has a similar meaning when it occurs in vocal music.

Divotaménte (It.) (dē-vō-tä-*men*-tĕ.) } See *Devoto*.
Divóto (It.) (dē-*vō*-to.)

Dixième (Fr.) (dēz-ĭ-ãm.) The *tenth*, or octave to the third.

D moll (Ger.) (dä-môll.) The key of D minor.

Do (It.) (dō.) A syllable applied to the first note of a scale in solfaing. In the "fixed Do" system, Do is always C, but in the "movable Do," it always represents the key-note, whether that note is C or not. In the "tonic-sol-fa" system it is movable and is spelt "Doh." See *Tonic Sol-fa*, and *Aretinian Syllables*.

Doctor of Music. The highest musical degree conferred by the universities. This degree is not conferred in Germany. See *Grove's Dictionary*, article "Degrees in Music."

Doigt (Fr.) (dwä.) Finger.

Dolcan. An organ-stop of 8-foot scale, the pipes of which are of larger diameter at the top than at the bottom. The dulciana.

Dólce (It.) (*dōl*-tshĕ.) Sweetly, softly, delicately.

Dolcézza (It.) (dōl-*tshet*-zä.) Sweetness; softness of tone.

Dolciáno (It.) (dōl-tshē-*ä*-nō.) } A small bassoon,
Dolcíno (It.) (dōl-*tshē*-nō.) } formerly much used as a tenor to the oboe. A reed-stop (8 or 16-foot tone) in the organ.

Dolent (Fr.) (dō-länh.) } Sorrowful, mournful,
Dolénte (It.) (dō-*len*-tĕ.) } pathetic.

Dolenteménte (It.) (dō-län-tĕ-*men*-tĕ.) Sorrowfully, mournfully.

Dolóre (It.) (dō-*lō*-rĕ.) Grief, sorrow.

Dolorosaménte (It.) (dō-lō-rō-zä-*men*-tĕ.) } Dolor-
Doloróso (It.) (dō-lō-*rō*-zō.) } ously, sorrowfully, sadly.

Dominant. The name applied by theorists to the *fifth* note of the scale.

Dominant chord. A chord founded on the dominant or *fifth* note of the scale.

Dominant harmony. Harmony on the dominant or *fifth* of the key.

Dona nóbis pacem (Lat.) (*dō-nä nō-bĭs pät-sĕm.*) The concluding movement of the Mass.

Dónna (It.) (*dŏn-nä.*) Lady; applied to the principal female singers in an opera.

Dópo (It.) (*dō-pō.*) After.

Doppel (Ger.) (*dŏp-p'l.*) Double.

Doppel-Be (Ger.) (*dŏp-p'l bā.*) A double flat (♭♭); lowering a note two half-steps.

Doppelgriffe (Ger.) (*dŏp-p'l-grĭf-fĕ.*) Double-stop on the violin, etc.

Doppelkreuz (Ger.) (*dŏp-p'l-kroitz.*) A double sharp ✕ or ×, raising a note two half-steps.

Dóppio (It.) (*dŏp-pē-ō.*) Double; twofold; sometimes indicating that octaves are to be played.

Dóppio moviménto (It.) (*dŏp-pē-ō mō-vē-mĕn-tō.*) Double-movement, of time, that is, *twice as fast.*

Dóppio pedále (It.) (*dŏp-pē-ō pĕ-dä-lĕ.*) Playing two notes on the pedals of organ at same time, generally octaves.

Dot. A mark which, when placed *after* a note, increases its duration one-half. When the dot is placed *over* a note it signifies that the note is to be played *staccáto.*

Double (Fr.) (dooblh.) The old name for a *variation;* used by Handel, Scarlatti, etc.

Double bar. Two strokes drawn down through the staff, to divide one strain or movement from another. The heavy double bar terminates the piece finally.

Double-bass. See *Contra-bass.*

Double-bassoon. See *Contra-bassoon;* also, a 16 or 32-foot organ reed-stop, of smaller scale and softer tone than the double trumpet.

Double counterpoint. A counterpoint which admits of the parts being inverted.

Double diapason. An organ-stop tuned an octave below the diapasons. It is called a 16-foot stop on the manuals; on the pedals it is a 32-foot stop.

Double dot. Two dots placed after a note increase its duration by three-fourths of its original value.

Double flat. A character (♭♭) which, placed before a note, signifies that it is lowered two half-steps.

Double note. A breve; a note twice the length of a whole note.

Double quartet. A composition written for eight instruments or voices.

Double reed. The mouth-piece of the hautboy bassoon, etc., formed of two pieces of cane joined together.

Double sharp. A character which when placed before a note, raises that note two half-steps. It is usually written as follows: × or ×.

Double stem. When two voice parts written on one staff sound the same note in unison, the note is stemmed up and down.

Double-stopped diapason. An organ-stop of 16-foot tone on the manuals; the pipes are stopped or covered at the top.

Double stopping. The stopping of two strings simultaneously with the fingers in violin, etc., playing.

Double tierce. An organ-stop tuned a tenth above the diapasons, or a major third above the principal.

Double-time. A time in which every measure is composed of two equal parts.

Double-tonguing. A method of articulating quick notes used by flute and brass instrument players.

Doucement (Fr.) (doos-mänh.) Sweetly, softly, pleasingly.

Douleur (Fr.) (doo-lŭr.) Grief, sorrow, pathos.

Doux (Fr.) (doo.) Sweet, soft, gentle.

Down bow sign. A sign used in violin music indicating that the bow is to be drawn down; thus, ⌐

Doxology. A form of praise sung in divine service, usually at the close of a prayer, psalm, or hymn; the Gloria Patri, used at the end of the psalms in the Christian Church; also any metrical form of the same.

Drammático (It.) (dräm-mä-tē-kō.) Dramatic.

Draw-stops. In an organ, stops placed on each side of the rows of keys by moving which the player opens or closes the stops within the organ.

Drei (Ger.) (drī.) Three.

Dreifach (Ger.) (drī-fäkh.) Three-fold, triple.

Dreist (Ger.) (drīst.) Brave, bold, confident.

Drítta (It.) (drĭt-tä.) } Right; máno drítta, the
Drítto (It.) (drĭt-tō.) } right hand.

Drítte (Ger.) (drĭt-tĕ.) Third.

Droite (Fr.) (drwät.) Right; main droite, the right hand.

Drone. The largest of the three tubes of the bagpipe. It only sounds one deep note, which answers as a perpetual bass to every tune. *Drone-bass,* a bass on the tonic, or tonic and dominant, which is persistent throughout a movement or piece, as in the *Musette.*

Drum. An instrument of percussion formed of a cylinder made of thin wood or metal, over each end of which is drawn a skin tightened by means of cords. There are three kinds of drums: 1. The bass drum, held laterally and played with a stuffed knob drumstick. 2. The side-drum having two heads, the upper one only being played upon by two sticks of wood; the lower head has occasionally strings of catgut stretched over its surface, and then it is called a *snare-drum.* 3. The kettledrum, always employed in pairs or threes.

Drum, kettle. A drum consisting of a cup-shaped shell of copper, over which a parchment head is stretched. It is used as an instrument of definite pitch, tuning keys being provided to raise or lower the sound by tightening or loosening the parchment head. Two or three drums are used and between them have a compass of

. See Prout's "The Orchestra"

or Arthur Elson's "Orchestral Instruments."

D. S. The initials of *Dal Segno.*

Dúe córde (It.) (*doo-ĕ kōr-dĕ.*) Two strings. See *A due Corde.*

Dúe pedáli (It.) (*doo-ĕ pĕ-dä-lē.*) The two pedals are to be used.

Duet. A composition for two voices or instruments.

Dúe volte (It.) (*doo-ĕ vōl-tĕ.*) Twice.

Dulciana-stop. An 8-foot organ-stop of a soft and sweet quality of tone.

Dulciana principal. A 4-foot organ-stop of delicate tone.

Dulcimer. An instrument usually of a triangular shape, the strings of which are struck with little rods held in each hand.

Dumka (Bohem.) (*doom-kah.*) A dirge, an elegy, or a funeral song. It has been introduced into the symphony by Dvorák. It possibly gave rise to the early English slow dance called the *dump* or *dumpe*, and mentioned by Shakespeare.

Dump or Dumpe. The name of an old dance in slow time with a peculiar rhythm, usually in $\frac{4}{4}$ rhythm. See Elson's "Shakespeare in Music."

Dúo (It.) (doo-ō.) Two; in two parts; a composition for two voices or instruments; a duet.

Duodécima (It.) (doo-ō-dĕ-tshē-mä.) The twelfth note from the tonic; also an organ-stop tuned a twelfth above the diapasons.

Duólo (It.) (dwō-lō.) Sorrow, sadness, grief.

Duplication. Doubling; where one or more of the intervals of a chord are repeated in different parts.

Dur (Ger.) (doer.) *Major*, in speaking of keys and modes; as C *dur*, C *major*.

Dur (Fr.) (dür.) Hard; harsh of tone.

Duraménte (It.) (doo-rä-*men*-tĕ.) Harshly; roughly; also meaning that the passage is to be played in a firm, bold style and strongly accented.

Durchspielen (Ger.) (*doorkh*-spē-l'n.) To play to the end.

Dúro (It.) (doo-ro.) Rude, harsh.

Düster (Ger.) (*düs*-tĕr.) Gloomy.

Dynamics. This term in music has reference to expression and the different degrees of power to be applied to notes.

E

E called in France and Italy *mi;* the third note of the scale of C. Name of a string on the violin and guitar.

E. Ed (It.) And.

Ebollimento or Ebollizione (It.) (eh-bol-litz-ee-*o*-neh.) Boiling over; sudden expression of passion.

Eccheggiáre (It.) (ĕk-kĕd-jē-*ä*-rĕ.) To resound, to echo.

Ecclésia (It.) (ĕk-*klä*-zē-ä.) Church.

Ecclesiastical modes. See *Gregorian modes.*

Échelle (Fr.) (ā-shĕll.) The scale, or gamut.

Écho (Fr.) (ā-kō.) ⎱ In music, this term means
Eco (It.) (*ä*-kō.) ⎰ a repetition, or imitation

of a previous passage, with much less force **than** the original passage.

Echo cornet. An organ-stop, the pipes of which are of small scale, with a light, delicate tone. It is usually placed in the swell.

Éclat (Fr.) (á-klä.) With dash; brilliancy; an outburst.

Eclogue or Eglogue (from Greek, to select.) A pastoral; a poem, or song, in which shepherds and shepherdesses are the actors.

École (Fr.) (ā-kōl.) A school; a method or course of instruction; a style formed by some eminent artist.

École de chant (Fr.) (ā-kōl dŭh shänh.) A singing-school.

Écossais (Fr.) (ā-kŏs-sā.) } Scotch; a dance, tune
Écossaise (Fr.) (ā-kŏs-sāz.) } or air, in the Scotch style. A contra-dance of lively tempo in $\frac{2}{4}$ rhythm.

Edel (Ger.) ($\bar{a}y$-del.) Noble and distinguished.

E dur (Ger.) (ā doer.) The key of E major.

Effétto (It.) (ĕf-*fet*-to.) Effect; the effect of music upon an audience.

Eguále (It.) (ā-*gwä*-lĕ.) Equal; even; alike, also applied to a composition for several voices or instruments of one kind, as, male voices only, trombones only.

Egualménte (It.) (ā-gwäl-*men*-tĕ.) Equally, evenly, alike.

Eighth. An octave.

Eilen (Ger.) (ī-len.) To hasten; accelerate; go faster . . . *Eilend*, hastening; *accelerando, stringendo* . . . *Eilig*, hasty; in a hurried style; rapid; swift.

Ein (Ger.) (eyn.) }
Eine (Ger.) (*eyn*-ĕ.) } A, an, one.

Einen (Ger.) (*eyn*-en.) A, one.

Einfach (Ger.) (*eyn*-fäkh.) Simple, plain, ornamented.

Eingang (Ger.) (*eyn*-gäng.) Introduction, preface, prelude.

Einhalt (Ger.) (*eyn*-hält.) A pause.

Einheit (Ger.) (*eyn*-hīt.) Unity.

Einigkeit (Ger.) (*eyn*-nig-kīt.) Concord, harmony, unity.

Einklang (Ger.) (*eyn*-klăng.) Consonance, harmony.

Einlage (Ger.) (*eyn*-lähge.) An inserted piece, an interpolation.

Einleitung (Ger.) (*eyn*-lī-toong.) Introduction, prelude.

Einmal (Ger.) (*eyn*-mäl.) Once.

Einschlafen (Ger.) (*eyn*-shlä-f'n.) To die away, to slacken the time and diminish the tone; to fall asleep.

Einschmeichelnd (Ger.) (*eyn*-shmī-khĕlnd.) Flattering, insinuating.

Einstimmen (Ger.) (*eyn*-stĭm-m'n.) To agree in tune; to be concordant; to join in.

Eintönig (Ger.) (*eyn*-tô-nĭg.) Monotonous.

Eintracht (Ger.) (*eyn*-träkht.) Concord, unity.

Eintretend (Ger.) (*eyn*-trä-tĕnd.) Entering, beginning.

Eintritt (Ger.) (*eyn*-trĭt.) Entrance, entry, beginning.

Eis (Ger.) (āis.) The note E sharp.

Éisis. E double sharp.

Eisteddfod (ais-*tedh*-vōd.) (Welsh.) A bardic congress; an assemblage of bards.

Elegánte (It.) (ā-lä-*gän*-tĕ.) Elegant, graceful.

Elegánza (It.) (ā-lä-*gän*-tsä.) Elegance, grace.

Elegía (It.) (ā-lä-*jē*-ä.) An elegy, or monody music of a mournful or funereal character.

Elegiáco (It.) (ā-lä-jē-ä-kō.) Mournful, plaintive.

Elegy. A mournful or plaintive poem, or a funeral song.

Elementary music. Exercises and studies specially adapted to beginners in the study of music.

Elevation. A motet or organ piece played or sung, in the Catholic service, during the elevation of the Host, in the Mass.

Eleváto (It.) (ā-lä-*vä*-tō.) Elevated, exalted, sublime.

Elevazióne (It.) (ā-lä-vä-tsē-ō-nĕ.) Elevation, grandeur.

Eleventh. An interval measuring eleven diatonic degrees.

Embellishments. See *Grace*.

Embouchure (Fr.) (änh-boo-shür.) The mouthpiece of a flute, oboe, horn, or other wind instrument. The part of the lips brought in contact with the mouth-piece; also called *Lip*.

E moll (Ger.) (ā mŏll.) The key of E minor.

Emozióne (It.) (ā-mo-tse-ō-nĕ.) Emotion, **agitation.**

Empfindung (Ger.) (ĕmp-*fĭn*-doong.) Emotion, passion, feeling.

Emphase (Ger.) (ĕm-*fä*-zĕ.) Emphasis.

Emphatique (Fr.) (änh-fä-tēk.) } Emphatical.
Emphatisch (Ger.) (ĕm-*fä*-tĭsh.) }

En (Fr.) (änh.) In.

Encore (Fr. ang-kor; It. *Ancora*.) Again; a demand for the reappearance of a performer; the piece sung or played on the reappearance of the performer.

Ende (Ger.) (ĕnd-ĕ.) End; conclusion; concluding piece.

Energicaménte (It.) (ā-nair-jē-kä-*men*-tĕ.) Energetically, forcibly.

Enérgico (It.) (ā-*nair*-jē-kō.) Energetic, vigorous, forcible.

Énergique (Fr.) (ā-nair-zhēk.) } Energetic; with
Energisch (Ger.) (en-*ār*-ghĭsh.) } emphasis.

Enfático (It.) (ĕn-*fä*-tē-kō.) Emphatical; with earnestness.

Enfler (Fr.) (änh-flā.) To swell; to increase the tone.

English fingering. In pianoforte music the use of a sign (×) to designate the thumb, in distinction from the German fingering, where the thumb is designated as the first finger. Erroneously called *American* fingering. See *Fingering*.

English horn. See *Cor Anglais*.

Enharmonic. In modern music it means writing the *same sound* in two different ways when changing from one key to another, thus: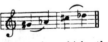

Enharmonic change. A passage in which the notation is changed, but the same keys of the instrument are employed:

etc.

Ensemble (Fr.) (änh-*sänh*-bl.) *Together; the whole,* applied to concerted music when the whole is given with perfect smoothness of style. It means precision of attack; unity of shading. A *morceau d'ensemble* is a composition for two or more parts, more especially quintets, sextets, septets, etc., in an opera, oratorio, or similar work.

Entr' acte (Fr.) (änh-tr' äkt.) Between the acts; music played between the acts of a drama.

Entscheidung (Ger.) (ĕnt-*shī*-doong.) Decision, determination.

Entschlafen (Ger.) (ĕnt-*shlä*-f'n.) See *Einschlafen*.

Entschlossen (Ger.) (ĕnt-*shlōs*-s'n.) Determined, resolute.

Entschluss (Ger.) (ĕnt-*shlooss*.) Resolution.

Entusiasmo (It.) (ĕn-too-zē-*äs*-mō.) Enthusiasm.

Entwurf (Ger.) (ĕnt-*voorf*.) Sketch; outline of a composition. The exposition of a fugue.

Enunciáre (It.) (ā-noon-tshē-*ä*-rĕ.) To enunciate; to declare; to proclaim.

Epico (It.) (*ā*-pē-kō.) Epic, heroic.

Epilogue. A speech or short poem addressed to the spectators by one of the actors, after the conclusion of the play. A concluding piece.

Episode. An incidental narrative or digression. A portion of a composition not founded upon the principal subject or theme. An accessory part of a composition, as contrasted with the themes and their development. An intermediate division. The parts of a fugue that intervene between the repetitions of the main theme.

Equábile (It.) (ĕ-*quä*-bē-lĕ.) Equal, alike, uniform.

Equabilménte (It.) (ĕ-quä-bēl-*men*-tĕ.) Equally, smoothly, evenly.

Equal counterpoint. A composition in two, three, four, or more parts, consisting of notes of equal duration.

Equal temperament. That equalization, or tempering, of the different sounds of an octave which renders them all of an equal degree of purity; the imperfection being divided among the whole. The division of the octave into *twelve equal semitones*. See *Temperament*.

Erhaben (Ger.) (er-*hä*-b'n.) Elevated; sublime; in a lofty and exalted style.

Erklingen (Ger.) (er-*klĭng*-ĕn.) To ring; to resound.

Ermattet (Ger.) (er-*mäh*-tet.) Wearied, exhausted.

Ermunterung (Ger.) (er-*moon*-tĕ-roong.) Animation, excitement.

Ernst (Ger.) (*airnst*.) } Earnest; serious; in
Ernsthaft (Ger.)(*āirnst*-häft.) } a grave and earnest style.

Erntelied (Ger.) (*ārn*-tĕ-lēd.) Harvest song.

Eroica (It.) (ĕ-*rō*-ē-kä.) Heroic.

Erotic (ĕr-*ot*-ĭk.) An amorous composition, a love song.

Erst (Ger.) (ārst.) First.

Erweckung (Ger.) (er-*vĕk*-oong.) Animation, excitement.

Erweitert (Ger.) (er-*vī*-tert.) Expanded, developed, extended.

Es (Ger.) The note E flat.

Es dur (Ger.) (ess dœr.) The key of E flat major.

Es es (Ger.) (ess ess.) The note E double-flat (E♭♭).

Esitaménto (It.) (ā-zee-tä-*men*-tō.) Hesitation.

Es moll (Ger.) (ess mōll.) The key of E flat minor.

Espagnol (Fr.) (ĕs-pän-*yōl*.) } Spanish; in
Espagnuólo (It.) (ĕs-pän-yoo-ō-lō.) } the Spanish style.

Espirándo (It.) (ĕs-pee-*rän*-do.) Breathing deeply; gasping.

Espressióne (It.) (ĕs-pres-sē-ō-nĕ.) Expression, feeling.

Espressívo (It.) (ĕs-pres-*see*-vō.) Expressive; to be played or sung with expression.

Estínto (It.) (ĕs-*tēn*-tō.) Becoming extinct; dying away in time and strength of tone; extinguished.

Estravagánte (It.) (ĕs-träv-ä-*gän*-tĕ.) Extravagant; a fanciful and extravagant work.

Estremaménte (It.) (ĕs-trä-mä-*men*-tĕ.) Extremely.

Esultazióne (It.) (ay-zool-tät-sē-ō-nĕ.) Exultation.

Et (Lat. ĕt; Fr. ā.) And.

Et incarnatus (Lat.) (ĕt ĭn-kär-*nä*-tüs.) A portion of the Credo, in the Mass.

Et resurrexit (Lat.) (ĕt ray-zur-*rex*-it.) A brilliant part of the Credo, in the Mass.

Etta (It.) (ĕt-tä.) } Little; an Italian final diminutive; as *Trombétta*, a little
Etto (It.) (ĕt-tō.) } trumpet, *Adagietto*, a little adagio.

Étude (Fr.) (ā-*tüd*.) A study; an exercise. An étude usually furnishes technical difficulties of

some description. *Étude de concert* is a very difficult study for concert performance. Chopin's *Études* are among the most famous.

Et vitam (Lat.) (ĕt-*vēe*-tăm.) A part of the Credo, in the Mass.

Etwas (Ger.) (*ĕt*-väs.) Some; somewhat; a little.

Euphonium. A modern Sax-horn; see *Baritone.*

Euphony. Agreeable sound; an easy, smooth enunciation of sounds.

Exaltation (Fr.) (ĕx-ăl-tä-sē-ŏnh.) In an exalted, dignified manner.

Exercise. A musical composition calculated to improve the technique of the performer. Exercises for the purpose of imparting instruction in musical execution.

Expression. That quality in a composition or performance which appeals to our feelings, taste or judgment displayed in rendering a composition and imparting to it the sentiment of the author. *Expression marks* are signs, words or phrases, written against the music to direct the performer in giving its proper expression.

F

F. The fourth note in the diatonic scale of C. It was the note first used as a clef sign to give definite pitch to the mediæval notation (Neumes) because " small f " was a good medium note in the baritone voice in the chants, which were therefore almost always composed around this note. f is also the abbreviation of *Forte;* ff, *fortissimo;* fff, *fortississimo:* ffff is rarely used.

Fa. The name applied to F in France and Italy; the fourth note of the syllables used in solfeggio. In the " fixed do " system it is always F; in the " movable do " it is the fourth note of *any* diatonic scale. In " Tonic sol-fa " it is spelled " Fah."

Fabliau (Fr.) (fah-blee-oh.) A fable.

Facile (Fr.) (fä-sēl.) ⎰
Facile (It.) (*fä*-chee-lay.) ⎱ Light, easy.

Facilità (It.) (fä-tshēl-ē-tä.) Facility.

Fackel-tanz (Ger.) (*fäk*-'l-tänts.) Dance with torches.

Fagott (Ger.) (fä-*gŏtt*.) A bassoon.

Fagótto (It.) (fä-*gôt*-tō.) A bassoon; also an organ-stop.

Fagótto contra (It.) (fä-*gôt*-tō *kôn*-trä.) The contra-bassoon.

Faiblement (Fr.) (fäy-bl-mänh.) Feebly, weakly.

False accent. When the accent is removed from the first beat of the measure to the second or fourth, it is called *false* accent.

False relation. When a note which has occurred in one chord is found chromatically altered in the followed chord, but in a *different part*.

Falsetto. The male head-voice as distinguished from the chest-voice. A false or artificial voice; that part of a person's voice that lies above its natural compass.

Fandángo (Spa.) (fän-*dän*-gō.) A dance much used in Spain, in ¾ or ⅜ time, generally accompanied with castanets and having a strong emphasis upon the second beat of each measure.

Fanfare (Fr.) (fänh-fär.) A short, lively, loud and warlike piece of music, composed for trumpets and kettledrums. A flourish of trumpets or hunting-horns.

Fantaisie (Fr.) (făn-tä-zēe.) ⎫ *Fancy*, imagination,
Fantasía (It.) (fän-tä-*zēe*-ä.) ⎬ caprice; a species
Fantasie (Ger.) (fän-tä-zēe.) ⎭ of music in which the composer yields to his imagination and gives free scope to his ideas, without regard to restrictions in *form*.

Fantasiren (Ger.) (fän-tä-*zēe*-r'n.) To improvise; to play extemporaneously.

Fantástico (It.) (fän-*täs*-tē-kō.) Fantastical; whimsical; capricious in relation to style, modulation, etc.

Farandole (Fr.) (fă-ränh-dōl.) A lively dance in ⅜ or ¼ time, peculiar to Provence.

Fársa (It.) (*fär*-sä.) Farce.

Fastosaménte (It.) (fäs-tō-zä-*men*-tĕ.) Pompously, proudly.

Fastóso (It.) (fäs-*tō*-zō.) Proudly; stately; in a lofty and pompous style.

F clef. The bass clef; a character placed on the fourth line of the staff so that the two dots are in the third and fourth spaces. See *Clefs*.

F dur (Ger.) (f doer.) The key of F major.

Feier (Ger.) (*fī*-ĕr.) Festival, celebration.

Feierlich (Ger.) (*fī-ĕr-līkh.*) Solemn, festive.

Férma (It.) (*fār*-mä.) Firm, resolute, steady.

Fermaménte (It.) (fär-mä-*men*-tĕ.) Firmly, steadily.

Fermáta (It.) (fār-*mä*-tä.) } A pause or hold
Fermáte (Ger.) (fār-*mä*-tĕ.) } marked thus, ⌒. Its length can be varied by the words, *lunga* (long), *piccola* (a little), *G. P.* (*grosse pause*, great pause), and other signs. Over a double bar it usually signifies the end of the composition.

Fermáto (It.) (fār-*mä*-tō.) Firmly, steadily, resolutely.

Férmo (It.) (*fār*-mō.) Firm, resolute.

Feróce (It.) (fā-rō-tshĕ.) Fierce; with an expression of ferocity.

Ferocità (It.) (fā-rō-tshē-*tä*.) Fierceness, roughness.

Fertig (Ger.) (*fĕr*-tĭg.) Quick, nimble, dexterous.

Fervénte (It.) (fār-*ven*-tĕ.) Fervent, ardent.

Férvido (It.) (*fār*-vē-dō.) Fervent, vehement.

Fes (Ger.) (fĕs.) The note F flat.

Fest (Ger.) A festival; firm; steady. *Music fest*, a musical festival.

Festiglich (Ger.) (*fĕs*-tĭg-līkh.) Firmly, steadily.

Festivaménte (It.) (fĕs-tē-vä-*men*-tĕ.) Gayly, brilliantly.

Festívo (It.) (fes-*tē*-vō.) Merry, cheerful, gay.

Festlich (Ger.) (*fĕst*-līkh.) Festive, solemn.

Festóso (It.) (fes-*tō*-zō.) Merry, cheerful, gay.

Feuer (Ger.) (*foi*-ĕr.) Fire, ardor, passion.

Feurig (Ger.) (*foi*-rĭg.) Fiery, ardent, passionate.

F holes. The sound holes on a violin are so called because of their resemblance to an *f*.

Fiácco (It.) (fē-*äk*-kō.) Feeble, weak, languishing.

Fiáto (It.) (fē-*ä*-tō.) The breath; the voice.

Fiducia (It.) (fē-*doo*-tshē-ä.) Confidence.

Field music. Music for military instruments, martial music. Fife and drum.

Fieraménte (It.) (fē-ĕr-ä-*men*-tĕ.) Proudly, vehemently, boldly.

Fiéro (It.) (fē-*ä*-rō.) Bold, energetic, proudly.

Fife. A small, shrill-toned flute, used only in martial music, together with drums. It has six holes and from one to six keys — compass about An organ-stop of 2-foot pitch; a piccolo-stop.

Fifteenth. An interval measuring fifteen diatonic degrees. Also an organ-stop tuned two octaves above the diapasons, and of 2-foot pitch.

Fifth. An interval measuring five diatonic degrees.

Figuration. An ornamental treatment of a passage; a mixture of concords and discords.

Figuráto (It.) (fē-goo-*rä*-tō.) Figured florid.

Figured. A free and florid melody.

Figured bass. A bass with figures placed over or under the notes to indicate the harmony. See *Thorough bass.*

Filár la vóce (It.) (fē-lär lä *vō*-tshě.) To spin out; to prolong the tone; gradually augmenting and diminishing the sound of the voice.

Fin al (It.) (fē näl.) End at; play as far as.

Finále (It.) (fi-*nä*-lě.) Final; concluding; the last piece of any act of an opera or of a concert; or, the last movement of a sonata or symphony, etc.

Fíne (It.) (*fee*-nay.) The end; the termination.

Finement (Fr.) (feen-mänh.) Finely, acutely.

Fingering. 1. The method of applying the fingers to the keys, strings, or holes, of different instruments. 2. The figures which are written in music to show the performer which finger to use in sounding a note. (See *English fingering.*) In Germany, as early as the time of Bach, the figures were used as they are to-day — 1, 2, 3, 4. 5.

Fingering, American. The use of the sign (×) to indicate the thumb in pianoforte playing, in distinction from the German or foreign fingering, in which the thumb is called the first finger.

Fingering, foreign. } A method of fingering
Fingering, German. } piano music which designates the thumb as the first finger.

Finger-satz (Ger.) (*fĭng*-ěr-sätz.) Fingering.

Fino al (It.) (fē-nō äl.) See *Fin al.*

Fioritúre (It.) (fē-ō-rē-*too*-rě.) } Literally, *little flowers;*
Fioritúri (It.) (fē-ō-rē-*too*-rē.) } graces and embellishments in singing.

Fis (Ger.) (fĭs.) The note F sharp *Fis-is.* F double sharp.

Fis dur (Ger.) (fĭs doer.) The key of F sharp major.

Fis moll (Ger.) (fĭs-mŏll.) The key of F sharp minor.

Fixed syllables. Vocal syllables which do not

change with the change of key. The Italians and French use fixed syllables. The *fixed-Do* system is that in which the tone C and all its chromatic derivatives (C♯, C×, and ♭ C♭♭) are called *Do*, D and its derivatives *Re*, etc., in whatever key or harmony they may appear.

Fixed-tone instruments. The piano, organ and harp have a fixed scale of steps and half-steps where no difference can be made in pitch between sharp and flat notes, for instance C♯ and D♭, which is possible and sometimes indulged in on the violin and other fingered string instruments. See *Temperament.*

Flageolet (Fr.) (flä-zhĕ-ō-lā.) ⎱ 1. An instrument
Flageolet (Ger.) (flä-ghĕ-ō-*lĕt.*) ⎰ similar to the flute in construction, but played through a small bone or ivory mouth-piece (artificial *embouchure*) which renders the tone shrill and unsuited for combination with other instruments. It is comparatively easy to play. The compass is slightly over two octaves extending from about " g " on treble staff upwards. The flageolet is analogous to the *flûte á bec.* 2. An organ stop of 2-foot tone and wooden pipes.

Flageolet tones. See *Harmonics.*

Flat (Ger., *Be;* Fr., *Bémol;* It., *Bemolle.*) The sign ♭, which lowers the pitch of the note following it by a semi-tone. It came originally from the letter *b*, as its shape and its foreign names indicate. See *Chromatic signs.*

Flat, double. A character composed of two flats which lowers a note two semi-tones, (♭♭).

Fláuto (It.) (flä-*oo*-tō.) A flute. Flauto coupled with *amabile, amoroso, di Pan, dolce, grave, traverso,* etc., constitutes names of various organ stops of generally soft and agreeable tone.

Flautóne (It.) (flä-oo-*tō*-nĕ.) A 16-foot pedal-stop in an organ, of soft tone.

Fláuto píccolo (It.) (flä-*oo*-tō *pik*-kō-lō.) An octave flute, a small flute of very shrill tone. See *Piccolo.*

Fláuto transverso (It.) (flä-*oo*-tō träns-*vāir*-sō.) ⎱
Fláuto travérso (It.) (flä-*oo*-tō trä-*vāir*-sō.) ⎰ The old designation of the flute now in use (blown at the side) in contradistinction to the *flûte à bec,* flageolet, recorder, etc., blown through a mouth-piece affixed to the end. The so-called

German flute. The name is also applied to an organ-stop.

Flébile (It.) (*flā-bē-lĕ.*) Mournful, sad, doleful.

Flessíbile (It.) (*flĕs-see-bē-lĕ.*) Flexible; pliant.

Florid. Ornamental, figured, embellished.

Florid counterpoint. Free counterpoint.

Flourish. A fanfare of trumpets or brass instruments.

Flüchtig (Ger.) (*flükh-tĭg.*) Lightly, nimbly.

Flügel (Ger.) (*flü-g'l.*) A grand piano, so called because it is shaped like a "wing," or "flügel."

Flügelhorn. Similar to the cornet, but of larger caliber and bell. The tone is soft and velvety and best adapted to sustained, expressive melodies.

Fluit. (Dut.) (floit.) } A flute.
Fluta (Lat.) (*floo-tä.*) }

Flute. A well-known wind-instrument, generally made of wood, but sometimes of metal, consisting of a tube closed at one end and being furnished with holes and keys. It is also called *Traverse flute*, *German flute*, and *D flute*. It was greatly improved by Theobald Boehm about 1834, and flutes with his system of keys attached are also called *Boehm flutes* or *concert flutes*. The usual compass of the flute is: although the instrument may, exceptionally, have an added semi-tone above and below. It is generally a non-transposing instrument, although transposing flutes are sometimes used in military bands. The *piccolo* or octave flute sounds an octave higher than the ordinary flute. Consult Prout's "Orchestra" and A. Elson's "Orchestral Instruments and their Use."

Flute. An organ-stop of the diapason species, the tone of which resembles that of the flute.

Flûte à bec (Fr.) (flüt ä bĕk.) *Flute with a beak;* the old English flute, with a lip or *beak;* it was blown at the end. The *Recorders* used in England in the Elizabethan era.

Flute, Boehm (bôm.) See *Boehm Flute.*

Flute-work. In the organ, the *flute-work* includes all flue-stops not belonging to the *principal-work* and *gedackt-work*, as well as various modifications of these two groups.

F moll (Ger.) (ĕf mōll.) The key of F minor.

Fois (Fr.) (fwä.) Time.

Foot. 1. A certain number of syllables constituting a distinct metrical element in a verse. In very old English music it was a kind of drone accompaniment to a song which was sustained by another singer. 2. That part of an organ-pipe below the mouth. 3. The unit of measure in organ-pipes. An open pipe 8-foot long sounds, and if a series of organ-pipes begin with this tone given by such a pipe, we call the series "8-foot tone." Any stop sounding its actual pitch (as a piano-key would do) is called "8-foot." If sounding an octave higher, "4-foot," two octaves higher, "2-foot," an octave lower "16-foot," etc. The sound-waves of being eight feet long, of the octave lower sixteen feet, the octave higher four feet, etc.

Forlána (It.) (fŏr-lä-nä.) ⎱ A lively Venetian
Forlane (Fr.) (fŏr-län.) ⎰ dance in $\frac{6}{8}$ time, used by the gondoliers. It is introduced in Ponchielli's "La Gioconda."

Form. Although modern music has become very vague in its shapes and frequently eludes analysis, yet there is in most music a definite architecture that can be studied as readily as the shape of a building.

Fórte (It.) (fŏr-tĕ.) Loud, strong.

Fortement (Fr.) (fŏrt-mänh.) ⎱ Loudly, power-
Forteménte (It.) (fŏr-tĕ-men-tĕ.) ⎰ fully, vigorously.

Fortézza (It.) (fŏr-tet-zä.) Force, power, strength.

Fórte-piáno (It.) (fŏr-tĕ-pē-ä-nō.) Attack the note strongly, but diminish instantly.

Fórte possíbile (It.) (fŏr-tĕ-pŏs-sē-bē-lĕ.) As loud as possible.

Fortíssimo (It.) (fŏr-tēs-sē-mō.) Very loud.

Fortsetzung (Ger.) (fŏrt-sĕt-soong.) A continuation.

Fórza (It.) (fŏrt-sä.) Force, strength, power.

Forzándo (It.) (fŏr-tsän-dō.) ⎱ Forced; laying a
Forzáto (It.) (fŏr-tsä-tō.) ⎰ stress upon one note or chord; sometimes marked ∧ or >.

Fourth. An interval measuring four diatonic degrees.

Française (Fr.) (fränh-săyz.) 1. A graceful dance in ¾ time. 2. In the French style.

Franchézza (It.) (frän-*ket*-zä.) Freedom, confidence, boldness.

Freddaménte (It.) (fred-dä-*men*-tĕ.) Coldly; without animation.

Freddézza (It.) (frĕd-*de*-tsä.) Coldness, frigidity.

Free composition. In a free style; a composition not in strict accordance with the rules of musical form.

Free reed. A reed-stop in an organ, in which the tongue by a rapid vibratory motion to and fro produces the sound. The tone of a *free* reed is smooth and free from rattling, but not usually so strong as that of the *beating* reed.

Frei (Ger.) (frī.) Free; unrestrained as to style.

French horn. See *Horn*.

French Sixth. One form of an augmented sixth; a chord composed of a major third, augmented fourth, and augmented sixth.

Frescaménte (It.) (frĕs-kä-*men*-tĕ.) } Freshly, vig-
Frésco (It.) (*frĕs*-kō.) } orously, lively.

Frétta (It.) (*fret*-tä.) Increasing the time; accelerating the movement.

Frets. Narrow strips of wood, ivory, or metal, set across the fingerboard of mandolin, banjo, guitar, etc., to mark the exact points for "stopping" the strings and serving as temporary bridges to render the tone of "plucked" strings more brilliant.

Freudig (Ger.) (*froy*-dĭg.) Joyfully.

Frisch (Ger.) (frĭsh.) Freshly, briskly, lively.

Fröhlich (Ger.) (*frö*-lĭkh.) Joyous, gay.

Frosch (Ger.) (frōsh.) Literally *Frog*. The lower part or nut of a violin bow.

Frühlingslied (Ger.) (*frü*-lĭngs-lēd.) Spring song.

F-schlüssel (Ger.) (ĕf-*shlüs*-s'l.) The F or bass clef.

Fúga (It.) (*foo*-gä.) A *flight;* a chase. See *Fugue*.

Fugara (Lat.) (foo-*gä*-rä.) An organ-stop of the gamba species.

Fugáto (It.) (foo-*gä*-tō.) In the style of a fugue.

Fuge (Ger.) (*foo*-ghĕ.) } A fugue.
Fugha (It.) (*foo*-gä.) }

Fughétta (It.) (foo-*get*-tä.) A short fugue.

Fugitive pieces. Ephemeral compositions.

Fugue (fūg.) A term derived from the Latin word *fuga*, a flight. It is a composition in the strict style, in which a subject is proposed by one part and answered by other parts, according to certain rules. A fugue may be strict or free, according to the style of its treatment. Fugues differ greatly in their construction, but in one point they are all alike; every fugue is a contrapuntal development of the subject which is announced quite alone at the beginning. Most fugues use more than this material; they develop the entire *exposition*. This exposition is made up of: 1st. The subject, which is a figure or phrase, *not* a complete melody. 2d. The answer, which is the subject reproduced on the degree of the dominant, either above or below. 3d. The counter-subject, which is a contrasted phrase, accompanying the subject or the answer, from the entrance of the second voice. See Prout's "Fugue" and "Fugal Analysis."

Fugue, double. A fugue on two subjects.

Full. For all the voices of instruments.

Full anthem. An anthem in four or more parts, without verses or solo passages: to be sung by the whole choir in chorus.

Full orchestra. An orchestra in which all the orchestra stringed and wind instruments are employed.

Full organ. An organ with all its registers or stops in use.

Full score. A complete score of all the parts of a composition, vocal or instrumental, or both combined, written on separate staves placed under each other.

Fundamental. 1. A tone producing a series of *harmonics*. 2. The root on which any chord is built.

Fundamental Chord. 1. The chord founded on the key-note. 2. A chord founded on one of the *Fundamental tones*. See *Fundamental Position*.

Fundamental Key. Original Key.

Fundamental Note. The root of any chord.

Fundamental Position. Applied to any *chord* when the root is the lowest note sounded. See *Inversions*.

Fundamental Tones. The *tonic*, *dominant*, and *sub-dominant* of any *scale* or *key*.

Funèbre (Fr.) (fü-nābr.) ⎫
Funerále (It.) (foo-ně-*rä*-lě.) ⎬ Funereal, mournful.
Funéreo (It.) (foo-*nā*-rě-ō.) ⎭

Fünf (Ger.) (fünf.) Five.

Fünf-fach (Ger.) (*fünf* fakh.) *Fivefold;* five ranks; speaking of organ-pipes.

Fuóco (It.) (foo-ō-kō.) Fire, energy, passion.

Fuocóso (It.) (foo-ō-*kō*-zō.) Fiery, ardent, impetuous.

Für (Ger.) (für.) For.

Fúria (It.) (*foo*-rē-ä.) Fury, passion, rage.

Furiosaménte (It.) (foo-rē-ō-zä-*men*-tě.) Furiously, madly.

Furióso (It.) (foo-rē-ō-zō.) Furious, vehement, mad.

Furniture stop. An organ-stop consisting of several ranks of pipes, of very acute pitch. A mixture-stop.

Furóre (It.) (foo-*rō*-rě.) Fury, rage, excitement.

G

G. The fifth note of the normal scale of C, called *Sol.* The lowest or fourth string of a violin, the third of the viola and violoncello. The keynote of the major scale, having one sharp in the signature. The letter-name of the treble clef.

G. (Fr) (*abb.* for *gauche.*) *Left;* as, *m. g.,* with the left hand.

Gagliardaménte (It.)(gäl-yē-är-dä-*men*-tě.) Briskly, gayly.

Gai (Fr.) (gā.) Gay, merry.

Gaiement (Fr.) (gā-mänh.) ⎫
Gaiment (Fr.) (gā-mänh.) ⎬ Merrily, lively, gaily.

Gaio (It.) (*gä*-ē-ō.) With gayety and cheerfulness.

Galánte (It.) (gä-*län*-tě.) ⎫ Gallantly,
Galanteménte (It.) (gä-län-tě-*men*-tě.) ⎬ boldly.

Galliard. A lively old dance in triple time, formerly very popular.

Galop (Fr.) (gäl-ō.) A quick dance, generally in ¾ time

Gamba, Viola da (It.) (vee-*o*-lä dä gäm-bä.) A knee or leg (*gamba*) viol, a predecessor of violoncello

Gamba-bass. A 16-foot organ-stop, on the pedals.

Gamme (Fr.) (gäm.) The gamut or scale.

Gang (Ger.) (gäng.) Pace; rate of movement **or** motion.

Ganz (Ger.) (gänts.) Whole, entire; also, all very.

Garbataménte (It.) (gär-bä-tä-*men*-tĕ.) Gracefully.

Garbáto (It.) (gär-*bä*-tō.) Graceful.

Gárbo (It.) (*gär*-bō.) Simplicity, grace, elegance.

Gauche (Fr.) (gōsh.) Left.

Gaudioso (It.) (gä-oo-dē-ō-zō.) Merry, joyful.

Gavot (Eng.) (gă-*vŏt*.) ⎫
Gavótta (It.) (gä-*vŏt*-tä.) ⎬ A dance of even rhythm,
Gavotte (Fr.) (gä-*vŏt*.) ⎭ generally quadruple, or duple (*alla breve*). The character of this dance should be graceful and elegant, though animated.

G clef. The treble clef; a character representing the letter G which invariably turns on the second line of the staff. It determines the position of one-lined G (g¹) upon the staff. See *Clef*.

G dur (Ger.) (gä doer.) The key of G major.

Gebrochen (Ger.) (ghĕ-*brō*-kh'n.) Broken.

Gebunden (Ger.) (ghĕ-*boon*-d'n.) Connected, in regard to the style of playing or writing.

Gedackt (Ger.) (ghĕ-*däkht*.) Stopped; in opposition to the open pipes in an organ.

Gedehnt (Ger.) (ghĕ-*dänt*.) Lengthened.

Gefällig (Ger.) (ghĕ-*fĕl*-lĭg.) Pleasingly, agreeably.

Gefühl (Ger.) (ghĕ-*fühl*.) Sentiment, expression.

Gehalten (Ger.) (ghĕ-*häl*-ten.) Sustained.

Gehaucht (Ger.) (ghĕ-*howcht*.) Whispered, sighed out.

Gehend (Ger.) (gä-ĕnd.) The same as *andánte*.

Geige (Ger.) (*ghī*-ghĕ.) The violin.

Geistlich (Ger.) (*ghīst*-lĭkh.) Ecclesiastical, clerical, spiritual.

Geistvoll (Ger.) (*ghīst*-fŏl.) Full of soul and of sentiment.

Gelassen (Ger.) (ghĕ-*läs*-s'n.) Calmly, quietly.

Geläufig (Ger.) (ghĕ-*loy*-fĭg.) Easy, fluent, rapid.

Gelinde (Ger.) (ghĕ-*lĭn*-dĕ.) Softly, gently.

Gemächlich (Ger.) (ghĕ-*mäkh*-lĭkh.) Quietly; in a calm, slow manner.

Gemählig (Ger.) (ghĕ-*mä*-lĭg.) Gradually; by degrees.

Gemisch (Ger.) (gĕ-*mĭsh*.) Mixed; mixture, or compound stops in an organ.

Gems-horn (Ger.) (*ghĕms* hōrn.) In the organ, a metal flue-stop having tapering pipes of 8, 4, or 2-foot pitch on the manuals and of 16-foot pitch on the pedal, with mellow horn-like timbre. The tone is light, but very clear.

Gemüth (Ger.) (ghĕ-*müt*.) Mind, soul.

Gemüt(h)lich (Ger.) (ghĕ-*müt*-lĭkh.) Agreeable, expressive, genial.

General bass (Ger.) (ghä-ner-*ahl* bass.) Thorough bass; figured bass.

General-pause (Ger.) (ghä-ner-*ahl* pow-seh.) A general cessation or silence of all the parts.

Generoso (It.) (je-nĕ-*rō*-zō.) Noble; in a dignified manner.

Genre (Fr.) (zhänhr.) Style, manner.

Gentile (It.) (jĕn-*tē*-lĕ.) Pleasing, graceful, elegant.

Gentilézza (It.) (jĕn-tee-*lĕt*-zä.) Grace; elegance; refinement of style.

Gentilménte (It.) (jĕn-tēl-*men*-tĕ.) Gracefully, elegantly.

German fingering. See *Fingering*.

German flute. See *Flute*.

German scale. A scale of the natural notes, consisting of A, H, C, D, E, F, G, instead of A, B, C, etc., the B being always reserved to express B flat.

German sixth. A name given to a chord composed of a major third, perfect fifth, and augmented sixth, as —

Ges (Ger.) (ghĕs.) The note G flat.

Gesang (Ger.) (ghĕ-*säng*.) Singing; the art of singing; a song; melody; air.

Geschick (Ger.) (ghĕ-*shĭk*.) Skill, dexterity.

Geschleift (Ger.) (ghĕ-*shlīft*.) Slurred, legato.

Geschwind (Ger.) (ghĕ-*shvĭnd*.) Quick, rapid.

Ges dur (Ger.) (ghĕs doer.) The key of G flat major.

Gestossen (Ger.) (ghĕ-*stōs*-s'n.) Separated, detached.

Getheilt (Ger.) (gĕ-*tīlt*.) Divided, separated; *Getheilte Violinen*, violini divisi; *Getheilte Stimmen*, partial stops (organ).

Getragen (Ger.) (ghĕ-*trä*-g'n.) Well-sustained; carried.

Gewiss (Ger.) (ghĕ-*vĭss*.) Firm, resolute.

Gíga (It.) (*jee*-gä.)　⎱ A jig, or lively species of
Gigue (Fr.) (zhĕg.)　⎰ dance. The name is sup-
Gige (Ger.) (ghē-geh.)
posed to be derived from the German word *geig*,
or *geige*, meaning a fiddle, as the music is partic-
ularly adapted to instruments of that class. It
is in ¾, ⅜, ¹²⁄₄, ⁴⁄₄ and sometimes even ¼ rhythm.

Giochévole (It.) (jē-ō-kĕ-vō-lĕ.)　Merry, sportive.
Giocóndo (It.) (jē-ō-kŏn-dō.)　Cheerful, merry.
Giocosaménte (It.) (jē-ō-kō-zä-*men*-tĕ.)　⎱ Humor-
Giocoso (It.) (jē-ō-*kō*-sō.)　⎰ ously, sportively.
Giója (It.) (jē-ō-yä.)　Joy, gladness.
Giojóso (It.) (jē-ō-*yō*-zō.)　Blithe, joyful, gay.
Giojosaménte (It.) (jē-ō-yō-zä-*men*-tĕ.)　Joyfully,
merrily.
Gioviále (It.) (jē-ō-vē-*ä*-lĕ.)　Jovial.
Giovialita (It.) (jē-ō-vē-ä-lē-*tä*.)　Joviality, gayety.
Gis (Ger.) (ghĭs.)　The note G sharp.
Gis moll (Ger.) (ghĭs mŏll.)　The key of G♯
minor.
Gitana (It.) (jē-*tä*-nä.)　A Spanish dance.
Giubilóso (It.) (joo-bē-*lō*-zō.)　Jubilant, exulting.
Giúbilazione (It.) (joo-bē-lät-sē-ō-nĕ.)　⎱ Jubilation,
Giúbilio (It.) (joo-*bē*-lē-ō.)　⎰ rejoicing.
Giúbilo (It.) (*joo*-bē-lō.)
Giustaménte (It.) (joos-tä-*men*-tĕ.)　Justly; with
precision.
Giústo (It.) (*joos*-tō.)　A term signifying that the
movement indicated is to be performed in an
equal, steady, and exact time. *Giusto* is sometimes used to indicate moderation, as *Allegro
giusto*, a moderate allegro.
Giustezza (It.) (joos-*tet*-zä.)　Precision.
Glee. A vocal composition in three or four parts,
generally consisting of more than one movement,
the subject of which may be grave, tender, or gay,
and bacchanalian. The glee was less intricate
than the madrigal, and was frequently accompanied, while the madrigal was sung *a cappella*.
It is a composition peculiar to England.
Gleich (Ger.) (glĭkh.)　Equal, alike, consonant.
Gleiten (Ger.) (glī-t'n.)　To slide the fingers.
Glissando.
Gli (It. pl.) ('l *yee*.)　The (masculine plural), as
gli strumenti, the instruments.
Glide. Portamento.

Glíding. In flute playing, a sliding movement of the fingers for the purpose of blending the tones.

Glissándo (It.) (glēs-*sän*-dō.) Slurred; smooth; in a gliding manner. Sliding the finger.

Glocke (Ger.) (glôk-ĕ.) A bell.

Glockenspiel (Ger.) (glôk-ĕn-spēl.) A stop in imitation of bells, in German organs. A set of small bars of polished steel, used in the orchestra, which, on being struck with a mallet, give forth tinkling tones of definite pitch.

Gloria (Lat.) (glō-rĭ-a.) A movement in a Mass, following the Kyrie.

Glottis (Gr.) (glŏt-tĭs.) The narrow opening in the larynx, forming the mouth of the windpipe, which by its dilation and contraction contributes to the modulation of the voice.

G moll (Ger.) (gä môl.) The key of G minor.

Gondellied (Ger.) (gōn-d'l-lēd.) A gondolier song.

Gong. A Chinese instrument consisting of a large, circular plate of metal, which, when struck, produces an exceedingly loud noise, not of definite pitch. Also called *Tam-tam.*

Grace. ⎱ Ornamental notes and embellish-
Grace-note. ⎰ ments, either written by the composer, or introduced by the performer. See Dannreuther's "Musical Ornamentation" (2 vols.). Many of the signs are becoming obsolete, and it has become the custom to write the notation in full, in modern editions, avoiding the signs altogether. The chief embellishments used at present are the *Trill, Turn, Mordent, Appoggiatura and Acciaccatura,* which will be found defined under their respective names.

Gradévole (It.) (grä-dā-vō-lĕ.) ⎱ Grace-
Gradevolménte (It.) (grä-dā-vōl-*men*-tĕ.) ⎰ fully, pleasingly.

Grádo (It.) (*grä*-dō.) A degree, or single step on the staff.

Gradual. 1. That part of the Roman Catholic service that is sung between the Epistle and the Gospel. The name comes from *Gradus,* a step. 2. A *cantatorium* (book of chants) containing the graduals, introits, and other antiphons of the Catholic Mass.

Gradualménte (It.) (grä-doo-äl-*men*-tĕ.) Gradually; by degrees or steps.

Gran (It.) (grän.) Great, grand.

Grand-barré (Fr.) (gränh bär-rā.) In guitar-playing this means laying the first finger of the left hand upon all the six strings of the guitar at once.

Grand bourdon. Great or double bourdon; an organ-stop of 32-foot tone in the pedal.

Grand choir. In organ-playing, the union of all the stops of the choir-organ.

Grandézza (It.) (grän-*det*-sä.) Grandeur, dignity.

Grandióso (It.) (grän-dē-ō-zō.) Grand, noble.

Grand opera. See *Opera*.

Grand orgue (Fr.) (gränh dōrg.) Great organ.

Graphophone. See *Phonograph*.

Gratias agimus (Lat.) (*grä*-shĭ-ăs ä-jee-mŭs.) Part of the Gloria in a Mass.

Grave (It.) (*grä*-vĕ.) A slow and solemn movement; also a deep low pitch in the scale of sounds. The slowest tempo in music.

Gravità (It.) (grä-vē-*tä*.) Gravity. majesty.

Grázia (It.) (*grä*-tsē-ä.) Grace, elegance.

Graziosaménte (It.) (grä-tsē-ō-zä-*men*-tĕ.) Gracefully, smoothly.

Grazióso (It.) (grä-tsē-ō-zō.) In a graceful style.

Great octave. See *Tablature*.

Great organ. In an organ with three rows of keys, usually the middle row, so-called because containing the most important stops and having its pipes voiced louder than those in the swell or choir organ.

Gregorian chant. A style of choral music, according to the eight celebrated church modes introduced by Pope Gregory in the sixth century.

Gregorian modes. } Those chants or melodies
Gregorian tones. } used for the psalms in the Roman Catholic service, and also in many English churches. They are taken from the ancient Greek modes, and the sounds are supposed to have been somewhat similar to those in the modern or natural scale of C; but with different orders of progression. See the "Oxford History of Music," Vol. I.

Grob-gedackt (Ger.) (grŏb ghĕ-*däkht*.) An organ-stop. Large stopped diapason of full tone.

Grossartig (Ger.) (grōs-är-tĭg.) Grand.

Gross-gedackt (Ger.) (grōs ghĕ-*däkht*.) Double stopped diapason of 16-foot tone in an organ.

Grôsso (It.) (grŏs-sō.) Full, great, grand.

Grottésco (It.) (grō-*tes*-kō.) Grotesque.

Group. Several short notes tied together.

Gruppetto (It.) (groo-*pet*-to.) A turn. Also, a collective term applied loosely to various "groups," or grace-notes, such as:

etc.

G-schlüssel (Ger.) (gä-shlüs-ʂ'l.) The G, or treble clef.

Guarácha (Spa.) (gwär-*ăk*-ä.) A Spanish dance.

Guarnerius (gwär-*nā*-rĭ-ŭs.) A make of violin highly prized, so-called from the name of the manufacturer.

Guerriéro (It.) (gwĕr-rē-*ā*-rō.) Martial, warlike.

Guída (It.) (*gwē*-dä.) *Guide;* also, the mark called a *direct.* The subject of a fugue.

Guidonian syllables. See *Solfaing.*

Guitar (ghit-*är*.) A "plucked" string instrument of great resonance; body and neck similar to the violin though considerably larger, the top and back however being flat. The six strings of gut, silk or wire vibrating over a circular sound-hole. While of Spanish invention and most popular in that country, modified types have long existed in Germany and Italy and the instrument may be said to be universally known and popular. Originally intended for accompaniment only, it has become an acceptable solo instrument in the hands of a capable performer.

It is generally tuned as below, the intervals being for the most part *fourths.*

While played from the Treble staff the actual sounds are an *octave lower;* the written compass being from E below the staff to the second A above the staff.

Gústo (It.) (*goos*-tō.) Taste, expression.

H

H. This letter is used by the Germans for B natural. Also stands for heel in organ music.

Habanera (Spa.) (hä-bän-*yĕ*-rä.) A slow Spanish dance in $\frac{2}{4}$ or $\frac{6}{8}$ time.

Halb (Ger.) (hälb.) Half.

Half-cadence. An imperfect cadence; a close on the dominant.

Half-note. A minim, ♩.

Half-rest. A pause equal in duration to a half-note, ▬.

Half-step. The smallest interval used in our musical system. For other applications of *half* in music see second word.

Hallelujah (Heb.) (hăl-lĕ-*loo*-yäh.) *Praise ye the Lord;* a song of thanksgiving.

Hardiment (Fr.) (är-dee-mänh.) Boldly, firmly.

Harfe (Ger.) (*här*-fĕ.) A harp.

Harmonica. A musical instrument invented by Benjamin Franklin, consisting of glasses, sometimes globular and sometimes flat. The tone is produced by rubbing the edge of the globular glasses with a moistened finger, or striking the flat ones with small hammers. The name is also applied to an organ-stop of delicate tone. See *Mouth-harmonica.*

Harmonic figuration. Broken chords.

Harmonic flute. An open metal organ-stop, of 8 or 4-foot pitch; the pipes are of double length, that is, 16 or 8 feet, and the bodies have a hole bored in them, midway between the foot and the top; the tone is exceedingly full, fluty, and powerful.

Harmonic mark. A sign used in violin, harp music, etc., to indicate that certain passages are to be played upon such parts of the open strings as will produce the harmonic sounds, marked Ö.

Harmonic modulation. A change in the harmony from one key to another.

Harmonics. 1. A term applied to those concomitant, accessory sounds or over-tones, accompanying a principal, and apparently simple tone. 2. *Harmonics* is also the name given to certain tones produced on the violin, harp, and other stringed instruments, by lightly touching the string at various points and causing it to vibrate in two, three, or more sections. Also called *Flageolet tones* owing to their peculiar character. 3. The *Harmonics* of a sounding tube (wind instruments) are a series of over-tones resulting from a division of the vibrating air column. The following series of harmonics is based on a deep fundamental, but the same ratio is preserved, taking the pitch of any open string or tube as the fundamental and transposing the series accordingly. The notes marked × are generally faulty.

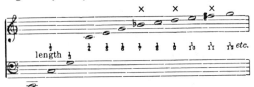

Fundamental

Harmonium. A small reed-organ.

Harmony. The agreement or consonance of two or more united sounds. The art of combining sounds into chords and treating those chords according to certain rules.

Harmony, close. A harmony whose tones are compact, the upper three voices lying within the compass of an octave.

Harmony, dispersed. A harmony in which the notes forming the different chords are separated by wide intervals.

Harmony, figured. Harmony in which, for the purpose of melody, one or more of the parts of a composition move, during the continuance of a chord, through certain notes that do not belong to that chord.

Harp. A stringed instrument of very ancient origin, consisting of a triangular frame, having strings extended in parallel sections from the upper part to one of its sides, and played with the fingers. The perfection of the harp did not occur until 1810, when Sebastian Erard introduced a system of double-acting pedals by which any note could be raised either a semi-tone or a whole tone, at will. The harp has very nearly the compass of the piano, starting with the lowest C♭ of that instrument, and ending with its highest, F♯. It is notated as the piano, on two staves, one treble and one bass. Its strings are of catgut in the upper octaves, of catgut wired, or of heavy wire, in the lower. The harp sounds best in flat keys. It has usually forty-six strings. See Flood's "Harp."

Harp, Œolian. See *Œolian Harp*.

Harpsichord. An instrument much used before the invention of the pianoforte. In shape it resembled the grand pianoforte and had sometimes two rows of keys, but it was very inferior to that instrument in capacity for power and expression. Its wires were not struck by hammers, but plucked by quills. See *Piano*. The compass was about four octaves, but sometimes more.

Haupt (Ger.) (houpt.) Head, principal.

Haupt-satz (Ger.) (*houpt* sätz.) Principal theme, or subject; the *motive*, or leading subject.

Haupt-werk (Ger.) (*houpt*-värk.) Chief work, or manual; the great organ.

Hautbois (Fr.) (ō-bwä.) The *oboè* or hautboy.

H dur (Ger.) (hä doer.) B major.

Head. 1. The membrane stretched over drum, tambourine or banjo. 2. The scroll and peg box of violin. 3. Point of violin bow.

Head voice. The upper or highest register of the voice; the falsetto in men's voices.

Heftig (Ger.) (*hĕf*-tig.) Vehement, boisterous.

Heftigkeit (Ger.) (*hĕf*-tĭg-kīt.) Vehemence, impetuosity.

Helicon (Eng.) (hĕl-ĭ-kŏn.) A tuba made in such shape as to circle the body and rest on the shoulder, for marching or mounted band use.

Hell (Ger.) (hĕl.) Clear, bright.

Hemidemisemiquaver. A sixty-fourth note. Term obsolete.

Hervortretend (Ger.) (hār-*fŏr*-trā-tund.) Prominently and distinctly.

Herzlich (Ger.) (*hĕrts*-lĭkh.) Tenderly, heartfelt.

Hidden. A term applied to *resultant* fifths or octaves when the two harmonic voices move in parallel motion from a position where they do not define the interval of fifth or octave. Hidden fifths and octaves are allowable.

High Mass. The Mass celebrated in the Roman Catholic churches by the singing of the choristers, distinguishing it from the low Mass in which the prayers are read without singing.

Hilfs (Ger.) (Auxiliary; *ilfslinie*, legerline. *Hilfsnote*, auxiliary note; *Hilfsstimme*, mutation-stop (often *Hülfs*).

Hirtlich (Ger.) (*hĭrt*-lĭkh.) Pastoral, rural.

His (Ger.) (hĭs.) The note B sharp.

H moll (Ger.) (hä-mōl.) The key of B minor.

Hoboe (Ger.) (hō-bō-ĕ.) Oboè, hautboy.

Hochzeits-lied (Ger.) (*hōkh*-tsĭts lēd.) Wedding-song.

Hohl-flöte (Ger.) (hōl-flō-tĕ.) *Hollow-toned flute;* an organ-stop producing a thick and powerful hollow tone.

Hohl-quinte (Ger.) (hōl quĭn-tĕ.) A *quint* stop of the *hohl-flute* species sounding a fifth higher.

Hold. A character (⌢) indicating that the time of a note or rest is to be prolonged. See *Fermata.*

Holding-note. A note that is sustained or continued while the others are in motion.

Holz-flöte (Ger.) (hōlts flō-tĕ.) *Wood flute;* an organ-stop.

Homophony. Unison; two or more voices singing in unison. In modern music, a style in which *one melody* or part, supported to a greater or less extent by chords (an *accompanied melody*) predominates. It is the opposite of polyphony, where different melodies are heard simultaneously.

Hook. A stroke attached to the stems of eighth notes, sixteenth notes, etc., (♪ 𝅘𝅥𝅯)

Horn. See *Horn, French.*

Horn, English. See *Cor Anglais.*

Horn, French. An orchestral instrument of brass, consisting of a long tube from 9 to 18 feet long twisted into several circular folds, and gradually increasing in diameter from the mouth-piece to the end. This instrument is most frequently called simply *the horn*. There are horns in all the different keys, but it is not necessary to have a special instrument in each key, for, by the addition of sections of tubing, called *crooks*, the horn can be lengthened and set in another key than its natural one. The horn generally used in the orchestra is the one in F, which, in its natural state, sounds a perfect fifth lower than its notation. The original (Wald-horn) could yield only the natural *harmonics* (which see) of its tube. A few of these tones could be flatted by partially *stopping* the bell. The modern F horn with valves gives the full chromatic scale from

Written   Sounding

The few notes above or below this compass are rarely used. The quality of the horn is mellow and tender, its tone-color suiting it to romantic effects, and woodland and forest pictures, but the *stopped* tones are the reverse of this, and are the most repulsive tone-color that can be produced in the orchestra. See Prout's "The Orchestra," and A. Elson's "Orchestral Instruments and their Use."

Hornpipe. An old dance in triple time, peculiar to the English nation. It is supposed to have received its name from the instrument played during its performance. Modern hornpipes are usually in common time and of a more lively character than the ancient hornpipe.

Hosanna (Lat.) (hō-*zăn*-nä.) Part of the Sanctus in a Mass.

Hurdy-gurdy. An old instrument consisting of four strings, which are acted upon by a wheel rubbed in resin powder, which serves as a bow. Two of the strings are affected by certain keys, which stop them at different lengths and produce the *tune*, while the others act as a drone bass. This instrument was imitated by Schubert in his song, *Der Leiermann*.

Hurtig (Ger.) (*hoor*-tĭg.) Quick; swiftly; same meaning as *Allégro*.

Hydraulic organ. An organ whose motive power was water, and the invention of which is of much greater antiquity than the pneumatic or wind-organ. It is supposed to have been invented by Ctesibius, a mathematician of Alexandria.

Hymn. A song of praise or adoration to the Deity; a short, religious lyric poem intended to be sung in church. Anciently, a song in honor of the gods or heroes.

Hymn, vesper. A hymn sung in the vesper service of the Catholic Church.

Hyper (Gr.) (*hī̆-pĕr.*) *Above.*

Hyper-ditonos (Gr.) (*hĭ-pĕr-di-tō̆-nŏs.*) The third above.

Hypo. *Below.*

I

I (It.) (masculine plural.) (ē.) The.

Iambic. ⎱ A poetical and musical foot, consisting
Iambus. ⎰ of one short unaccented and one long accented note or syllable, ⏑ —.

Idyl. A short poem in pastoral style; an eclogue.

Il (It.) (ēl.) The.

Ilarita (It.) (*ē-lär-ē-tä.*) Hilarity, cheerfulness, mirth.

Il più (It.) (eel pĕ-*oo*.) The most.

Im (Ger.) (ēm.) In the.

Imitándo (It.) (ee-mee-*tän*-dō.) Imitating.

Imitation (Lat., *imitatio;* Fr., *imitation;* It., *imitazione;* Ger., *Nachahmung.*) The repetition of a motive, phrase, or theme proposed by one part (the *antecedent*) in another part (the *consequent*), with or without modification.

Immer (Ger.) (*ĭm*-mĕr.) Always, ever.

Impaziénte (It.) (im-pä-tsē-*en*-tē.) Impatient, hurried.

Impazienteménte (It.) (im-pä-tsē-ĕn-tĕ-*men*-tĕ.) Impatiently, hurriedly.

Imperfect cadence. See *Cadence, imperfect.*

Imperfect intervals. See *Intervals.*

Imperióso (It.) (im-pä-rē-ō-zō.) Imperious, pompous.

Impeto (It.) (*im*-pä-tō.) Impetuosity, vehemence.

Impetuóso (It.) (im-pä-too-ō-zō.) Impetuous, vehement.

Imponénte (It.) (im-pō-*nen*-tĕ.) Imposingly, haughtily.

Impresário (It.) (im-prĕ-*zä*-rē-ō.) A term applied by the Italians to the manager or conductor of operas or concerts.

Imprómptu (Fr.) (ăhn-pron-tü.) An extemporaneous production.

Improperia (Lat.) (*reproaches.*) In the Roman ritual, a series of antiphons and responses forming part of the solemn service substituted, on the morning of Good Friday, for the usual daily Mass.

Improvisation. The art of singing, or playing music without preparation; extemporaneous performance. Also a form of composition.

In (It. and Lat.) (ēn.) In, into, in the.

In alt (It.) (in ält.) See *Alt.*

Incalzando (It.) (in-cal-*tsan*-do.) With growing warmth and fervor.

Incarnatus (Lat.) (in-car-*nä*-tus.) Part of the *Credo* of the Mass.

Inconsoláto (It.) (ēn-kŏn-sō-*lä*-tō.) In a mournful style.

Inconsonant. Discordant.

Incordaménto (It.) (ēn-kŏr-dä-*men*-tō.) Tension of the strings of an instrument.

Incordáre (It.) (in-kŏr-*dä*-rě.) To string an instrument.

Incidental music. Descriptive music, generally orchestral, accompanying a drama. Played independently in the form of overture, entr'acte, etc., or during spoken dialogue or pantomime. Vocal music is sometimes introduced *incidentally* during the action of a play.

Inflection. Any change or modification in the pitch or tone of the voice.

Innig (Ger.) (*ĭn*-nĭg.) Sincere; cordial; with depth of feeling.

Innocenteménte (It.) (in-nō-tshen-tě-*men*-tě.) Innocently; in an artless and simple style.

Ino (It.) (*ē*-nō.) An Italian final diminutive. As *Scherzo, Scherzino.* The feminine is *Ina,* as *Sonata, Sonatina*

Inquiéto (It.) (in-quē-*ä*-tō.) Restless, uneasy, agitated.

Insensíbile (It.) (in-sĕn-*see*-bi-lě.) } In**Insensibilménte** (It.) (in-sĕn-sē-bēl-*men*-tě.) } sensibly; by small degrees; by little and little.

Instanteménte (It.) (in-stän-tě-*men*-tě.) Vehemently, urgently.

Instrumentation. The act of writing for an orchestra or band with a practical knowledge of each instrument, and of the distribution of harmony among the different instruments.

Instruments

String Instruments.

Percussion —
  Pianoforte.
  Schlagzither.
Friction (Bowing) —
  Violin.
  Viola.
  Violoncello.
  Contrabass.
  Viol d'Amore.
Plucking —
  Harp.
  Guitar.
  Mandolin (plectrum or pick).
  Banjo.
  Zither.

Wind-instruments of Wood.

With open mouth-piece —
  Flute.
  Piccolo.
  Fife.
Single reed —
  Clarinet.
  Bass clarinet.
  Basset-horn.
  Pedal Clarinet.
Double Reed —
  Oboe.
  English Horn.
  Bassoon.
  Contrabassoon.

Brass Instruments.

With cup mouth-piece —
  Cornet.
  Trumpet.
  French Horn.
  Trombone (keyed).
  Trombone (slide).

Tuba.
Saxhorns.
Bugle.
Post-horn.
Ophicleide.
With single reed —
Saxophone.
With double reed —
Sarussophone.

Instruments of Percussion.

With definite pitch —
Kettle drum.
Xylophone.
Glockenspiel.
Bells.
Celesta.
Without pitch —
Bass drum.
Military drum.
Cymbals.
Gong.
Tambourine.
Castanets.
Triangle.

The organ combines most of the effects of the above-given wind-instruments, and there are also obsolete instruments, such as the clavichord, harpsichord, oboe di caccia, etc., which are not given in the above list.

Interlude. A short musical representation, introduced between the acts of any drama or between the play and afterpiece; an intermediate strain or movement played between the verses of a hymn, or of a song.

Intermezzo (It.) (In-tĕr-*mēt*-sō.) An interlude, intermediate, placed between two others; detached pieces introduced between the acts of an opera. Also a short movement in the symphony taking the place of the Scherzo. In the old Suite, the *Intermezzi* were from two to four short movements, of moderate tempo (generally minuets or gavots), placed between the sarabande and the finale, — the *gigue*.

Interval (Lat., *intervallum;* Ger., *Intervall;* Fr., *intervalle;* It., *intervallo.*) The difference between any two notes, measured by degrees on the staff. The interval is counted from the lowest note to the highest. Two notes on the same degree constitute a Prime, etc.

Apart from numerical designation, Intervals are classified as *Diminished, Minor, Major, Augmented* and *Perfect.*

The above are only samples of *qualifications,* there are Major, Minor and Augmented Seconds, etc. Each Interval is limited to *certain* qualifications, which can properly be explained only in the theory and practice of Harmony.

Chromatic Alteration.

Each *major* or *perfect* interval when widened by *raising* the upper note a half-step, becomes *augmented.* Each *major* interval contracted by *lowering* the upper note a half-step, becomes *minor.* Each *minor* or *perfect* interval contracted by *raising* the lower note a half-step, becomes *diminished.*

Inversion of Intervals.

Writing the lower note an octave higher, or the upper note an octave lower, is called inverting the interval. Using the intervals last given, we obtain

Aug.   Maj.   Min.   Dim.   Per.

Note that apart from the change in numerical designation, the character of the interval is also changed in the first four. The *Diminished* Third becomes an *Augmented* Sixth, etc. The last, the Fifth, however does not change its *character*, hence it is called a *Perfect* Interval.

General Rule in Inversions.

Perfect	intervals remain perfect (Primes, Fourths, Fifths, and Octaves)
Major	intervals become minor,
Minor	intervals become major,
Augmented	intervals become diminished,
Diminished	intervals become augmented.

Intimo (It.) (in-*tē*-mō.) Inward feeling; expressive. See *Innig*.

Intonation. A word referring to the proper emission of the tone (voice or instrument) so as to produce any required note in exact tune; the act of modulating the voice. The chanting of *Plain-song*.

Intráda (It.) (in-trä-dä.) A short prelude or introductory movement.

Intrepidaménte (It.) (in-trĕ-pē-dä-*men*-tĕ.) Boldly; with intrepidity.

Intrepidezza (It.) (in-trĕ-pē-*det*-sä.) Intrepidity, boldness.

Intrépido (It.) (ēn-*trä*-pē-dō.) Intrepid, bold.

Introduction. That movement in a composition the design of which is to prepare the ear for the movements which are to follow. It may be a mere phrase, or an entire division of a work. See *Beethoven's* 1st, 2d, and 7th Symphonies.

Introduzione (It.) (ēn-trō-doo-tsē-ō-nĕ.) An introduction.

Introit (Eng.) (In-*trō*-It.) ⎱ *Entrance;* a hymn or
Introit (Fr.) (ănh-twä.) ⎰ antiphonal chant sung
while the priest approaches the altar at the
commencement of the Mass. In the Anglican
Church, a short anthem, psalm, or hymn, sung
while the minister proceeds to the table to ad-
minister the Holy Communion. Formerly, in
some English cathedrals, the Sanctus was sung
as an Introit.

Invention (Fr.) (ănh-vänh-sĭ-ŏnh.) An old name
for a species of prelude or short fantasia: a
short piece in free contrapuntal style.

Inversion. A change of position with respect to
intervals and chords; the lower notes being
placed above, and the upper notes below. See
Interval. A *chord* is inverted when a note other
than the fundamental appears as the lowest note.

Chord. Inversions. Chord. Inversions.

Inverted turn. A turn which commences with the
lowest note instead of the highest.

Invocazióne (It.) (in-vō-kä-tsē-ō-nĕ.) An invo-
cation, or prayer.

Ira (It.) (ē-rä.) Anger, wrath. Ire.

Iráto (It.) (i-*rä*-tō.) Irate. Angrily, passionately.

Irlandais (Fr.) (ir-länh-dä.) An air, or dance
tune, in the Irish style.

Ironicaménte (It.) (i-rŏn-ē-kä-*men*-tĕ.) Ironically.

Irónico (It.) (i-*rŏ*-nē-kō.) Ironical.

Irresolúto (It.) (ir-rĕ-zō-*loo*-tō.) Irresolute, wavering.

Issimo (ēs-sē-mō.) An Italian final, superlative,
as *Fortissimo*.

Istésso (It.) (ees-*tes*-sō.) The same.

Istésso tempo (It.) (ees-*tes*-sō tĕm-pō.) The same
time.

Italian sixth. A name sometimes given to a chord
composed of a major third and an
augmented sixth.

Ite missa est (Lat.) (ē-tä *mĭs*-sä est.) The termination of the Mass sung by the priest to

Gregorian music. It means " Go, ye are dis-missed," and gave the name *Missa* or *Mass* to the entire service.

J

Jack. The quill which strikes the strings of a harpsichord, or the upright lever in piano action.

Jagd-horn (Ger.) (*yägd*-hŏrn.) Hunting-horn.

Jagd-stück (Ger.) (*yägd*-stük.) A hunting-piece.

Jäger-chor (Ger.) (*yä*-ghĕr-kōr.) See *Jaegerchor.*

Jaléo (Spa.) (hä-lā-ō.) A Spanish national dance.

Janko keyboard. A system of pianoforte key, invented by a Hungarian, Paul von Janko, in 1882. It is two series of keys (each key repre-senting a step of one whole tone), set in three different positions (six ranks of keys in all), and presents the following advantages: 1. The same fingering of scales and runs in any key. 2. The widest intervals are brought within the compass of a small hand. 3. Octave passages are made especially easy. There are other ad-vantages, but, as yet, very few prominent artists have used the ingenious invention.

Jarábe (Spa.) (hä-*rä*-bĕ.) A Spanish dance.

Jeu (Fr.) (zhŭh.) Play; the style of playing on an instrument; also a register in an organ or harmonium; also *Grand jeu, plein jeu,* full organ; full power; *demi-jeu,* half-power.

Jeu d'anche (Fr.) (zhŭh d'änsh.) A reed-stop in an organ.

Jew's harp. A small instrument of brass or steel, and shaped somewhat like a *lyre* with a thin, vibrating tongue of metal: when played, it is placed between the teeth, and struck with the forefinger. The initial tone wave produced by the reed may be varied in pitch according to the position of the mouth (acting as a resonance chamber), the breath controlling the force of tone.

Jig. See *Gigue.*

Jodeln (Ger.) (yō-d'ln.) A style of singing peculiar to the Tyrolese peasants, the natural voice, and the falsetto, being used alternately. A warble.

Jóta (Spa.) (*hō*-tä.) A Spanish national dance in triple time and rapid movement.

Jovialisch (Ger.) (yō-fĭ-ä-lĭsh.) Jovial, joyous, merry.

Jubel-lied (Ger.) (*yoo*-b'l-lēd.) Song of jubilee.

Jubilate. In the Anglican liturgy, the one hundredth psalm, following the second lesson in the morning service.

Jubilee. A season of great public joy and festivity. Among the Jews, every *fiftieth* year was a jubilee.

Jubilóso (It.) (yoo-bē-*lō*-zō.) Jubilant, exulting.

Just. A term applied to all consonant intervals, and to those voices, strings, and pipes that give them with exactness.

K

Kammer (Ger.) (*käm*-měr.) Chamber.

Kanon (Ger.) (*kä*-nōn.) A canon.

Kapelle (Ger.) (käp-*pěl*-lě.) Chapel.

Keck (Ger.) (kěk.) Pert, fearless, bold.

Keckheit (Ger.) (*kěk*-hīt.) Boldness, vigor.

Kent bugle. A bugle having six keys (soundholes and pads), four of which are commanded by the right hand and two by the left. Obsolete.

Keraulophon (Ger.) (kě-*rou*-lō-fōn.) An 8-foot organ-stop, of a reedy and pleasing quality of tone; its peculiar character being produced by a small round hole bored in the pipe near the top.

Kettledrum. See *Drum, Kettle*.

Key. 1. The lever by which the sounds of a pianoforte, organ, or harmonium are produced. 2. An arrangement by which certain holes are opened and closed in flutes, oboes, and other wind-instruments. 3. A scale, or series of notes progressing diatonically, in a certain order of tones and semi-tones, the first note of the scale being called the *Key-note*.

Keyboard. (Ger., *Klaviatur,* Fr., *Clavier,* It., *Tastatura.*) The rows of keys upon a pianoforte, organ, or similar instrument. The keyboard as at present arranged for piano, or organ, is very ancient. The oldest actually existing keyboard of the present style is on a spinet in the Paris *Conservatoire,* which is dated 1523. It is probable that the shape of the piano keyboard has not materially changed in the last five hundred years.

For various compound words or expressions containing *Key* or *Keys*, look under separate headings, *Fundamental Key*, etc.

Key-note. The tonic, or first note of every scale.

Keys, pedal. That set of keys belonging to an organ which are acted upon by the feet.

Kirchen-musik (Ger.) (*kĭr-kh'n-moo-zĭk.*) Church music.

Kit. The name of a small pocket-violin formerly used by dancing masters. Its length is about sixteen inches, and that of the bow about seventeen.

Klagend (Ger.) (*klä-g'nd.*) Plaintive.

Klang (Ger.) (*kläng.*) Sound, tune, ringing.

Klangfarbe (Ger.) (*kläng-*fahrbeh.) Tone-color; quality of tone; clang-tint.

Klappe (Ger.) (*kläp-pĕ.*) Key of any wind-instrument; a valve.

Klar (Ger.) (klär.) Clear, bright.

Klavier (Ger.) (klä-*fēr.*) Pianoforte, harpsichord. See *Clavier.*

Klaviermässig (Ger.) (klä-*fēer*-may-sig.) Suited to the piano.

Klein (Ger.) (klīn.) Minor; speaking of intervals.

Klein-gedackt (Ger.) (*klīn-ghĕ-däkht.*) A small covered stop in an organ; a stopped flute.

Klingbar (Ger.) (*klīng-*bär.) ⎫
Klingen (Ger.) (*klīng-*'n.) ⎬ Sonorous, resonant, ringing.
Klingend (Ger.) (*klīng-*ĕnd.) ⎭

Knabenstimme (Ger.) (*knä-*b'n-*stĭm-*mĕ.) A boy's voice; a counter tenor.

Knee-stop. A knee-lever under the manual of the reed-organ; there are three kinds, used (*a*) to control the supply of wind; (*b*) to open and shut the swell box; (*c*) to draw all the stops.

Konzert-meister (Ger.) (kŏn-*tsĕrt*-mīs-tĕr.) See *Concert-meister.*

Kräftig (Ger.) (*kräf-*tĭg.) Powerful; vigorous; full of energy.

Krakoviak (krä-*kō*-vĭ-äk.) The *Cracovienne,* a Polish dance in ¾ time.

Kreuz (Ger.) (kroits.) A *sharp.*

Kreuz-doppeltes (Ger.) (kroits *dop-*pĕl-tĕs.) A *double sharp* ✲.

Kriegerisch (Ger.) (*krĕ-*ghĕr-ĭsh.) War-like, martial.

Kurz (Ger.) (koorts.) Short, detached staccato.

Kyrie eleison (Gr.) (kē-rē-ā ā-lā-ee-son.) *Lord have mercy upon us.* The first movement in a Mass.

L

L. Left hand. Notes to be played with the left hand are sometimes written with an L over them. (Ger., *Links;* Eng., *Left.*)

La. (It. Fr.) (lä.) A syllable applied in *solfa-ing;* to the note A; the sixth sound in the scale of Guido. In Italy and France, the note A is always called *La.* The article *the.*

Labial. Organ-pipes with *lips,* called also *flue* pipes.

Lacrimosa (Lat.) (lah-cree-*mo*-zah.) A division of the Requiem Mass.

Lage (Ger.) (*lä*-ghĕ.) Position of a chord, or of the hand.

Lagrimóso (It.) (lä-grē-*mō*-zō.) Weeping; tearful; in a sad and mournful style.

Lamentándo (It.) (lä-mĕn-*tän*-dō.) Lamenting, mourning.

Lamentations. The funeral music of the ancient Jews was called by this name.

Lamentévole (It.) (lä-mĕn-*tā*-vō-lĕ.) Lamentable, mournful, plaintive.

Lamentóso (It.) (lä-mĕn-*tō*-zō.) Lamentable, mournful.

Ländler (Ger.) (*länd*-lĕr.) A country dance, or air in a rustic and popular style, in ⅜ or ¾ time. It is like the *Tyrolienne.*

Ländlich (Ger.) (*länd*-lĭkh.) Rural.

Land-lied (Ger.) (*länd*-lēd.) Rural song; rustic song.

Lang (Ger.) (läng.) Long.

Langsam (Ger.) (*läng*-säm.) Slowly; equivalent to *Lento.*

Langsamer (Ger.) (*läng*-sä-mĕr.) More slowly.

Languéndo (It.) (län-*guen*-dō.) ⎫
Languénte (It.) (län-*guen*-tĕ.) ⎬ Languishing; feeble; with languor.
Lánguido (It.) (län-guē-dō.) ⎭

Largaménte (It.) (lär-gä-*men*-tĕ.) ⎫ Broadly. Fully
Largaménto (It.) (lär-gä-*men*-tō.) ⎭

Larghetto (It.) (lär-*ghet*-tō.) A word specifying a time not quite so slow as that denoted by *largo,* of which word it is the diminutive.

Lárgo (It.) (*lär*-gō.) A slow and solemn degree of movement. *Largo* is often combined with modifying words. It may be introduced for temporary effect only in otherwise faster movements.

Larigot (Fr.) (lä-ree-go.) Shepherd's flageolet or pipe; an organ-stop tuned an octave above the twelfth.

Larynx. The upper part of the *trachea.* It is composed of five annular cartilages, placed above one another and united by elastic ligaments, by which it is so dilated and contracted as to be capable of varying the tones of the voice.

Laryngoscope, an instrument for examining the larynx. Devised in 1854 by Manuel Garcia the celebrated singing-master. With modern development it is one of the most important aids in vocal physiology.

Láuda (It.) (lä-*oo*-dä.) Laud; praise; hymn of praise.

Laudamus te (Lat.) (lou-*dä*-mŭs tä.) *We praise Thee;* part of the Gloria.

Läufer (Ger.) (*loi*-fĕr.) A flight or run of rapid notes; a roulade.

Launig (Ger.) (*lou*-nĭg.) Humorous, capricious.

Le (Fr.) (lŭh.) }
Le (It. pl.) (lĕ.) } The.

Leader. The first or principal violin in an orchestra; a director of a choir, or of a military band, generally the first cornet. Sometimes used for *conductor*.

Leading-note. The major seventh of any scale, the semi-tone below the key-note.

Leaning-note. See *Appoggiatura.*

Leap. See *Skip.*

Leben (Ger.) (*lä*-b'n.) Life, vivacity.

Lebhaft (Ger.) (*läb*-häft.) Lively, vivacious, quick.

Leçon (Fr.) (lŭs-sŏnh.) A lesson; an exercise.

Ledger lines. } The short extra or additional lines
Leger lines. } drawn above or below the staff, for the reception of such notes as are too high or too low to be placed on the staff proper.

Legatíssimo (It.) (lĕ-gä-*tēs*-sē-mō.) Exceedingly smooth and connected.

Legáto (It.) (lĕ-*gä*-tō.) In a close, smooth, graceful manner; the opposite to *staccato.* It is often indicated by a sign called a slur ⌒.

Légende (Fr.) (lay-zhänd.) A legend; a piece written in a romantic, narrative style.

Léger (Fr.) (lä-zhair.) Light, nimble.

Légèrement (Fr.) (lä-zhair-mänh.) Lightly, nimbly, gayly.

Leggerezza (It.) (lĕd-jĕr-*et*-tsä.) Lightness and agility.

Leggiadra (It.) (lĕd-jĕ-ä-drä.) Graceful, elegant

Leggiéro (It.) (lĕd-jē-ā-rō.) Light, swift, delicate.

Leichen-musik (Ger.) (lī-kh'n-moo-*zĭk*.) Funeral music.

Leicht (Ger.) (likht.) Light, easy, facile.

Leichtfertig (Ger.) (*līkht*-fär-tĭg.) Lightly, carelessly.

Leidenschaftlich (Ger.) (lī-den-shäft-lĭkh.) Impassioned, passionate.

Leise (Ger.) (*lī*-ze.) Low, soft, gentle.

Leitmotif (Ger.) (*līt*-mo-*teef*.) A well-marked theme or phrase associated with a character, thought or action in the modern music-drama. It renders the orchestral accompaniment of greater value and meaning. These characteristic themes are seldom varied except by harmonic coloring as the situation may demand. Richard Wagner may be said to have developed the *leitmotif* to its present significance.

Léno (It.) (*lāy*-nō.) Weak, feeble, faint.

Lentaménte (It.) (lĕn-tä-*men*-tĕ.) Slowly

Lentándo (It.) (lĕn-*tän*-dō.) With increased slowness.

Lentézza, con (It.) (lĕn-*tĕt*-tsa, kŏn.) With slowness and delay.

Lénto (It.) (*len*-tō.) Slow.

Lestaménte (It.) (lĕs-tä-*men*-tĕ.) Quickly, lively.

Lestézza (It.) (lĕs-tĕt-tsä.) Agility, quickness.

Lésto (It.) (lĕs-tō.) Lively, nimbly, quick.

Libero (It.) (lē-bĕ-rō.) Free, unrestrained.

Librétto (It.) (lē-*brĕt*-tō.) The text of an opera or other extended piece of music.

Lieblich (Ger.) (*lēb*-lĭkh.) Lovely, charming.

Lieblich-gedackt (Ger.) (*lēb*-lĭkh ghĕ-*dä̆kht*.) A stopped diapason organ-register of sweet tone.

Lied (Ger.) (leed.) A song; a ballad; a lay.

Lieder ohne Worte (Ger.) (*lee*-dĕr ō-nĕ *Vōr*-tĕ.) Songs without words.

Ligature. A slur; an old name for a *tie* or *bind*. A group of notes executed in one breath or phrase.

Linke Hand (Ger.) (*lĭn*-kĕ händ.) The left hand.

Lip. 1. The lips of a flue-pipe are the flat surfaces above and below the mouth, called the *upper* and *lower* lip. 2. (Ger., *Ansatz;* **Fr.,** *embouchure;* It., *imboccatura.*) The art or faculty of so adjusting the lips to the mouth-piece of a wind-instrument as to produce artistic effects of tone. Also *lipping.*

Líscio (It.) (*lee-shē-ō.*) Simple, unadorned, smooth.

Lispelnd (Ger.) (*lts-pĕlnd.*) Lisping, whispering.

L'istésso (It.) (*lees-tes-sō.*) The same.

Litany. A solemn form of supplication used in public worship.

Liturgy. The ritual for public worship in those churches which use written forms.

Lob-gesang (Ger.) (*lŏb-ghĕ-zäng.*) A hymn, or song of praise.

Lóco (It.) (*lō-kō.*) *Place;* a word used to indicate a return to the written register after a series of notes have been executed an octave higher through use of 8ᵛᵃ. In modern music the termination of a dotted line following 8ᵛᵃ indicates point of return to written register.

Long metre. A stanza of four lines in iambic measure, each line containing eight syllables.

Long mordent. See *Mordent (double).*

Lontáno (It.) (*lŏn-tä-nō.*) Distant; remote; a great way off.

Loure (Fr.) (loor.) An old dance of slow time and dignified character, either three or six quarter notes to the measure.

Lugúbre (It.) (loo-*goo*-brĕ.) Lugubrious, sad, mournful.

Lullaby. A cradle song; a soft, gentle song.

Lúnga páusa (It.) (*loon*-gä pä-*oo*-zä.) *A long pause*, or rest. Sometimes written *Lunga.*

Lusingándo (It.) (loo-zēn-gän-do.) }
Lusinghévole (It.) (loo-zēn-*gë*-vō-lĕ.) } Soothing; coaxing; persuasively; insinuatingly.

Lustig (Ger.) (*loos*-tĭg.) Merrily, cheerfully, gayly.

Lute. A very ancient stringed instrument, formerly much used, and containing at first only five strings, but to which more were afterwards added.

Luttuóso (It.) (loot-too-ō-zō.) Sorrowful, mournful.

Lyre. One of the most ancient of stringed instruments, a species of harp.

M

M. This letter is used as an abbreviation of mezzo, also of various other words, as *metronome*, *mano*, *main*, *manual*, and also in connection with other letters.

M. M. The abbreviation for *Maelzel's Metronome*.

Ma (It.) (mä.) *But*, as *Allégro ma non tróppo*, quick, but not too much so.

Madrigal. An elaborate vocal composition, in three, four, five, or six parts, without accompaniment, in the strict or ancient style, with imitation; the parts or melodies moving in that conversational manner peculiar to the music of the sixteenth and seventeenth centuries. The madrigal is generally sung in chorus.

Maestévole (It.) (mä-ĕs-*tē*-vò-lĕ.) Majestic, majestical.

Maestóso (It.) (mä-ĕs-*tō*-zō.) Majestic, stately, dignified.

Maéstro (It.) (mä-*es*-trō.) Master, composer; an experienced, skilful artist.

Maggióre (It.) (mäd-jē-ō-rĕ.) The major key.

Magnificat (Lat.) (mág-*nee*-fee-kăt.) A part of the vespers, or evening service at the Roman Catholic Church.

Main (Fr.) (mănh.) The hand.

Main droite (Fr.) (mănh drwät.) Right hand.

Main gauche (mănh gōsh.) The left hand.

Majeur (Fr.) (mä-zhŭr.) Major; major key.

Major. *Greater*, in respect to intervals, scales, etc. It is used in combination with many other words. See *Intervals*.

Major scale. The scale in which the half-steps fall between the third and fourth, and seventh and eighth tones, both in ascending and descending. Also in which the intervals reckoned from the key-note are either *major* or *perfect*.

Malincólico (It.) (mä-lēn-*kō*-lē-kō.) ⎫ Melancholy.
Malinconia (It.) (mä-lēn-*kō*-nī-ä.) ⎭

Malincónico (It.) (mä-lēn-*kō*-nē-kō.) In a melancholy style.

Mancándo (It.) (män-*kăn*-dō.) Decreasing; dying away.

Mandola (It.) (män-dō-lä.) A mandolin of large size.

Mandolin(e). A pear-shaped instrument of the lute species, with four strings (generally doubled.) Tuned like the violin. The fingering is the same as that of violin, but the fingerboard is fretted like that of guitar. It is played with a *pick* or *plectrum*. While originating in Spain and Italy, the mandolin has become popular everywhere. The compass is about three octaves extending upward from " G " below the treble staff.

Maniéra (It.) (*mä-nē-ä-rä.*) Manner, style.

Máno (It.) (*mä-nō.*) The hand.

Máno destra (It.) (*mä-nō des-*trä.) The right hand.

Máno sinistra (It.) (*mä-nō sē-nis-*trä.) The left hand.

Manual. The key-board; in organ music it means that the passage is to be played by the hands alone without using the pedals.

Manualiter (Ger.) (mä-noo-*ä-*lĭ-tĕr.) Organ pieces to be played by the fingers alone without the pedals.

Marcándo (It.) (mär-*kän-*dō.) } Marked; accented;
Marcáto (It.) (mär-*kä-*tō.) } well-pronounced.

March. A military air or movement especially adapted to martial instruments; it is generally written in $\frac{2}{4}$, ₵ or $\frac{4}{4}$ rhythm.

Márcia funebre (It.) (*mär-*tshē-ä fōo-*nä-*brĕ.) Funeral march.

Martelláto (It.) (mär-tĕl-*lä-*tō.) *Hammered,* strongly marked.

Marziále (It.) (mär-tsē-*ä-*lĕ.) Martial; in the style of a march.

Mask. } A species of musical drama,
Maske (Ger.) (*mäs-*kĕ.) } or operetta, including sing-
Masque (Fr.) (mäsk.) } ing and dancing, performed by characters in masks. The masque was the predecessor of the opera.

Mass. A vocal composition performed during the celebration of High Mass, in the Roman Catholic Church, and generally accompanied by instruments. The Mass contains the following numbers: " Kyrie," " Gloria " (containing also the " Qui Tollis," " Gratias," " Quoniam," and " Cum Sancto Spirito "), " Credo " (with " Et Incarnatus," " Et Resurrexit," and " Amen," as subdivisions), " Sanctus," " Benedictus," " Agnus Dei," and " Dona Nobis." These are in beautiful contrast in the emotions they express, and therefore the Mass has always been a favorite form of composition.

Mässig (Ger.) (*mäs*-sĭg.) Moderate, moderately.

Mazurka (Ger.) (mä-*tsoor*-kä.) A lively Polish dance of a skipping character in 3/8 or 3/4 time, of a peculiar rhythmic construction, quicker than the Polonaise or Polácca.

Measure. That division of time by which the air and movement of music are regulated; the space between two bar lines on the staff. The measure is often miscalled a *bar*, but the terms should not be confused. See *Time*.

Mediant (Lat.) (*mā*-dĭ-ănt.) The third note of the scale; the *middle note* between the tonic and the dominant.

Medley. A mixture. A *Potpourri.*

Mehr (Ger.) (mār.) More.

Melodeon. See *Reed-organ.*

Melodía (It.) (mä-lō-*dē*-ä.) Melody, tune.

Melodrama. In modern music the term is applied to a declamation, recited (not sung) to a musical accompaniment. The "Manfred" music of Schumann is a fine example with orchestral accompaniment, while Richard Strauss has made a most effective modern setting or "background" (for piano) to Tennyson's "Enoch Arden." Reciting to music is sometimes called *Cantillation.*

Melody. 1. A succession of sounds so arranged as to produce a pleasing effect upon the ear; distinguished from *harmony* where two or more tones are sounded simultaneously. 2. By *the melody* the leading part in a harmonized composition is meant.

Melos (Gr.) (*mā*-lŏs.) Song. *Melos* is the name which Wagner applies to the vocal progressions of his later operas, which have not the form or symmetry of regular tunes.

Même (Fr.) (mām.) The same.

Méno (It.) (*mā*-nō.) Less.

Menuet (Fr.) (mŭn-ü-ay.) } A minuet; a slow
Menuetto (It.) (mĕ-noo-*ĕt*-tō.) } dance in 3/4 time.
See *Minuet.*

Méssa (It.) (*mes*-sä.) }
Messe (Fr.) (mäss.) } A Mass.
Messe (Ger.) (*mĕs*-sĕ.) }

Méssa di vóce (It.) The gradual swelling and diminishing of the vocal tone generally written thus: The *Méssa di Voce* requires thorough control of the breath.

Mésto (It.) (mes-tō.) Sad, mournful, melancholy.

Mestóso (It.) (mes-tō-zō.) Sadly, mournfully.

Mesure (Fr.) (muz-zür.) The measure; strict time.

Meter, Metre. Measure; verse; arrangement of poetical feet, or of long and short syllables in verse. The succession of accents in music. Meter is the rhythm of the *phrase*, not of the *measure*.

Metre, common. A stanza of four lines in iambic measure, the syllables of each being in number and order as follows: 8, 6, 8, 6.

Metre, eights and sevens. Consists of four lines usually in trochaic measure, designated thus, 8s and 7s, the syllables as follows: 8, 7, 8, 7. A few exceptions are found in iambic verse.

Metre, hallelujah. A stanza of six lines in iambic measure, the syllables of each being in number and order as follows: 6, 6, 6, 6, 8, 8.

Metre, long. Four lines in iambic measure, each line containing eight syllables.

Metre, particular or peculiar. This means that the poem has peculiarities or irregularities which prevent its being classified. Such poems generally require their own especial tunes.

Metre, sevens. Consists of four lines in trochaic measure, each line containing seven syllables.

Metre, sevens, and sixes. Consists of four lines, 7, 6, 7, 6, properly iambic, but a few exceptions (trochaic) are found.

Metre, short. Consists of four lines in iambic measure, the syllables in number and order as follows: 6, 6, 8, 6.

Metronom (Ger.) (mĕt-rō-nŏm.) } A machine in-
Metronome (Ger.) (mĕt-rō-nō-mĕ.) } vented by John Maelzel (in 1815), for measuring the time or duration of notes by means of a graduated scale and pendulum, which may be shortened or lengthened at pleasure. It is a pendulum with a movable counterweight which can be set at any designated figure and which will then swing to and fro that number of times per minute an audible click accompanying each oscillation

When made with a bell, the sound of this appliance denotes the beginning of each measure. The words of *tempo* on the metronome, such as *Andante*, *Largo*, etc., are entirely misleading; the teacher must be guided by the numerals only. Beethoven and Czerny were the first composers to use the metronome.

Metronomic marks. Figures appended to pieces of music, referring to corresponding figures on a metronome: The " M. M." employed in this connection means " Maelzel's Metronome," *not* " Metronome Mark." The following are examples of metronome marks: 1. M. M. ♩ = 112. 2. M. M. ♩ = 60. These would mean: 1. That the counterweight of the metronome is to be set at 112, and that each click is to represent the speed of a quarter-note, or in other words, that the speed is to be at the rate of 112 quarter-notes a minute. 2. This signifies that the metronome is to be set at sixty, and each click is to represent a dotted quarter.

Mézza (It.) (*met*-tsä.) ⎫
Mézzo (It.) (*met*-tsō.) ⎬ Medium, half.

Mézza vóce (It.) (*met*-tsä vō-tshĕ.) Half the power of the voice; softly.

Mézzo soprano (It.) (*met*-tsō sō-*prä*-nō.) A female voice of lower pitch than the soprano, or treble, but higher than the contralto. The general compass is See *Voice*.

Mi (It.) (mē.) A syllable used in solfa-ing to designate E, or the third note of the major scale.

Middle C. That C which is between the bass and treble staves.

Militáre (It.) (mē-lē-*tä*-rĕ.) Military, in a warlike, martial style.

Military band. An aggregation of performers on wood-wind, brass, and percussion instruments. The New York Twenty-second Regiment Band is composed of sixty-six instruments as follows:

2 piccolos	1 contra-bassoon
2 flutes	1 E♭ cornet
2 oboes	2 1st B♭ cornets

1 Ab piccolo clarinet	2 2nd Bb cornets
3 Eb clarinets	2 trumpets
8 1st Bb clarinets	2 flügelhorns
4 2nd " "	4 French horns
4 3rd " "	2 Eb alto horns
1 alto "	2 Bb tenor horns
1 bass "	2 euphoniums
1 sopr. saxophone	3 trombones
1 alto "	5 bombardons or tubas
1 tenor "	3 drums
1 bass "	1 pair cymbals
2 bassoons	

The military band is composed, therefore, of the orchestral wind-instruments plus saxophones, cornets and drums. The oboe is often omitted. The clarinets are made very prominent, taking the place of the strings. Instruments of high pitch are used, such as the E flat clarinet, the A flat clarinet, the tierce flute, and others, that would be too shrill for orchestral use. A military band has sometimes as many performers as a full orchestra.

Military music. Music intended for military bands, marches, quicksteps, etc.

Minacciándo (It.) (mē-nät-tshē-*än*-dō.) ⎫
Minacciévole (It.) (ınē-nät-tshē-*ch*-vō-lĕ.) ⎬
Minaccióso (It.) (mē-nät-tshē-*ō*-zō.) ⎭
Threatening, menacing.

Minim. A half-note; a note equal to one-half of a semibreve.

Minim rest. A half rest.

Minnesinger (Ger.) (min-nĕ-*sĭng*-ĕr.) Minstrels of the twelfth and thirteenth centuries, who wandered from place to place singing a great variety of songs and melodies. They were *love-singers* (the word *Minne* meaning homage to woman) and generally of high rank. Wagner's opera *Tannhäuser* is founded upon the epoch of the minnesingers. The minnesingers were the troubadours of Germany.

Minor. Less; smaller; in speaking of intervals, etc.

Minor scale. There are two kinds, *Harmonic* and *Melodic;* in the first variety the half-steps fall between the second and third, fifth and sixth, and seventh and eighth degrees, both in

101

ascending and descending; in the other the half-step falls between the second and third, and seventh and eighth degrees ascending, and between the sixth and fifth, and third and second, descending. Also the scale form in which the majority of intervals reckoned from the key-note are either *minor* or *perfect*.

Minuet. The minuet is always in triple rhythm, and of slow tempo as a dance, but it has been so freely treated by the classical composers that its tempo is very often rapid. *Tempo di Minuetto* has come to mean an *allegretto*, or even a quicker speed.

Minuétto (It.) (mē-noo-*et*-tō.) A minuet.

Miserere (Lat.) (mee-zay-*ray*-ray.) *Have mercy;* a psalm of supplication, especially used during Holy Week.

Missa (Lat.) (*mis*-sä.) A Mass.

Misterióso (It.) (mees-tay-ree-ō-zo.) Mysteriously; in a mysterious manner.

Misuráto (It.) (mee-soo-rä-tō.) Measured; in strict, measured time.

Mit (Ger.) (mǐt.) With, by.

Mixture stop. An organ-stop consisting of three or more ranks of pipes. These are not intended to sound alone. They are voiced an octave, a fifth, a twelfth, etc., above the regular stops and they add the harmonics to the diapasons. See *Acoustics* and *Harmonics.*

Móbile (It.) (mō-bē-lĕ.) Movable, changeable.

Mode. A particular system or constitution of sounds, by which the octave is divided into certain intervals, according to the genus. The arrangement of notes in a scale, — major, minor, etc.

Mode, major. That in which the third degree from the key-note forms a major interval.

Mode, minor. That in which the third degree from the key-note forms a minor interval.

Moderáto (It.) (mō-day-rä-tō.) Moderately; in moderate time.

Modes, church. The ancient modes called by the following names: *Dorian, Phrygian, Lydian, Mixo-Lydian, Œolian, Ionian,* or *Iastian.* The Gregorian tones. See Ritter's "History of Music," William's "Story of Notation," and the "Oxford History of Music."

Modes, ecclesiastical. The ancient church modes. The Gregorian tones.

Modulation. A transition of key; going from one key to another, by a certain succession of chords, either in a natural and flowing manner, or sometimes in a sudden and unexpected manner. As applied to the voice, modulation means to accommodate the tone to a certain degree of intensity, or light and shade.

Modulation, abrupt. Sudden modulation into keys which are not closely related to the original key.

Modulation, deceptive. Any modulation by which the ear is deceived and led to an unexpected harmony.

Modulation, enharmonic. A modulation effected by altering the *notation* of one or more intervals belonging to some *characteristic* chord, and thus changing the key and the harmony into which it would naturally have resolved.

Moll (Ger.) (mŏll.) Minor.

Mólto (It.) (*mól*-to.) Much; very much; extremely; a great deal.

Monody (Eng.) (mŏn-ō-dy.) A composition for a single voice. The term originally applied to those solos which were used in the earliest operas and oratorios, A.D. 1600 (*circa*); for before that time solos did not exist in any large work. Monody, was homophony, as opposed to counterpoint or polyphony.

Monodic. For *one* voice; a solo.

Morbidezza, con (It.) (mŏr-bē-*det*-sä.) Morbidly.

Morceau (Fr.) (mŏr-sō.) A musical piece, or composition.

Mordént (It.) (mŏr-*dänt*.) A group of two or more grace notes played rapidly before a principal note; consisting of the principal note itself and the note above or below. The sign ∿ over the principal note calls for the upper auxiliary, (Ger. *Pralltriller*) the same sign with a vertical line through it, ∿ for the lower auxiliary. Mordents are notated and executed as follows:

The accent comes on the first note of group.

103

For detailed description see *Elson's Music Dictionary.*

Moréndo (It.) (mō-*ren*-dō.) Dying away; expiring; gradually diminishing the tone and the time.

Mormorándo (It.) (mŏr-mō-*rän*-dō.) ⎱ With a gentle,
Mormoróso (It.) (mŏr-mō-*rō*-zō.) ⎰ murmuring sound.

Mósso (It.) (*mòs*-sō.) Moved, movement, motion. *Meno mosso*, less movement, slower. *Più mosso*, more movement; quicker.

Motet. ⎱ A sacred composition of the anthem
Motett. ⎰ style, for several voices. The words are taken from the Scriptures. The motet is generally contrapuntal, and it is possible that the word is derived from *moto* (motion), because of the constant motion of all the parts.

Motif (Fr.) (mo-*teef*.) A motive, or figure. The term *Leitmotif* (which see) was used by Wagner for his guiding-figures.

Motion. The progression of a melody, or part.

Motive. The characteristic and predominant passage of an air; the theme or subject of a composition; a figure.

Móto (It.) (*mō*-tō.) Motion, movement; *con móto*, with motion; rather quick.

Móto perpetuo (It.) (mo-tō pair-*pay*-too-oh.) Perpetual motion; a study in rapidity of execution and endurance.

Mouth-harmonica. A set of graduated metal reeds mounted in a narrow frame, blown by the mouth, and producing different tones on expiration and inspiration.

Mouth-piece. That part of a trumpet, horn, etc., which is applied to the lips.

Mouvement (Fr.) (moov-mänh.) ⎱ Motion; move-
Movimento (It.) (mō-vĕ-*men*-tō.) ⎰ ment; impulse; the time of a piece.

Movement. The name given to any portion of a composition comprehended under the same general measure or time; a composition consists of as many *movements* as there are positive changes in time and style.

Munter (Ger.) (*moon*-tĕr.) Lively, sprightly.

Murmelnd (Ger.) (*moor*-mĕlnd.) Murmuring.

Mus. Bac. An abbreviation of *Bachelor of Music.* (Little used.)

Mus. Doc. An abbreviation of *Doctor of Music.*

Musetta (It.) (moo-zĕt-tä.) ⎱ A species of small
Musette (Fr.) (mü-zet.) ⎰ bagpipe. An air or
dance composed for the musette. A primitive
oboe. A composition, or movement in a composition, with a drone-bass.

Mutation. Change, transition; the transformation
of the voice occurring at the age of puberty.

Mutation, or *filling-up stops* are those which do not
give a tone corresponding to the key pressed
down; such as the quint, tierce, twelfth, etc.

Mute. A small clamp of brass, ivory, or wood,
sometimes placed on the bridge of a violin, viola,
or violoncello, to diminish the tone of the instrument by damping or checking its vibrations.
The direction for using it is *Con sordino,* for removing it *Senza sordino.* In brass instruments
the mute is a pear-shaped, leather-covered pad
introduced into the bell of the horn, trumpet or
trombone to modify the tone.

Muthig (Ger.) (*moo-tĭg.*) Courageous, spirited.

N

Nacaire (Fr.) (nä-kār.) ⎱ A brass drum with a loud
Nacara (It.) (nä-kä-rä.) ⎰ metallic tone, formerly
much used in France and Italy.

Nachahmung (Ger.) (*nakh*-ä-moong.) Imitation.

Nach (Ger.) (näkh.) After.

Nachdruck (Ger.) (*näkh*-drook.) Emphasis, accent.

Nachdrücklich (Ger.) (*näkh*-drük-lĭkh.) ⎱ Energetic,
Nachdrucksvoll (Ger.)(*näkh*-drooks-fōl.) ⎰
emphatic, forcible.

Nacht-horn (Ger.) (*näkht*-hōrn.) *Night-horn;* an
organ-stop of 8-foot tone, nearly identical with
the *Quintaton* but of larger scale and more horn-
like tone.

Nacht-musik (Ger.) (*näkht*-moo-zĭk.) *Night-music;*
serenade.

Narrator. A name given to the character which
gives Scriptural story, generally in recitative,
in an oratorio, or Passion-music.

Natural. A character ♮, used to contradict a sharp,
or flat. See *Flat.*

Natural horn. The old French horn, called also
Waldhorn, without any keys.

Natural keys. Those which have no sharp or flat at the signature, as C major and A minor.

Neapolitan sixth. A chord composed of a minor third and minor sixth, and occurring on the sub-dominant, or fourth degree of the scale. In the key of C (major or minor) this chord is really the same as the first inversion of the triad of Db.

Neck. That part of a violin, guitar, or similar instrument, extending from the head to the body, and on which the fingerboard is fixed.

Negligénte (It.) (nāl-yē-*jen*-tĕ.) Negligent, unconstrained.

Negligénza (It.) (nāl-yē-*jen*-tsä.) Negligence, carelessness.

Negli (It. pl.) (*nāl*-yē.) } In the, at the.
Nei (It. pl.) (*nā*-ē.)

Nel (It.) (nĕl.)
Nella (It.) (*nĕl*-lä.)
Nelle (It. pl.) (*nĕl*-lĕ.) } In the, at the.
Nello (It.) (*nĕl*-lō.)
Nell' (It.) (nĕl.)

Nétto (It.) (*net*-tō.) Neat, clear, quick, nimble.

Neu (Ger.) (noi.) New.

Nicht (Ger.) (nĭkht.) Not.

Nineteenth. An organ-stop, tuned a nineteenth above the diapasons. See *Larigot.*

Ninth. An interval consisting of an octave and a second. Nine diatonic intervals.

Nóbile (It.) (*nō*-bē-lĕ.) Noble, grand, impressive.

Nobilità, con (It.) (nō-bē-lē-*tä*, kŏn.) With nobility; dignified.

Nocturn. } A composition of a dreamy and ro-
Nocturne. } mantic character suitable for evening recreation; also, a piece resembling a serenade, to be played at night in the open air.

Nodal points. } In *music,* the fixed points of a
Nodes. } sonorous cord, or string, at which it divides itself, when it vibrates, by aliquot parts and produces the harmonic sounds. See *Harmonics.*

Noël (Fr.) (nō-ĕl.) A Christmas carol, or hymn. The word had its origin in *Nouvelles* or *News, i.e.,* good tidings.

Non (It.) (nŏn.) Not, no.

Non troppó (It.) (nŏn *trŏp*-pō.) Not too much; moderately.

106

Notation. The art of representing tones by written or printed characters.

Notehead. The *head* or principal part of the note as distinguished from the stem and hook.

Notturno (It.) (nŏt-*toor*-nō.) A nocturne.

Novelette. A name bestowed by Schumann (Op. 21) on instrumental compositions free in form, romantic in character, and characterized by a variety of contrasting themes.

Nuances (Fr. pl.) (nü-änhs.) Lights and shades of expression; variety of intonation.

Nuóvo (It.) (noo-ō-vō.) New; *di nuóvo*, newly, again.

Nuptial songs. Wedding-songs; marriage-songs.

Nut. The small bridge at the upper end of the fingerboard of a guitar or violin, over which the strings pass to the pegs, or screws.

O

O. This letter, forming a circle or double C, was used by the mediæval monks as the sign of triple time from the idea that the *ternary*, or number *three*, being the most perfect of all numbers, and representing the *Trinity*, would be best expressed by a circle, the most perfect of all figures. The imperfect, or common time, was designated by a C, or semicircle — a broken circle.

O, before a consonant (It.) (ō.) } Or, as, either.
Od, before a vowel (It.) (ōd.) }

The sign O is placed over notes in violin, 'cello, etc., music to indicate "open string," or as a *harmonic* mark. It is also used in the figuration of the *Diminished Triad* in Harmony.

Obbligáto (It.) (ōb-blē-*gä*-tō.) | Obligatory, *in-*
Obbligáti (It. pl.) (ōb-blē-*gä*-tē.) | *dispensable, nec-*
Obligé (Fr.) (ō-blee-zhä.) | *essary;* a part,
Obligat (Ger.) (ōb-lĭ-*gät*.) | or parts, which cannot be omitted, being indispensably necessary to a proper performance; a temporary solo in a concerted work, often misspelled *Obligato.*

Ober. (Ger.) (ō-bĕr.) Upper, higher.

Ober-manual (Ger.) (ō-bĕr mä-noo-*äl*.) The upper manual.

Oblique motion. When one part ascends, or descends, whilst the others remain stationary.

Oboe (Ger.) (ō-bō-ĕ.) } The hautboy; an instru-
Oboé (It.) (ō-bō-ā.) } ment of great antiquity,
consisting of a conical tube with various sound
holes and keys, played with a double reed.
The tone is small and nasal, often reedy in effect.
While capable of expressing grief and pathos
under certain conditions, it is more often used in
pastoral scenes to suggest rural simplicity and
gayety. The compass is from B♭ below the treble
staff to E or F above, with all the chromatic
intervals. The orchestra is always tuned to the
" a " sounded by the oboe. For detailed information see A. Elson's " Orchestral Instruments " or Prout's " Orchestra." A characteristic stop on the organ is called Oboe or Hautboy.

Oboé da caccia (It.) (ō-bō-ā dä kät-tshē-ä.) A
larger species of *oboe* with the music written in
the alto clef. Its place is taken, in the modern
orchestra, by the English horn.

Ocarina. A simple wind instrument made of
terra-cotta, in shape like an elongated egg,
sharply pointed at one end. There are sound
holes for fingers and thumbs and the tone is
produced through a mouthpiece of whistle principle. It is limited to the diatonic scale and
comes in various keys and sizes. The tone is
soft and veiled.

Octave. An interval measuring eight diatonic
degrees; also the name of an organ-stop.

Octave, Contra. See *Tablature.*

Octave coupler. A device used on organs to add
the upper or lower octave as may be needed to
the notes actually played.

Octave fifteenth. An organ-stop of bright, sharp
tone, sounding an octave above the fifteenth.

Octave flute. See *piccolo.*

Octave hautboy. A 4-foot organ reed-stop; the
pipes are of the hautboy species.

Octave, great. See *Tablature.*

Octave-marks. The abbreviation 8va or 8, followed by a dotted line, indicates that the note
or notes over which it is placed are to be played
an octave *higher* until the end of the dotted line
or the word *loco* is reached. When the *lower*
octave is desired the dotted line, etc., is placed
under the notes, generally with the addition of
words " bassa." Often the higher or lower oc-

tave is to be played *with* the printed note, in which case the term *col* 8va or *col* 8 is used.

Octet. } A composition for eight parts, or for
Octett. } eight voices.

Oder (Ger.) (ō-dĕr.) Or, or else.

Œuvre (Fr.) (üvr.) See *Opus*.

Off. In organ music, a direction to push in a stop, or coupler; as *choir to Gt.* off

Offertory (Eng.) (ŏf-fĕr-tō-ry.) A hymn, prayer, anthem, or instrumental piece sung or played during the collection of the offering. It follows the *Credo* in the Mass.

Ohne (Ger.) (ō-nē.) Without.

One-lined octave. See *Tablature*.

Open diapason. An organ-stop, generally made of metal, and thus called because the pipes are open at the top. It commands the whole scale, and is the most important stop of the instrument.

Open pedal. The right-hand pedal of a pianoforte; that which raises the dampers and allows the vibrations of the strings to continue.

Open string. The string of a violin, etc., when not pressed by the finger.

Open unison stop. The open diapason stop.

Oper (Ger.) (ō-pĕr.) } A drama set to music, for
Opera (It.) (ō-pĕ-rä.) } voices and instruments, and with scenery, decorations and action. The term is also applied to any *work*, or publication of a composer. (See also *Opus*.) The chief parts of the opera, apart from the overture, are the recitative, aria, chorus, and the various kinds of *ensemble* — duet, trio, quartet, quintet, sextet, etc. — of which the *finale* is the most important. In France operas are classified as follows: Grand Opéra, in which the plot is throughout earnest, and there are no spoken passages. Opéra Bouffe, a comic opera, but one of a much lighter character than an *opéra comique*. Opéra Comique, an opera with spoken dialogue, as distinguished from the *grand opéra*, which has no spoken dialogue. Opéra Lyrique, a lyric opera. Consult A. Elson's "Critical History of Opera," and Grove's Dictionary.

Operetta. A little opera, generally in a light and playful vein.

Ophicleide (ŏf-ĭ-klīd.) A large bass wind instrument of brass, sometimes used in large orches tras, but chiefly in military music. It has a compass of three octaves, and the tone is loud and of deep pitch. This instrument is now practically obsolete. The bass-tuba takes the place of the ophicleide in almost all modern works, but does not reproduce its peculiarly raucous tone.

Ophicleide stop. The most powerful manual reed-stop known, in an organ, of 8 or 4-foot scale, and is usually placed upon a separate sound-board, with a great pressure of wind.

Oppure (It.) (ōp-*poo*-ray.) Or; or else. See *ossia*.

Opus (Lat.) (ō-pŭs.) ⎱ Work, composition; as, Op.
Opus (Ger.) (ō-poos.) ⎰ 1, the first work, or publication of a composer. An *opus* may include several numbers or may consist of a single piece.

Oratório (It.) (ō-rä-*tō*-rĭ-ō.) ⎫
Oratorium (Lat.) (ō-rä-*tō*-rĭ-oom.) ⎬ Oratorio. A
Oratorium (Ger.) (ō-rä-*tō*-rĭ-oom.) ⎭ species of musical drama consisting of airs, recitatives, trios, choruses, etc. It is founded upon some Scriptural narrative, and performed without the aid of scenery and action. Consult Naumann's "History of Music," Ritter's "Students' History of Music," Dickinson's "Music in the History of the Western Church," and Upton's "Standard Oratorios."

Orchester (Ger.) (ōr-*khĕs*-tĕr.) ⎫ A body of perfor-
Orchéstra (It.) (ōr-*käs*-trä.) ⎬ mers on string in-
Orchestre (Fr.) (ōr-kĕs-tr.) ⎭ struments, or string instruments in conjunction with various wood-wind, brass and percussion instruments. Orchestras are large or small according to the number or variety of instruments employed. The modern opera or symphony orchestras consist of from 60 to 116 performers. The Boston Symphony orchestra (1909) consists of 98 performers as follows:

30 Violins	1 Bass Clarinet
10 Violas	3 Bassoons
10 'Cellos	1 Contra Bassoon
8 Basses	8 Horns
4 Flutes	4 Trumpets
3 Oboes	3 Trombones
1 Cor Anglais	1 Tuba
3 Clarinets	1 Harp
2 Tympani, and 4 other Percussion.	

Prout's "The Orchestra," or A. Elson's "Orchestral Instruments and their Use."

Orchestration. The arranging of music for an orchestra; scoring; instrumentation.

Orchestrion (ŏr-kĕs-trĭ-ŏn.) A large mechanical instrument consisting of various organ pipes, reeds, bells, etc.

Organ. This term in modern phraseology applies only to the instrument known also as the "pipe-organ." It is of very ancient origin, and from a crude instrument of less than a dozen pipes in a row like a "Pan's Pipe" it has grown into the massive instrument of to-day, containing thousands of open flue, stopped and reed pipes of every conceivable tone color, and ranging from the deep 64-foot tone to the highest harmonic. The pitch of these extreme tones is almost indistinguishable. The organ varies in power from a thunderous fortississimo to a faint pianississimo scarcely audible.

The pipes are made to sound through the medium of compressed air supplied by bellows. The organ is played from a key-board like that of a piano, but called *manual*. The various ranks or sets of pipes are controlled by stops placed within reach. On large modern organs there are three to five manuals. Great, Choir, Swell, Solo, Echo, beside a Pedal key-board (played by the feet). The organ is unquestionably the king of all instruments. Consult Stainer's *The Organ*, Ed. by J. H. Rogers, Audsley's *Art of Organ Building*.

Organ-point. A long pedal note, or stationary bass, upon which is formed a series of chords, or harmonic progressions. Also a *Cadenza*.

Organum. (or-*gah*-num.) The Latin word for organ. Also the term applied to the first crude attempts at harmony in ancient times, when the chords were only formed of fourths and fifths and always moved in parallel motion.

Ornamental notes. All notes not forming an essential part of the harmony, but introduced as embellishments. See *Trill, Turn, Grace-notes, Appoggiatúra, Acciaccatúra.*

Osservánza (It.) (ōs-sĕr-*vän*-tsä.) Observation; attention; strictness in keeping time.

Ossía (It.) (ŏs-sē-ä.) Or; otherwise; **or else.** Indicating another way of playing a passage.

Ostinato (It.) (ŏs-tēe-*nah*-tō.) Obstinate, continuous, unceasing; adhering to some peculiar melodial figure, or group of notes.

Ottáva (It.) (ŏt-*tä*-vä.) An octave; an eighth.

Ottáva álta (It.) (ŏt-*tä*-vä äl-tä.) The octave above an octave higher; marked thus, 8va.

Ottáva bássa (It.) (ŏt-*tä*-vä *bäs*-sä.) The octave below, marked thus, 8va bássa.

Ou (Fr.) (oo.) Or.

Outer voices. The highest and lowest voices.

Ouvert (Fr.) (oo-vair.) Open.

Ouverture (Fr.) (oo-vair-*tür*.) } An introductory
Overtúra (It.) (ō-vĕr-*too*-rä.) } part to an ora-
Ouvertüre (Ger.) (ō-fĕr-*too*-rĕ.) } torio, opera, etc.;
Overture (Eng.) (ō-vĕr-tshŭr.) } also an independent piece for a full band or orchestra, in which case it is called a *concert overture*.

P

P. Abbr. of *Pedal* (P. or Ped.); *piano* (*p*), *pp*, *pianissimo*; *ppp*, *pianississimo*; Verdi and Tschaikowsky have employed *ppppp* several times. P. F., *pianoforte*; *più forte* (louder); *poco forte* (rather loud); *fp*, *fortepiano* (*i.e.* loud, instantly diminishing to soft); *mp*, *mezzo-piano* (half-soft); and in Fr. organ-music, *P* stands for *Positif* (choir-organ.)

Pandean pipes. } One of the most ancient and
Pan's pipes. } simple of musical instruments; it was made of reeds or tubes of different lengths fastened together and tuned to each other, stopped at the bottom and blown into by the mouth at the top.

Pantomime. An entertainment in which not a word is spoken or sung, but the sentiments are expressed by mimicry and gesticulation accompanied by instrumental music.

Parallel intervals. Intervals passing in two parallel parts in the same direction; consecutive intervals.

Parallel keys. The major and minor founded on same key note.

Parallel motion. When the parts continue on the same degree, and only repeat the same sounds;

also, two parts continuing their course and still remaining at exactly the same distance from each other.

Paraphrase. A transcription or rearrangement of a vocal or instrumental composition for some other instrument or instruments, with more or less brilliant variations.

Parlándo (It.) (pär-*län*-dō.) } Accented; in a de-
Parlánte (It.) (pär-*län*-tĕ.) } clamatory style; in a recitative, or speaking style.

Part. The music for each separate voice or instrument.

Partial tone. See *Harmonics.*

Partita (It.) (par-*tee*-ta.) The earliest form of the instrumental suite.

Partition (Fr.) (pär-tē-sǐ-ŏnh.) } A *score; a full score,*
Partitur (Ger.) (pär-tē-*toor.*) } or entire draft of
Partitúra (It.) (pär-tē-*loo*-rä.) } a composition for voices, or instruments, or both.

Part-song. An unaccompanied choral composition for at least three voices or parts. A melody harmonized by other parts more or less freely, but from which counterpoint is for the most part excluded.

Pas (Fr.) (*pah.*) A step, or a dance in a ballet.

Passacáglia (It.) (päs-sä-*kal*-yē-ä.) A species of chaconne, a slow dance with divisions on a ground-bass in triple rhythm. Rather bombastic in character.

Passage. Any phrase, or short portion of an air, or other composition. Every member of a strain, or movement, is a *passage.*

Passamézzo (It.) (päs-sä-*met*-sō.) An old slow dance, little differing from the *Pavane,* but somewhat more rapid. Generally in ⅔ rhythm.

Passecaille (Fr.) (pass-käh-ĕ.) See *passacaglia.*

Passepied (Fr.) (pass-pi-ay.) A sort of jig; a lively old French dance in ¾, ⅜, or ⅝ time; a kind of quick minuet, with three or more strains, or reprises. A *Paspy.*

Passing notes. Notes which do not belong to the harmony, but which serve to connect those which are essential.

Passionataménte (It.) (päs-sē-ō-nä-tä-*men*-tĕ.) } Passionate; im-
Passionáto (It.) (päs-sē-ō-*nä*-tō.) } passioned; with fervor and pathos.

113

Passióne (It.) (päs-sē-ō-ně.) Passion, feeling.

Passion music. ⎫ Music picturing the suffer-
Passions-musik (Ger.) ⎬ ings of the Saviour, and
(päs-sĭ-*ōns moo*-zĭk.) ⎭ his death.

Pasticcio (It.) (päs-*tĭt*-tshe-ō.) ⎱ A medley made up
Pastiche (Fr.) (päs-teesh.) ⎰ of songs, etc., by
various composers; the poetry being written to
the music.

Pastoral. A musical drama, the personages and
scenery of which are chiefly rural. An instrumental composition written in the pastoral
style.

Patética (It.) (pä-*tä*-tē-kä.) ⎱ Pathetic.
Patético (It.) (pä-*te*-tē-kō.) ⎰

Pateticaménte (It.) (pä-tä-tē-kä-*men*-tě.) Patheti-
cally.

Patiménto (pä-tē-*men*-tō.) Affliction, grief, suffering.

Pauken (Ger. pl.) (*pou*-k'n.) Kettledrums; also, to
thump.

Pausa (It.) (pä-*oo*-zä.) A pause.

Pause (Ger.) (*pou*-zě.) A rest.

Pause (Eng.) See *Hold, Fermata.*

Pavan (Eng.) ⎫ A grave, stately dance,
Pavána (It.) (pä-*vä*-nä.) ⎬ which took its name
Pavane (Fr.) (pä-*vänh*.) ⎭ from *pavano,* a peacock.
It is in quadruple rhythm.

Paventáto (It.) (pä-věn-*tä*-tō.) ⎰ Fearful; timorous;
Paventóso (It.) (pä-věn-*tō*-zō.) ⎱ with anxiety and
embarrassment.

Pavillon chinois (Fr.) (pä-vē-yǒnh she-noo-wä.)
An instrument with numerous little bells.

Peal. A set of bells tuned to each other; the
changes rung upon a set of bells.

Pedal. This word is used in many different ways
in music, but always has reference to some
mechanism moved by the foot. The most general usage of the word applies to the *piano pedals.*
The object of the right-hand piano pedal is to
raise the dampers from the wires, so that the
sound may be prolonged after the finger of the
player has left the key. On the organ *Pedal*
refers to the keyboard played with the feet,
also the *swell* and various combination stops and
couplers actuated by the feet. Some pianos are
fitted with *pedal keyboard;* others with extra pedals for *mandolin* and other imitative effects.

Pedals are also certain low foundation notes on *trombone*, *horn*, etc. On the *harp* the pedals raise the notes in pitch by semi-tones. See Elson's *Music Dictionary* or Mathews' *School of the Piano Pedal.*

Pedal point. A sustained bass, or pedal note, held on or sustained for several measures, while a variety of chords are introduced.

Pentatonic scale. A scale of five notes, the fourth and seventh degrees being omitted.

Per (It.) (*pair.*) For, by, from, in, through.

Percussion (Eng.) (pĕr-*kŭsh*-ŏn.) } A general
Percussióne (It.) (pār-koos-sē-ō-nĕ.) } name for all instruments that are struck, as a gong, drum, bell, cymbals, triangle, tambourine.

Perdendósi (It.) (pār-den-*dō*-zē.) Gradually decreasing the tone and the time; dying away, becoming extinct.

Perfect. A term applied to certain intervals and chords. See *Intervals.*

Perfect cadence. See *Cadence.*

Period (Eng.) A complete and perfect musical sentence, containing at least two phrases and bringing the ear to a perfect conclusion or state of rest.

Pesánte (It.) (pĕ-zän-tĕ.) Heavy, ponderous; with importance and weight, impressively.

Petit (Fr.) (pĕ-*tē*.) Little, small.

Peu (Fr.) (pŭh.) Little, a little.

Pezzo (It.) (*pet*-sō.) A detached piece of music.

Phantasie (Ger.) (fän-tä-zē.) See *Fantasia.*

Phonetic. Vocal, representing sounds.

Phonograph. An instrument invented in 1877, by Thomas A. Edison, by means of which sounds either vocal or instrumental, the tones of the speaking voice, and even noises, can be recorded and reproduced.

Phrase. The phrase in music may be regarded as a dependent division, like a single line in a poem. In simple music the phrases balance each other.

Phrasing. Dividing the musical sentences into rhythmical sections. The punctuation of music.

Piacére (It.) (pē-ä-*tshā*-rᵡ.) Pleasure, inclination, fancy; *a piacére*, at pleasure.

Piacévole (It.) (pē-ä-*tshe*-vō-lĕ.) Pleasing, graceful, agreeable.

Piagnévole (It.) (pē-än-*ye*-vō-lĕ.) Mournful, doleful, lamentable.

Piangéndo (It.) (pē-än-*jen*-dō.) Plaintively, sorrowfully, weeping.

Pianíssimo (It.) (pē-än-*is*-sē-mō.) Extremely soft.

Piano (It.) (pee-ä-no.) Soft.

Pianoforte or Piano. The piano comes from the combination of the two instruments of antiquity, the *Dulcimer*, and the *Monochord*. The immediate predecessors of the piano were the *Clavichord*, the *Harpsichord*, and the *Spinet* (see these words). The principle of striking the wires of the instrument with hammers was invented by Cristofori, a native of Padua, Italy, about 1710. Great improvements were made in the piano in Germany, Silbermann manufacturing very sweet-toned instruments, and Stein inventing the soft pedal. But the best pianos at the beginning of the nineteenth century were made in England, where an Alsatian, named Erhardt, afterwards changed into Erard, and a Scotchman, named Broadwood, made many improvements in the instrument, the latter inventing the damper-pedal Elson's "History of Music in America."

Piátti (It. pl.) (pē-*ät*-tē.) Cymbals.

Pibroch (pē-brŏk.) Music peculiar to Scotland performed on the bagpipe.

Picchiettáto (It.) (pē-kē-ĕt-*tä*-tō.) Scattered, detached; in violin-playing, it means that sort of staccáto indicated by dots under a slur.

Píccolo (It.) (*pē*-kō-lō.) Small; little.

Piccolo. A 2-foot organ-stop, of wood pipes producing a bright and clear tone in unison with the fifteenth.

Píccolo. A small flute. See *Flute*.

Picchettáto (It.) (pē-kĕt-*tä*-tō.) See *Picchiettáto*.

Piéna (It.) (pē-ä-nä.) } Full.
Piéno (It.) (pē-ä-nō.) }

Pietà (It.) (pē-ä-tä.) Pity.

Pietosaménte (It.) (pē-ä-tō-zä-*men*-tĕ.) } Compas-
Pietóso (It.) (pē-ä-*tō*-zō.) } sionately; tenderly; pitifully.

Pincé (Fr.) (pănh-say.) *Pinched.* See *Pizzicáto*.

Pipe. Any tube formed of a reed, or of metal, or of wood, which, being blown at one end, produces a musical sound. (See *Horn*, *Stop*, and *Organ*.) Organ-pipes divide into two classes the *reed* and the *flue-pipe*. The reed-pipe has its column of air set in vibration by means of a reed which is set in a box or reservoir. The *flue-pipe* is caused to sound by directing the wind against a thin edge in the mouth of the pipe, only a slight portion of the current of air entering the pipe, but this causes the column of air within to vibrate. Flue-pipes may be stopped or open. For description of the method of vibration of various kinds of pipes, see Blaserna's "Sound and Music," Zahm's "Sound and Music," and Pole's "Philosophy of Music."

Pitch. The acuteness or gravity of any particular sound, or of the tuning of any instrument. Pitch can most scientifically be defined as the *rate* of *vibration*. Rapid vibrations mean a high tone, slow vibrations a deep one. The standard of pitch has always been a variable one, thus the note A, which in Paris at present has 435 vibrations in 1858 was given 448, and in 1699 had only 404, while Handel's tuning-fork dated 1740 gives the same note 416 vibrations.

In 1859 France adopted a pitch of 435 vibrations per second for A (treble staff.) In 1891 the United States concurred in this pitch which is now called *International Pitch.* Germany uses a pitch slightly higher. *Concert Pitch* was indefinite, but generally higher than common pitch for the sake of brilliancy.

Più (It.) (pē-*oo.*) More.

Più mósso (It.) (*pēe-oo mŏs-sō.*) } More motion,
Più móto (It.) (*pēe-oo mō-to.*) } quicker.

Pizzicáto (It.) (pit-sē-kä-tō.) *Pinched;* meaning that the strings of the violin, violoncello, etc., are not to be played with the bow, but pinched, or snapped with the fingers, producing a *staccáto* effect.

Plácido (It.) (*plă-tshēe-dō.*) Placid, tranquil, calm.

Plagal cadence. A cadence in which the final chord on the tonic is preceded by the harmony of the sub-dominant. See *Cadence.*

Plagal mode. A church mode or scale in which the *final* or keynote was the fourth tone upward.

Plain chant. The plain-song. See *Cánto Férmo.*

Plain-song. The name given to the old ecclesias-

117

tical chant when in its most simple state and without harmony. See Stainer & Barrett, Dickinson's "Music in the History of the Western Church," or Helmore's "Plain-Song."

Plectrum (Lat.) (*plĕk-*trŭm.) A quill, or piece of ivory or hard wood used to twitch the strings of the mandolin, zither, etc. (It.) *Penna.*

Plein jeu (Fr.) (plänh zhü.) Full organ; the term is also applied to a mixture-stop of several ranks of pipes.

Plus (Fr.) (plü.) More.

Pochettíno (It.) (pō-kĕt-*tē-*nō.) } Very little, slower.
Pochétto (It.) (pō-*ket-*tō.)

Póco (It.) (*pō-*kō.) Little.

Póco a póco (It.) (*pō-*kō ä *pō-*kō.) By degrees, little by little.

Pói (It.) (*pō-*ē.) Then, after, afterwards; *piano pói forte,* soft, then loud.

Pói a pói (It.) (*pō-*ē ä *pō-*ē.) By degrees.

Pói a pói tútte le córde (It.) (*pō-*ē ä *pō-*ē *too-*tĕ lĕ *kōr-*dĕ.) Lift the soft pedal gradually. See *Pedal.*

Point (Fr.) (pwanh.) A dot.

Polácca (It.) (pō-*läk-*kä.) A Polish national dance in ¾ time. See *Polonaise.*

Polka. A lively Bohemian dance in ²⁄₄ time.

Polka mazurka (*pōl-*kä mä-*zŭr-*kä.) A dance in triple time, played slow, and having its accent on the last part of the measure.

Polka redowa (*pōl-*kä rĕd-ō-ä.) A dance tune in triple time, played faster than the polka mazurka, and having its accent on the first part of the measure.

Polonaise (Fr.) (pōl-ō-*nāz.*) A Polish dance written in ¾ rhythm, and containing every contrast possible. The melody contains runs, skips, and many artificial groupings, and syncopation occurs freely both in the melody and the accompaniment.

Polyphonic. *Polyphonic music* is *many voiced* or *plural-voiced* music, and is, where the music is formed of two or more different melodies going on simultaneously. Counterpoint.

Pompóso (It.) (pŏm-*pō-*zō.) Pompous, stately, grand.

Ponderóso (It.) (pŏn-dĕ-ɾō-zō.) Ponderously, massively, heavily.

Ponticéllo (It.) (pŏn-tē-*tshel*-lō.) The bridge of a violin, guitar, etc. The direction to bow near the bridge is *sul ponticello*, and the result is a thin, squeaky, but incisive tone.

Portaménto (It.) (pōr-tä-*men*-tō.) From *portare*, to carry. Indicates a carrying or gliding of the tone from one note to the next, but so rapidly that the intermediate notes are not defined, as would be the case in a *Legato* passage between two principal notes. The expression occurs generally in vocal music, but may be found in instrumental music.

Portunal-flaut (Ger.) (pōr-too-*näl*.) An organ-stop of the clarabella species, the pipes of which are larger at the top than at the bottom and produce a tone of clarionet quality.

Posaune (Ger.) (pō-*zou*-nĕ.) A trombone; also, an organ-stop. See *Trombone*.

Positif (Fr.) (pō-zē-*tēf*.) } The choir-organ, or low-
Positiv (Ger.) (pō-zĭ-*tĭf*.) } est row of keys with soft-toned stops in a large organ.

Position. 1. The point or place taken by the left-hand on fingerboard of any string instrument. 2. The disposition as to distance of the several notes of a chord; *close* or *open* position. 3. The point or place taken by the *slide* in Trombone playing.

Possíbile (It.) (pŏs-*si*-bē-lĕ.) Possible; *il più forte possibile*, as loud as possible.

Postlude (Lat.) (*pōst*-lūde.) } After-piece,
Postludium (Lat.) (pōst-*lū*-dĭ-ŭm.) } concluding voluntary.

Pot-pourri (pō-poor-*rē*.) A medley; a *capríccio*, or *fantásia* in which favorite airs and fragments of musical pieces are strung together and contrasted.

Pour (Fr.) (poor.) For.

Prall-triller (Ger.) (*präl*-trĭl-lĕr.) See *Mordent*.

Precentor. The appellation given to the master of the choir.

Precipitáto (It.) (pröy-tshē-pē-*tä*-tō.) In a precipitate manner; hurriedly.

Precipitándo (It.) (pröy-tshē-pē-*tän*-dō.) Hurrying.

Precipitóso (It.) (pröy-tshē-pē-*lō*-zō.) Hurrying, precipitous.

Precisióne (It.) (pröy-tshē-zē-ō-nĕ.) Precision, exactness.

119

Precíso (It.) (pray-*tshē*-zō.) Precise, exact, exactly.

Prelude. A short introductory composition, or *extempore* performance, to prepare the ear for the succeeding movements. The word *prelude* has been applied to compositions of a free and improvised character. In opera the distinction between *prelude* (or *vorspiel*) and *overture* lies in the fact that the overture is an independent piece while the *vorspiel* leads directly into the opera.

Preparation. That disposition of the harmony by which discords are lawfully introduced. A discord is said to be prepared, when the discordant note is heard in the preceding chord, and in the same part as a consonance.

Prestíssimo (It.) (près-*tis*-sē-mō.) Very quickly; as fast as possible.

Présto (It.) (*pres*-tō.) Quickly, rapidly.

Príma (It.) (*prēc*-mä.) First, chief, principal. See *Primo*.

Príma dónna (It.) (*prēe*-mä *dŏn*-nä.) Principal female singer in a serious opera.

Primary chord. The common chord; the first chord.

Príma vólta (It.) (*prēe*-mä *vōl*-tä.) The first time.

Príme. First note, or tone of a scale. Or the interval where two voices are on the same degree of the staff, a unison.

Prímo (It.) (*prēe*-mō.) Principal, first.

Principal, or octave. An important organ-stop, tuned an octave above the diapasons, and therefore of 4-foot pitch on the manual, and 8-foot on the pedals. In German organs the term *principal* is also applied to all the open diapasons.

Principal bass. An organ-stop of the open diapason species on the pedals.

Program-music. Instrumental music which either by its title, or by description printed upon the composition, gives a definite picture of events or objects. Beethoven was really the founder of the school with his "Pastoral Symphony." Berlioz in his "Symphonie Fantastique" and "Childe Harold" and Richard Strauss in his "Heldenleben" have given the largest examples of program music. See Hadow's "Studies in Modern Music," Weingartner's "Symphony since Beethoven," and Hanslick's "Beautiful in Music."

Progression. *Melodic* progression is the advance from one tone to another. *Harmonic* progression is the advance from chord to chord.

Pronunziato (It.) (prō-noon-tsē-ä-tō.) Pronounced.

Propósta (It.) (prō-*pōs*-tä.) Subject, or theme of a fugue.

Psalm. A sacred song or hymn.

Psaltery (Eng.) A stringed instrument much used by the Hebrews in ancient times. supposed to be a species of lyre, harp or dulcimer.

Púnta (It.) (*poon*-tä.) The point, the top; also a thrust, or push.

Pyramidon (Gr.) (pĭ-*răm*-ĭ-dŏn.) An organ-stop of 16- or 32-foot tone, on the pedals, invented by the Rev. F. A. G. Ouseley. The pipes are four times larger at the top than at the mouth, and the tone of remarkable gravity, resembling that of a stopped pipe in quality.

Q

Quadrat (Ger.) (quäd-*rät*.) The mark called a natural, ♮. See *Flat*.

Quadrille (Fr.) (kä-*drēl*.) A French dance, or set of five consecutive dance movements. Generally in $\frac{6}{8}$ or $\frac{2}{4}$ rhythm.

Quadruple counterpoint. Counterpoint in four parts, all of which may be inverted.

Quartet (Eng.) (quär-*tĕt*.) ⎫ A composition for
Quartett (Ger.) (quär-*tĕtt*.) ⎬ four voices or in-
Quartétto (It.) (quär-*tĕt*-tō.) ⎭ struments, or the group of players or singers.

Quási (It.) (*quä*-zi.) In the manner of, in the style of, or somewhat.

Quickstep. A lively march, generally in $\frac{6}{8}$ time.

Quiéto (It.) (quē-ä-tō.) Quiet, calm, serene.

Quint (Lat.) (quĭnt.) ⎫ A fifth; also the name of
Quínta (It.) (*quin*-tä.) ⎬ an organ-stop sounding a fifth (or twelfth) above the foundation stops.

Quintadena. An organ-stop. See *Quintaton*.

Quintaton (Ger.) (quĭn-tä-*tōn*.) A manual organ-stop of eight-foot tone; a stopped diapason of rather small scale producing the twelfth, as well as the ground tone; it also occurs as a pedal-stop of thirty-two and sixteen-foot tone.

Quintet. A composition for five voices or instruments.

Qui tollis (Lat.) (quē *tŏl*-lĭs.) A part of the *Gloria* in the Mass

Quoniam tu solus (Lat.) (*quō*-nĭ-äm tū *sō*-lŭs.) Part of the *Gloria* in the Mass.

R

R for *right* (Ger. *rechte*); *r. h.* = right hand (*Rechte Hand*); for *ripieno;* stands in Catholic church music for *Responsorium*, **R** in French organ-music, stands for *clavier de récit* (swell manual).

Rábbia (It.) (*räb*-bē-ä.) Rage, fury, madness.

Raddolcéndo (It.) (räd-dōl-*tshen*-dō.) } With increasing softness; becoming softer by degrees; gentler and calmer.
Raddolcénte (It.) (räd-dōl-*tshen*-tĕ.) }

Rallentándo (It.) (räl-lĕn-*tän*-dō.) The time gradually slower.

Rapidaménte (It.) (rä-pē-dä-*men*-tĕ.) Rapidly.

Rasch (Ger.) (räsh.) Swift, spirited.

Rattenúto (It.) (rät-tĕ-*noo*-tŏ.) Holding back; restraining the time.

Re (rā.) A syllable applied in solfaing to the note D. In France and Italy D is called *Re*.

Rebec. } An old Moorish instrument somewhat
Rebecca. } like a mandolin, with two strings, played on with a bow.

Recessional. The hymn sung at close of service in church as choir and clergy retire.

Recht (Ger.) (rĕkht.) Right.

Recitative (rĕ-sĭ-tä-*tēev*.) A species of musical declamation. There are two chief kinds of recitative, the free (*secco*) and the measured (*misurato* or *stromentato*).

Redowa (rĕd-ŏ-wä.) A Bohemian dance in $\frac{2}{4}$ and $\frac{3}{4}$ time alternately.

Reed. Primarily reeds are thin strips of reed, wood, or metal which, when set in vibration by a current of air, produce a musical sound. Reeds are classified as *Free* and *Beating*, the latter being sub-divided into *Single* and *Double*. The *Free* reed is used in instruments of concertina class and in reed organs, the length and thickness of the vibrating tongue itself giving the pitch. *Beating* reeds set an enclosed column of air in vibration, the length of the confining chamber giving the pitch. The *Single* beating reed is used on the clarinet, saxophone and large church organ (in reed pipes), and the *Double* beating reed is used on oboe, bassoon and sarrusophone.

Reed fifth. ⎱ A *stopped-quint* register in an organ,
Reed nasat. ⎰ the stopper of which has a hole or tube in it.

Reed stops. Those stops in an organ, the peculiar tone of which is produced by the wind having to pass against a reed placed at the bottom of the pipe and putting the *tongue* into vibration.

Reel. A lively Scotch and Irish dance. Originally the term *Rhay*, or *Reel*, was applied to a very ancient English dance, called *the Hay*. The reel is usually in $\frac{4}{4}$ or $\frac{6}{8}$ time.

Refrain. The *burden* of a song; a ritornel; a repeat. See *Burden*.

Register. The stops, or rows of pipes in an organ; also applied to the high, low or middle parts, or divisions of the voice; also the compass of a voice, or instrument.

Registering. ⎱ The proper management of the stops
Registration. ⎰ in an organ.

Related. A term applied to those chords, modes or keys, which, by reason of their affinity and close relation of some of their component sounds, admit of an easy and natural transition from one to the other.

Religiosaménte (It.) (rĕ-lē-jē-ō-zä-*men*-tĕ.) ⎱ Religiously; solemnly;
Religióso (It.) (rĕ-lē-jē-ō-zō.) ⎰ in a devout manner.

Remote keys. Those keys whose scales have few tones in common, as the key of C and the key of D♭.

Repeat. A character indicating that certain measures or passages are to be sung, or played twice. Written:

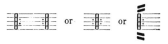

See also *Da Capo* and *Dal Segno*.

Repercussion. A frequent repetition of the same sound. The regular reëntrance, in a fugue, of the subject and answer after the episodes immediately following the exposition.

Replicazióne (It.) (rē-plĕ-kä-tsē-ō-nĕ.) Repetition.

Reprise (Fr.) (rŭh-preez.) The burden of a song.

Requiem (Lat.) (rā-kwee-em.) A Mass, or musical service for the dead. Its divisions are as follows: (1) Requiem, Kyrie; (2) Dies iræ. Requiem; (3) Domine Jesu Christe; (4) Sanctus, Benedictus; (5) Agnus Dei, Lux æterna.

Resolution. Resolving a discord into a concord according to the rules of harmony.

Response. Response, or answer of the choir. In a fugue the *response* is the repetition of the given subject by another part.

Rest. A character indicating silence. The following are the signs and names of the various rests:

➖	Whole rest.	⌐	16th-rest.
➖	Half-rest.	⌐	32nd-rest.
𝄽 or ⌡	Quarter-rest.	⌐	64th-rest.
⌐	Eighth-rest.		

Retardation. 1. Slackening, or retarding the time. 2. Delayed *ascent* of a harmonic voice, the reverse of *suspension*.

Réveille (Fr.) (ray-vā-yĕ.) Awakening, a military morning-signal.

Reverse motion. Imitation by contrary motion, in which the ascending intervals are changed into descending, and *vice versa*.

Rhapsody (Eng.) (răp-sō-dy.) A free, ecstatic composition.

Rhythm (Eng.) (rĭthm.) The division of musical ideas or sentences into regular metrical portions; musical accent and cadence as applied to melody. Rhythm represents the regular pulsation of music.

Ribs. The sides of a violin, etc.

Rigaudon (Fr.) (ree-go-don.) A lively French dance in ¾, sometimes in ⅜ time.

Rigóre (It.) (ree-*go*-rĕ.) Rigor, strictness; *al rigóre di témpo*, with strictness as to time.

Rigoróso (It.) (ree-gŏ-rō-zō.) Rigorous, exact, strict.

Rinforzándo (It.) (rin-fŏr-tsän-dō.)
Rinforzáre (It.) (rin-fŏr-tsä-rĕ.)
Rinforzáto (It.) (rin-fŏr-tsä-tō.)
Rinfórzo (It.) (rin-fór-tsō.)
} Strengthened; reinforced; a reinforcement

of tone, or expression; indicating that either a single note or chord, or *several* notes, are to be played with emphasis, although not with the suddenness of a *sforzando*.

Ripetizióne (It.) (ree-pĕ-tē-tsē-ō-nĕ.) Repetition.

Ripiéni (It. pl.) (ree-pē-ä-nē.)
Ripiéno (It.) (ree-pē-ä-nō.)
} The *tútti*, or full parts which fill up and augment the effect of the chorus of voices and instruments. The mass of instruments as against the solo or principal instrument in each group.

Risolúto (It.) (ree-zō-*loo*-tō.) Resolved, resolute, bold.

Risonáre (It.) (ree-zō-*nä*-rĕ.) To resound; to ring, or echo.

Risvegliáto (It.) (rees-väl-yē-ä-tō.) Awakened, re-animated.

Ritardándo (It.) (ree-tär-*dän*-dō.) Retarding; delaying the time gradually.

Ritenúto (It.) (ree-tĕ-*noo*-tō.) Detained; slower; kept back.

Ritmo (It.) (*reet*-mō.) Rhythm, cadence, measure.

Ritornéllo (It.) (ree-tōr-*nel*-lō.)
Ritournelle (Fr.) (ree-toor-nĕl.)
} The burden of a song; also, a short prelude or introduction to an air; and the postlude which follows an air; it is also applied to *tutti* parts, introductory to, and between, or after, the solo passages in a concerto.

Rohr-flöte (Ger.) (*rōr*-flŏ-tĕ.) *Reed-flute;* a stopped diapason in an organ.

Rohr-quint (Ger.) (rōr-quint.) *Reed-fifth;* an organ-stop, sounding the fifth above the diapasons.

Romance (Fr.) (rō-mänhs.)
Románza (It.) (rō-*män*-tsä.)
Romanze (Ger.) (rō-*män*-tsĕ.)
} Formerly the name given to the long lyric tales sung by the minstrels; now a term applied to an irregular, though delicate and romantic composition.

Róndo (It.) (*rōn*-dō.) A composition, vocal or instrumental, consisting of one prominent theme which reappears again and again in alternation with other contrasted themes.

Root. The fundamental note of any chord.

Roulade (Fr.) (roo-läd.) A florid vocal passage.

Round. A species of vocal canon in the unison, or octave; in three or more parts.

Rubáto (It.) (roo-bäh-tō.) *Robbed, stolen;* taking a portion of the duration from one note and giving it to another. See *Témpo Rubáto.*

Run. A rapid flight of notes introduced as an embellishment; a roulade.

Rústico (It.) (*roos*-tē-kō.) Rural, rustic.

S

S. As an abbreviation " S " means *Segno, Sinistra, Subito* or *Senza.*

Sackbut. An ancient bass wind-instrument, resembling a trombone.

Saite (Ger.) (zī-tĕ.) A string of a musical instrument.

Salcional (Fr.) (săl-sĭ-ō-näl.) ⎫ An 8 or 16-foot or-
Salicet (Fr.) (sä-lĭ-sā.) ⎬ gan-stop of small
Salicional (Fr.)(sä-lē-sĭ-ō-näl.) ⎭ scale and reedy tone.

Saltándo (It.) (säl-*tän*-dō.) Leaping, proceeding by skips, or jumps; *arco saltando*, in violin music, means skipping the bow upon the strings.

Saltarélla (It.) (säl-tä-*rel*-lä.) A Roman, or Italian dance, quick, skipping in character, and in $\frac{2}{4}$ or $\frac{6}{8}$ time.

Sanctus (Lat.) (*sănk*-tŭs.) Holy; a principal movement of the Mass.

Sanft (Ger.) (sänft.) Soft, mild, smooth; *mit sanften stimmen;* with soft stops.

Sans (Fr.) (sänh.) Without.

Saraband (Eng.) (*săr*-ă-bănd.) A dance said to be originally derived from the Saracens, and danced with castanets; it is in slow $\frac{3}{4}$ or $\frac{3}{2}$ time, and characterized by the second note of the measure being lengthened, which gives gravity and majesty to the movement.

Sarrusophone. A brass wind-instrument named after the band-master Sarrus, of Paris, with a *double reed* like the oboe and bassoon. It resembles the saxophone. The sarrusophone is made in various pitches.

Sax-horns. A group of brass wind instruments invented by Antoine (Adolphe) Sax, a Belgian, in 1842. Consisting of a tube of gradually widening calibre ending in a more or less flaring bell. Through a system of 3 to 5 piston valves the natural harmonics of the tube were lowered in pitch as needed, resulting in a complete chromatic scale. Broadly speaking, our modern brass instruments (with valves) are Sax-horns, variously modified.

Saxophone. Invented by M. Sax, in 1840. Consisting of a conical brass tube, key mechanism based on that of oboe and Boehm system, and played with a *single reed* like clarinet, to which instrument it is closely allied. Saxophones are made in six keys from high soprano to contra-bass, the lower instruments being most useful. The tone, while penetrating, is at the same time mellow and veiled in quality. They are used to best effect as a group in Military bands, but have been introduced successfully in Modern orchestral scores.

Scale. Primarily the " ladder " or succession of tones belonging to any key. Scales may be first divided into *Diatonic* and *Chromatic;* then the *Diatonic* into *Major* and *Minor,* the latter again into *Natural, Melodic* and *Harmonic.* The Major and Minor scales alternate between half and whole steps according to their individual characteristics. The Chromatic scale is made up entirely of half-steps. A so-called whole-tone (or step) scale has been introduced by ultra-modern composers. Apart from the general divisions, there are many special varieties of scales or modes used in the old Gregorian music, and scales peculiar to various countries.

In pipe organs, scale means the ratio between length and width of pipes; in piano the ratio between length and thickness of strings and method of stringing.

Scéna (It.) (*shāy-nä.*) The *scena* is the largest and most brilliant vocal solo form. It generally consists of *recitative, cavatina* and *aria.* It generally forms part of an opera, but it may be an independent composition.

Schalkhaft (Ger.) (*shällk-*häft.) Roguish, playful.

Scherzándo (It.) (skĕr-*tsän*-dō.)) Playful, lively,
Scherzhaft (Ger.) (*shĕrts*-häft.)) sportive, merry.
Scherzo (It.) (*skĕr*-tsō.) Play, sport, a jest; a piece of a lively, sportive character, and marked, animated rhythm; also one of the movements in a symphony. While the scherzo may be written in any rhythm and in almost any form, the great majority of scherzo movements are in triple rhythm, and possess a *trio*.
Schiétto (It.) (skē-*ĕt*-tō.) Simple, plain, neat.
Schleppend (Ger.) (*shlĕp*-pĕnd.) Dragging, drawling.
Schluss (Ger.) (shlooss.) The end; conclusion.
Schmachtend (Ger.) (shmäkh-tĕnd.) Languishing.
Schmerzhaft (Ger.) (*shmĕrts*-häft.) Dolorous, sorrowful.
Schnell (Ger.) (shnĕll.) Quickly, rapidly.
Schottisch (Ger.) (*shŏt*-tĭsh.) A modern dance, rather slow, in $\frac{2}{4}$ or $\mathbf{C}$ time.
Schreiend (Ger.) (*shrī*-ĕnd.) Acute, shrill, screaming.
Schwach (Ger.) (shväkh.) *Piáno*, soft, weak.
Schweige (Ger.) (*shvī*-ghĕ.) A rest.
Schwer (Ger.) (shvär.) Heavily, ponderously.
Schwermüthig (Ger.) (shvär-*mü*-tĭg.) In a pensive, melancholy style.
Scioltézza (It.) (shē-ōl-*tet*-sä.) Freedom, ease, lightness.
Sciólto (It.) (shē-*ōl*-tō.) Free, light.
Scordatúra (It.) (skŏr-dä-*too*-rä.) A special tuning scheme for string instruments, generally to simplify execution of some difficult passage.
Score. The whole instrumental and vocal parts of a composition, written on separate staves, placed under each other. (Ger., *Partitur*, Fr., *Partición*; It., *Partitura*.)
Score, full. A complete score of all the parts of a composition, either vocal or instrumental, or both.
Score, instrumental. A score in which the instrumental parts are given in full.
Score, piano. A score in which the orchestral accompaniments are compressed into a pianoforte part; an arrangement of music for the piano.
Score, short. An abbreviated, or a skeleton score.

Score, vocal. The notes of all the voice-parts placed in their proper order under each other for the use of the conductor.

Scoring. The forming of a score, by collecting and properly arranging the different parts of a composition.

Scorréndo (It.) (skŏr-*ren*-dō.) Gliding from one sound into another.

Scotch scale. A scale differing from that of the other nations of Europe by its omission of the fourth and seventh. See *Scale*.

Scotch snap. A rhythm common to Scottish music, where a quarter note or beat is divided unevenly into one sixteenth and a dotted eighth note.

Scozzése (It.) (skŏt-*sä*-zĕ.) In the Scotch style.

Sdégno (It.) (*sden*-yō.) Anger, wrath, passion.

Se (It.) (sā.) If; in case; provided; as.

Sec (Fr.) (sĕk.) } Dry, unornamented, coldly;
Sécco (It.) (*sĕk*-kō.) } the note, or chord, to be struck short or staccato.

Second. An interval measuring two diatonic degrees.

Section. A complete, but not an independent musical idea; a part of a musical period.

Secular music. Music which is intended for the theatre or concert hall; an expression used in opposition to *sacred* music.

Ségno (It.) (*sen*-yō.) A *sign*, :𝄋: *al ségno*, return to the sign; *dal ségno*, repeat from the sign.

Segue (It.) (*sā*-gwĕ.) Follows; now follows; as follows; it also means, go on, *in a similar, or like manner*, showing that a passage is to be played like that which precedes it.

Seguidilla (Spa.) (sā-guē-*dēl*-yä.) A favorite Spanish dance in $\frac{3}{4}$ time.

Sehnsucht (Ger.) (*sān*-sookht.) Desire, longing, ardor, fervor.

Sehr (Ger.) (zair.) Very, much, extremely.

Semibreve (Eng.) (*sĕm*-i-brēv.)

Half a breve; whole note. 

Semitone (Eng.) (*sĕm*-ī-tōn.) A half-tone, or half-step.

Sémplice (It.) (*sem*-plē-tshĕ.) Simple, pure, plain.

Sémpre (It.) (*sem*-prĕ.) Always, evermore, continually.

Sensibilità (It.) (sĕn-sē-bē-lē-tä.) Sensibility, expression, feeling.

Sentiménto (It.) (sĕn-tē-*men*-tō.) Feeling; sentiment; delicate expression.

Sénza (It.) (sen-tsä.) Without.

Septet (Eng.) (sĕp-*tĕt*.) A composition for seven voices, or instruments.

Séquence (Eng.) (sē-quĕns.) A series, or progression, of similar chords, or intervals, in succession.

Sérénade (Fr.) (say-ray-näd.) } Night music; an
Serenáta (It.) (say-ray-*nä*-tä.) } evening concert in the open air and under the window of the person to be entertained. This word is used in different senses in instrumental music. In the eighteenth century, it was used to denote a rather free suite of pieces, often orchestral, and forming a short program of music for an evening performance.

Seréno (It.) (say-*rä*-nō.) Serene, calm, tranquil, cheerful.

Sério (It.) (sä-rē-ō.) } Serious, grave; in a seri-
Serióso (It.) (sä-rē-ō-zō.) } ous, sedate style.

Serpent. An ancient bass wind instrument, so named on account of its resemblance to a serpent. The tone was rough and coarse, and the instrument has been happily replaced in modern bands and orchestras by the tuba. Also a reed-stop in an organ.

Sesquialtera (Lat.) (sĕs-quĭ-*ăl*-tĕ-rä.) An organ-stop, comprising two or more ranks of pipes, of acute pitch.

Seventeenth. An organ-stop. See *Tierce.*

Seventh. An interval measuring seven diatonic degrees.

Seventh chord. A chord composed of a root, its third, fifth and seventh.

Severita (It.) (sä-vä-rē-tä.) Severity, strictness.

Sextet. A composition for six voices or instruments.

Sextole (Lat.) (*sĕx*-tō-lĕ.) } A group of six
Sextuplet (Lat.) (*sĕx*-tū-*plĕt*.) } notes, having the value, and to be played in the time of four.

Sfogato (It.) (sfō-*gä*-tō.) A very high soprano or a direction to sing in a light manner.

Sforzándo (It.) (sfōr-*tsän*-dō.) } *Forced;* one par-
Sforzáto (It.) (sfōr-*tsä*-tō.) } ticular chord, or
note, is to be played with force and emphasis.

Sfumato (It.) (sfoo-*mäh*-tō.) Very lightly, like a
vanishing smoke-wreath.

Shake. See *Trill.*

Sharp. The sign ♯, which occurring either before
a note or in the signature, raises the pitch of a
tone one chromatic half-step. See *Accidentals*
and *Chromatics.*

Sharp, double. See *double sharp.*

Shift. A change of position of the left hand, in
playing the violin, etc.

Si (It.) (sē.) Applied in *solfáing* to the note B.

Siciliána (It.) (sē-tshē-lē-*ä*-nä.) } A dance of the
Siciliáno (It.) (sē-tshē-lē-*ä*-nō.) } Sicilian peasants,
a graceful movement of a slow, soothing, pastoral
character, in ⁶⁄₈ or ¹²⁄₈ time.

Side-drum. The common military drum so-called
from its hanging at the side of the drummer when
played upon.

Signature. The sharps, flats, or figures in frac-
tional form given at the beginning of a composition. The former constitue the *key signature*
and are placed at head of each staff; the latter
constitute the *time signature* and are placed at
beginning or where the time changes.

Signs. The following are the chief signs used in
music:

- (1) A dot above or below a note signifies
staccato. (2) After a note, or rest, it is a
sign of length.

- A dash above or below a note signifies *stac-
catissimo* (becoming obsolete at present).

- A slur, bind, tie.

- A slur and dots above or below two or more
notes (one dot to each note) indicate that
the latter have to be played somewhat
detached. See *Portamento.*

- Sustained. Horizontal dashes above or below a series of notes indicate that they
have to be sustained but not slurred.

- Accented and sustained, *ben pronunziato* or
marcato.

- With a weighty and well-sustained touch,
pesante, or *martellato.*

- *Crescendo.*

131

➤ *Diminuendo.*

> and < *Rinforzando,* accented.

∧ *Forzando,* or *sforzato,* accented. ∧ and ➤
    mean practically the same, unless used
    together, when the first has the stronger
    accent.

<> In vocal music would mean *Messa di Voce*
    (which see). In instrumental music it
    would also mean *crescendo* and *diminuendo*
    (a swell mark), but it is sometimes used
    over a single note, or chord, in piano
    music, in which case it means resonance
    without suddenness.

V Up-bow; ⊓ Down-bow.

⌒ Hold, or *Fermata.*

➤ Repeat preceding measure.

𝄋. :S: Segno. Repeat from this sign.

✳ ⤬· ♯♯ *Double sharp.*

 Repeat.

:‖: Repeat.

× or + Thumb (pfte-music.) *American Fingering.*

❜ Breathing-mark.

  Added lines to call attention to repetition
    dots. *Bis* is also sometimes used as a
    repeat-mark.

∿ ∿ Mordent and Praller.

∼ ∼ 𝄴 Turns.

𝗜 Repeat preceding figure of eighth notes.

𝗜𝗜 Repeat preceding figure of sixteenth notes.

𝗜𝗜𝗜 Repeat preceding figure of thirty-second notes.

∿∿∿ Indicates the continuation of a trill or
    an octave mark.

Arpeggio.

[Signifies sometimes in pianoforte music that
  two notes on different staves have to be
  played with one hand.

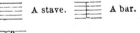 A stave. A bar.

A double bar

⊕   The coda mark. First time of playing disregard the sign. Second time (after D. C.) skip from this sign to the coda. Sometimes the sign is also placed at the coda.

Iᵐᵒ Iᵐᵃ : Primo, Prima (*prima volta*).

IIᵈᵒ IIᵈᵃ: Secondo, Seconda (*seconda volta*).

M. M. ♩ = 120. Refers to Maelzel's metronome. This or any other figure indicates to which part of the pendulum the regulator, is to be moved, and this or any other note indicates whether it beats halves, quarter-notes, or eighths, so many to the minute.

or A direct.

Ped. : The sign to *press down* the loud pedal on pianoforte.

✻ ⊕   These signs also refer to the pianoforte-pedal. The first is the only one now in use, and indicates where the foot is to be *raised* after the pedal has been pressed down. The second is sometimes found in German editions.

⌐⌐   An American pedal-mark, showing exactly how long to use the damper-pedal.

v   A breathing-mark in some *vocalises*.

⌞⌟ ⌐⌐   Organ-music, pedal; notes so connected are to be played with alternate toe and heel of same foot. Heel and toe are also sometimes marked ∧ v and also o, ∧ *over* the note, meaning right foot, and *under*, left foot.

∧ — v   Change toes on organ-pedal.

v‿v   Slide same toe to next note.

O   Thumb position (violoncello-playing).

{   Brace.

Tr. ∿∿ Trill.

♪ Short grace-note or acciaccatura.

♪ ♪ Long grace-note or appoggiatura.

133

Similar motion. Where two or more parts ascend, or descend, at the same time.

Simile (It.) (*sē-mē-lĕ.*) Similarly; in like manner.

Sín' al fine (It.) (*seen* äl *fēe-nĕ.*) To the end; as far as the end.

Síncopa (It.) (*sin-kō-pä.*) ⎱ See *Syncopation.*
Síncope (It.) (*sin-kō-pĕ.*) ⎰

Sinfonia (It.) (sin-fō-nē-ä.) ⎱ An orchestral com-
Sinfoníe (Fr.) (sin-fō-*nē.*) ⎰ position in many parts; used by Bach and others for *prelude.* See *Symphony.*

Síno (It.) (*see-*nō.) ⎱ To; as far as; until. *Con fuoco*
Sín (It.) (seen.) ⎰ *sin' al fine;* with spirit to the end.

Sixteenth note. A semiquaver, 𝅘𝅥𝅯.

Sixteenth rest. A pause equal in duration to a sixteenth note.

Sixth. An interval measuring six diatonic degrees.

Sixty-fourth note. A hemidemisemiquaver. 𝅘𝅥𝅰

Sixty-fourth rest. A pause equal in point of duration to a sixty-fourth note.

Skip. A term applied to any transition exceeding that of a whole step.

Slancio, con (It.) (kon *slan*-tshee-oh.) With vehemence; impetuously.

Slargándo (It.) (slär-*gän*-dō.) Extending, enlarging; the time to become gradually slower.

Slentándo (It.) (slĕn-*tän*-dō.) Relaxing the time; becoming gradually slower.

Slide. 1. A movable tube in the trombone (formerly in the trumpet), which is pushed in and out to alter the pitch of the tones while playing. 2. A rapid run of two or more notes.

Slur. A curved line drawn over or under two or more notes, signifying that they are to be executed *legato.* The slur is used also in modern piano music to indicate melodic phrasing.

Small octave. The name given in Germany to the notes included between C on the second space of the bass staff and the B above, these notes being expressed by small letters, as *a*, *b*, *c*, *d*, etc.

Smaniánte (It.) (smän-ē-*än*-tĕ.) ⎱ Furious; vehe-
Smaniáto (It.) (smä-nē-*ä*-tō.) ⎰ ment; frantic
Smanióso (It.) (smä-nē-*ō*-zō.) ⎰ with rage.

Smorzándo (It.) (smŏr-*tsän*-dō.) ⎰ Extinguished; put
Smorzáto (It.) (smŏr-*tsä*-tō.) ⎱ out; suddenly dying away.

Snare-drum. The commonly used small drum,
so named on account of the *snares* or strings of
raw-hide drawn over its lower head.

Soáve (It.) (sō-ä-vĕ.) A word implying that a
movement is to be played in a gentle, soft and
engaging style.

Sol (sŏl.) A syllable applied by the Italians and
French to G, the fifth sound of the diatonic scale
of C.

Solénne (It.) (sō-*len*-nĕ.) Solemn.

Solfaing. Singing the notes of the scale to the
monosyllables applied to them by Guido. *ut,
re, mi, fa, sol, la, si*; using *do* in place of *ut*.

Solfège (Fr.) (sŏl-fezh.) ⎫ Exercises for the voice
Solféggi (It. pl.) (sŏl-*fed*-ji.) ⎬ according to the rules
Solféggio (It.) (sŏl-*fed*-jē-ō.) ⎭ of *solfainɟ*.

Solmization. See *Solféggi.*

Sólo (It.) (sō-lō.) ⎫ A composition for a single
Solo (Fr.) (sō-lō.) ⎬ voice, or instrument, or a
Solo (Ger.) (sō-lō.) ⎭ passage for single voice or
instrument introduced in an ensemble composition.

Son (Fr.) (sŏnh.) Sound.

Sonábile (It.) (sō-nä-bē-lē.) Sonorous, resonant.

Sonáre (It.) (sō-nä-rĕ.) To sound; to have a
sound; to ring; to play upon.

Sonáta (It.) (sō-*nä*-tä.) ⎫ An instrumental com-
Sonate (Fr.) (sō-*nät*.) ⎬ position, usually of
Sonate (Ger.) (sō-*nä*-tĕ.) ⎭ three or four distinct
movements, each with a unity of its own, yet
all related so as to form a perfect whole. It
commonly begins with an allegro, sometimes
preceded by a slow introduction. Then come the
andante, adagio, or largo; then the minuet and
trio, or scherzo; and lastly the finale in quick
time. This form is applied, not only to large
piano sonatas, but to symphonies, string quartets,
etc.

Sonatína (It.) (sō-nä-*tē*-nä.) ⎰ A short, easy sonata,
Sonatine (Fr.) (sō-nä-*tēn*.) ⎱ generally two or
three movements. The *sonatina movement* differs
from the *sonata-allegro* in having no development,
or middle section, being merely an exposition,
followed by a recapitulation.

Song. 1. (Ger., *Gesang;* Fr., *chant;* It., *canto.*)
Vocal musical expression or utterance. 2. (Ger.,
Lied; Fr., *chanson;* It., *canzone.*) A lyrical
poem set to music. The *song* deals with emotions; the *ballad* tells a story. *Song form* is a
musical form originally derived from vocal music.
(See *Form.*) *Folk-song* is a simple song (frequently a ballad) which is popular with the
common people. *Songs* are chiefly of two styles
of composition. 1st. The *strophe form,* in which
the music is set to the first stanza and then repeated to each succeeding stanza. 2d. The *art-
song* (or *through-composed — Durch-componiert*
style), in which each stanza receives separate
musical treatment according to its contents.

Sóno (It.) (*soh-*no.) Sound, tone.

Sonore (Fr.) (sŏ-nōr.) } Sonorous, harmonious,
Sonóro (It.) (sō-nō-rō.) } resonant.

Sópra (It.) (sō-prä.) Above, upon, over, before.
See *Super.*

Sopráno (It.) (sō-prä-nō.) The treble; the highest kind of female voice; a treble,
or soprano singer. Normal compass about

Sordaménte (It.) (sōr-dä-*men*-tĕ.) Softly, gently;
also, damped, muffled.

Sordíno (It.) (sōr-*dēe*-nō.) *Sordine* or *mute.* A
contrivance to deaden the vibration and change
the natural sound of an instrument. On the
violin, etc., a piece of wood or metal is attached
to the bridge. The *mute* or *sordino* for brass wind
instruments is made of wood or metal, cone
shape, and is inserted in the bell of the instrument.
The *dampers* on a piano, actuated by the pedals
are *sordini.*

Sospirándo (It.) (sōs-pē-*rän*-dō.) Sighing; very
subdued; doleful.

Sostenúto (It.) (sōs-tĕ-*noo*-tō.) Sustaining the
tone; keeping the notes down their full duration.

Sotto (It.) (*sŏt*-tō.) Under, below.

Sótto vóce (It.) (*sŏt*-tō vŏ-tshĕ.) Softly; in a low
voice; in an undertone.

Sound post. A small tube, or prop, within a violin,
nearly under the bridge; it is not only to sustain
the tension but to carry the vibrations from the
frontboard, or *belly* to the back, thus making the
whole sound-box vibratory.

Space. The interval between the lines of the staff.

Spasshaft (Ger.) (*späss*-häft.) Sportively, playfully, merrily.

Spianáto (It.) (spē-ä-*na*-tō.) Smooth, even; *legáto*.

Spiccáto (It.) (spēk-*ka*-tō.) Separated, pointed, distinct, detached; in violin music it means that the notes are to be played with the point of the bow.

Spinet (Eng.) (*spĭn*-ĕt.) A stringed instrument formerly much in use, somewhat similar to the harpsichord.

Spírito (It.) (spee-rē-tō.) Spirit, life, energy.

Spitz-flöte (Ger.) (spĭtz-*flô*-tĕ.) } Pointed-flute; an
Spitz-flute (Eng.) } organ-stop of a soft, pleasing tone, the pipes of which are conical, and pointed at the top.

Squillánte (It.) (squeel-*yän*-tĕ.) Clear, plain, sounding, ringing.

Stabat mater (Lat.) (*stä*-băt *mä*-tĕr.) "The Mother stood." The first words of a Latin hymn on the Crucifixion.

Stábile (It.) (*stä*-bē-lĕ.) Firm.

Staccáto (It.) (stäk-*ka*-tō.) Detached; distinct; separated from each other.

Staccato marks. Small dots or dashes placed over or under the notes, thus: The wedge-shaped marks are shorter than the dots, but are little used by modern composers.

Staff. The five horizontal and parallel lines, on and between which the notes are written.

Stanchezza (It.) (stän-*ket*-za.) Weariness; *con st.*, wearily; very dragging.

Ständchen (Ger.) (*stend*-khĕn.) A serenade.

Stark (Ger.) (stärk.) Strong, loud, vigorous.

Stentándo (It.) (stĕn-*tän*-dō.) Heavy, and retarding.

Stentádo (It.) (stĕn-*tä*-tō.) Hard, forced, loud.

Step. The progression from one degree on the staff to the next above or below; the unit for measuring all intervals. The *whole-step* or simply *step* is equivalent to a major second (or tone) and the *half-step* to a minor second (or semitone). The word step is preferable to "tone" which literally means *sound* and cannot properly be divided or form a unit for measurement of distance.

Stésso (It.) The same; lo stesso *témpo*, in the same time.

Stîle (It.) (*stē-lĕ*.) Style.

Stimme (Ger.) (*stĭm-mĕ*.) The voice; sound; a sound-post; a part in vocal, or instrumental music; also an organ-stop, or register.

Stimmung (Ger.) (*stĭm-moong*.) Tuning, tune, tone.

Stop. A register, or row of pipes in an organ; on the violin, etc., it means the pressure of the finger upon the string. Double-stop, pressing two strings at once. Organ-stops are of two kinds, *flue*, and *reed-stops*. (See *Organ*.) The *flue-stops* are subdivided into, 1st, *principal*, or cylindrical pipes of diapason style; 2d, *gedackt* (or covered) pipes, which are stopped at the end, and give a hollow tone; 3d, *flute-work*, which includes pipes which are too narrow to sound their fundamental tones, stopped pipes, with chimneys, and three-sided or four-sided pipes. Mechanical-stops are those which do not give a tone, but work some mechanism, as the couplers, etc. Mixture-stops are those sounding more than one note to a single key. They are to add the harmonics to the *principals*. See *Harmonics*, *Acoustics*, *Organ*, *Pipe*.

Stopped diapason. A stop, the pipes of which are generally made of wood, and its bass, up to middle C, *always* of wood. They are only half as long as those of the open diapason, and are stopped at the upper end with wooden *stoppers*, or plugs which render the tone more soft and mellow than that of the open diapason, and lower it an octave.

Stop, salcional. A variety of Dulciana stop.

Stops, compound. An assemblage of several pipes in an organ, three, four, five or more to each key, all answering at once to the touch of the performer. *Mixture-stops*.

Stops, draw. See *Draw-stops*.

Stop, sesquialtera. A stop resembling the mixture, running through the scale of the instrument, and consisting of three, four, and sometimes five, ranks of pipes, tuned in thirds, fifths, and eighths.

Stops, mutation. In an organ, the twelfth, tierce, and their octaves.

Stop, solo. A stop which may be drawn alone, or with one of the diapasons.

Stops, reed. Stops consisting of pipes upon the end of which are fixed thin, narrow plates of brass, which, being vibrated by the wind from the bellows, produce a reedy thickness of tone. See *Pipes*.

Stop, stopped unison. The stopped diapason stop.

Stop, tierce. A stop tuned a major third higher than the fifteenth, and only employed in the full organ.

Stop, treble forte. A stop applied to a melodeon, or reed-organ, by means of which the treble part of the instrument may be increased in power, while the bass remains subdued.

Stop, tremolo. A contrivance, by means of which a tremulous effect is given to some of the registers of an organ.

Stop, trumpet. A stop, so-called, because its tone is imitative of a trumpet. In large organs it generally extends through the whole compass.

Stop, twelfth. A metallic stop, so denominated from its being tuned twelve notes above the diapason. This stop, on account of its pitch, or tuning, can never be used alone.

Stradivari. The name of a very superior make of violin, so-called from their maker, Stradivarius, who made them at Cremona, Italy, in the first part of the eighteenth century.

Strain. A portion of music divided off by a double bar. A period.

Strascináto (It.) (strä-shē-*nä*-tō.) Dragged along; played slowly.

Strathspey. A lively Scotch dance somewhat slower than the reel, and like it in ¼ time, but in dotted eighth notes alternating with sixteenths, producing the peculiar jerky rhythm of the Scotch snap. See *Scotch Snap*.

Strepitóso (It.) (strĕ-pē-tō-zō.) Noisy, boisterous.

Strétta (It.) (*strĕt*-tä.) A concluding passage, coda, or finale, taken in quicker time to enhance the effect.

Strétto (It.) (*strĕt*-tō.) *Pressed, close*, contracted; formerly used to denote that the movement indicated was to be performed in a quick, con-

cise style. In fugue-writing, that part where the subject and answer overlap one another.

Stridente (It.) (strē-*den*-tĕ.) Sharp, shrill, acute.

Stringed instruments. Instruments whose sounds are produced by striking, or plucking strings, or by the friction of a bow drawn across them.

Stringéndo (It.), (streen-*jen*-dō.) Pressing, accelerating the time.

String quartet. A composition for four instruments of the violin species, as two violins, a viola and violoncello; or the group of performers.

Strisciándo (It.) (strē-shē-*än*-dō.) Gliding; slurring; sliding smoothly from one note to another.

Stück (Ger.) (stük.) Piece, air, tune.

Stücken (Ger.) (*stük*-ĕn.) Pieces.

Studien (Ger. pl.) (*stoo*-dee-ĕn.) Studies.

Stufe (Ger.) (*stoo*-fĕ.) Step, degree.

Stürmisch (Ger.) (*stürm*-ĭsh.) Impetuously, boisterously, furiously.

Styrienne. (Fr.) (stee-ree-en.) An air in slow movement and $\frac{2}{4}$ time, often in minor, with *J odler* after each verse.

Su (It.) (soo.) Above, upon.

Suavita (It.) (soo-wä-vē-*tä*.) Suavity, sweetness, delicacy.

Sub (Lat.) (sŭb.) Under, below, beneath.

Sub-bass (Ger.) (soob-bäss.) } *Underbass;* an organ-register in the pedals, usually a double-stopped bass of 32 or 16-foot tone. The ground bass.
Subbourdon.

Subdominant. The fourth tone of any scale, or key. Tone below dominant.

Súbito (It.) (*soo*-bē-tō.) Suddenly; immediately; at once.

Subject. A melody, or theme; a leading-text, or *motivo*.

Submediant. The sixth tone of the scale. The *middle* note between tonic and sub-dominant (below).

Suboctave. An organ-coupler producing the octave below.

Subprincipal. *Under principal,* that is, below the pedal-diapason pitch; in German organs this is a double open bass-stop of 32-foot scale.

Subtonic. Under the tonic; the semitone immediately below the tonic.

Suite (Fr.) (swēet.) A series, a succession; *une suite de pièces*, a series of lessons, or pieces.

Suite de Danses. (Fr.) (sweet de dans.) A set of dances. It was generally known as the *suite*, and probably began not far from the year 1600 in the freer *Partita*. Both had their origin in dances. The contrasts of the suite were well-established by Bach, and the movements gradually assumed the following order in his suites: A prelude or not, as the composer desired, after which came the *allemande*, the *courante*, the *sarabande*, the *intermezzi*, and finally the *gigue*. The *intermezzi* were from two to four dances, or other movements, left to the choice of the composer, as *minuets, gavottes*, etc. The modern orchestral suite is of a much freer character and is practically a small symphony.

Suivez (Fr.) (swē-vā.) Follow, attend, pursue; the accompaniment must be accommodated to the singer, or solo player.

Súl (It.) (sool.)
Súll' (It.) (sool.) } On, upon the.
Súlla (It.) (*sool*-lä.)

Superdominant. The tone in the scale next above the dominant; also *sub-mediant*.

Superoctave. An organ-stop tuned two octaves, or a fifteenth, above the diapasons; also a coupler producing the octave above.

Supertonic. Tone above the tonic.

Supplichévole (It.) (soo-plē-*keh*-vō-lĕ.)
Supplichevolménte (It.) (soop-plē-keh-vŏl-*men*-tĕ.) } In a supplicatory manner.

Súr (It.) (soor.) } On, upon, over.
Sur (Fr.) (sür.)

Suspension. A theoretical expression applied to the retaining in any chord some note, or notes, of the preceding chord. A dissonant note which finally sinks into the harmony of the chord.

Süss (Ger.) (züss.) Sweetly.

Sussurándo (It.) (soos-soo-*rän*-dō.) Whispering, murmuring.

Svegliáto (It.) (svĕl-yē-*ä*-tō.) Brisk, lively, sprightly.

Svélto (It.) (*svel*-tō.) Free, light, easy.

Swell. A gradual increase of sound.

Swell-organ. In organs having three manuals, the third, or upper, controlling a number of pipes enclosed in a box, which may be gradually opened, or shut, and thus the tone increased, or diminished, by degrees. See *Organ*.

Swell-pedal. That which opens the shutters of the swell-organ, increasing the tone.

Symphonie (Fr.) (sănh-fō-nē.) ⎫ In the first half
Symphonie (Ger.) (sĭm-fō-nēe.) ⎬ of the eight-
Symphony (Eng.) ⎭ eenth century
symphony meant any instrumental prelude, or interlude, or postlude. It now means a grand composition of several movements, for a full orchestra. The symphony in its present form was introduced by Haydn, and generally consists of an allegro movement (sometimes with a slow introduction), a slow movement, a *minuet* or *scherzo*, and a *finale*. It is a *sonata for orchestra*. (See *Sonata*.) For further information regarding symphony see Grove's "Beethoven's Nine Symphonies," Weingartner's "Symphony since Beethoven," Elson's "Famous Composers and their Works."

Symphonic poem. A form of orchestral composition originated by Liszt and developed by Richard Strauss and other moderns. It is a musical illustration or setting of an episode or story. There is no set form, but the themes or *motives* are logically introduced and developed, and the opportunity for orchestral expression is unlimited.

Syncopation. A temporary displacement of the natural accent in music. For instance making the note attacks fall *between* the pulses or beats, or shifting the accent from the naturally strong first or third beat to the weak second or fourth beat. There are various forms of *syncopation*, but the principle is the same in all. The syncopation cannot be continued for too long a period without danger of entirely supplanting the original beat or pulse, especially when no part is sustaining the original accent against it.

T

T. An abbreviation of *Talon*, *Tasto* (*t.s.* = tasto solo), *Tempo* (*a.t.* = a tempo), *Tenor*, *Toe* (in organ-music), *Tre* (T.C. = tre corde), and *Tutti*

Tablatúra (It.) (täb-lä-*too*-rä.)
Tablature (Fr.) (tä-blä-tür.)
Tablature (Eng.) (*täb*-lä-tshūr.)
Tabulatur (Ger.) (tä-boo-lä-*toor*.)

} A term formerly applied to the general assemblage of the signs used in music; the method of notation for the lute, and other similar instruments, was also distinguished by this appellation. The musical rules of the master-singers were also called the *tablatur*. But the chief use of the word is to designate the *pitch* of different notes in different octaves by letters with numerals, accents, or adjectives attached. The principle of the tablature of pitches dates back to the time of Guido of Arezzo, about A. D. 1000. The chief system used by musicians is the following: (Note capitals or small letters.)

Sub-contra Octave.   Contra Octave.

Great Octave.   Small Octave.

One-lined Octave.   Two-lined Octave.

Three-lined Octave.

Four-lined Octave.

In many cases, however, the lines are made horizontal instead of vertical, thus, c̄, ē̄, etc., and sometimes the subcontra notes are written with three capitals (CCC, DDD, etc.), and the contra notes with two (CC, DD, etc.), instead of having lines attached.

Tacet (Lat.) (*tä*-set.) ⎫
Táce (It.) (*tä*-tshā.) ⎪ Be silent; a term
Táci (It.) (*tä*-tshē.) ⎬ found in the sepa-
Taciási (It.) (tä-tshē-ä-zē.) ⎭ rate vocal or in-
strumental parts of a composition to indicate that that particular voice or instrument has nothing to sing or play during a certain movement or period.

Takt (Ger.) (täkt.) Time, measure, beat.

Tambourine. A small drum, very shallow, with a single head of parchment. Around the narrow shell are metal jingles. It is beaten by the hand.

Tambourin (Fr.) (tänh-boo-rēn.) A species of dance accompanied by the tambourine; also a tambourine.

Tam-tam. The gong.

Tánto (It.) (*tän*-tō.) So much, as much; *allegro non tante*, not so quick; not too quick.

Tantum ergo (Lat.) (tăn-tüm air-gō.) A hymn sung at the benediction in the Roman Catholic service.

Tanz (Ger.) (tänts.) A dance.

Tarantélla (It.) (tä-rän-*tel*-lä.) A swift, delirious Italian dance in ⅜ time. The form has been adopted by many composers, for piano compositions.

Tardaménte (It.) (tär-dä-*men*-tĕ.) Slowly.

Tárdo (It.) (*tär*-dō.) Tardy, slow.

Tásto sólo (It.) (*täs*-tō sō-lō.) *One key alone;* in organ, or pianoforte music, this means a note without harmony; the bass notes over or under which it is written are not to be accompanied with chords.

Te. *Si* in Tonic Sol-fa.

Technic. The mechanical skill of playing or of singing.

Tedésca (It.) (tĕ-*des*-kä.) ⎱ German: *álla tedésca*,
Tedésco (It.) (tĕ-*des*-kō.) ⎰ in the German style.

Te Deum laudamus (Lat.) (tĕ *dā*-ŭm lou-*dä*-mŭs.) *We praise Thee, O God;* a canticle, or hymn of praise.

Tell-tale. A movable piece of metal, bone, or ivory, attached to an organ, indicating by its position the amount of wind supplied by the bellows.

Téma (It.) (*tāy*-mä.) A theme, or subject; a melody.

Temperament. The division of the octave into twelve *equal* semi-tones, in defiance of the law of nature, which demands a different proportion. The introduction of equal temperament was a modification of the scale of nature that alone made music on keyed instruments practicable. See *Pitch.* Consult Pole's "Philosophy of Music" and Zahm's "Sound and Music" for details of temperament; also see "Elson's Music Dictionary."

Tempestóso (It.) (tĕm-pĕs-*tō*-zō.) Tempestuous, stormy, boisterous.

Tempo (It.) (*tem*-pō.) The Italian word for *time.* Tempo is rather loosely defined as the speed of the music, but it ought rather to be regarded as the speed of the rhythm, the rapidity with which the natural accents follow each other. The chief terms used for speed are (from slowest to quickest) *grave, largo, larghetto, adagio, lento, andante, andantino, moderato, allegretto, allegro, presto,* and *prestissimo.* The words for *tempo* and expression are usually in Italian, although modern German and French composers use terms in their respective languages. *A tempo* means return to the original speed after a temporary variation.

Témpo giústo (It.) (*tem*-pō jē-*oos*-tō.) In just, exact strict time.

Témpo ordinário (It.) (*tem*-pō ōr-dē-*nä*-rē-ō.) Ordinary, or moderate time.

Témpo prímo (It.) (*tem*-pō *prē*-mō.) First, or original time; after an entire movement has been in a different *tempo.*

Témpo rubáto (It.) (*tem*-pō roo-*bä*-tō.) *Robbed* or *stolen* time; irregular time; meaning a slight deviation to give more expression by retarding one note, and quickening another, but so that the time of each measure is not altered as a whole.

Teneraménte (It.) (tĕ-nĕ-rä-*men*-tĕ.) Tenderly, delicately.

Tenerézza (It.) (tĕ-nĕ-*ret*-tsä.) Tenderness, softness, delicacy.

Tenor. That species of male voice next above the baritone, and extending from the C upon the second space in bass, to G on the second line in the treble. So-called from *teneo* (I hold), since it held the *melody* in olden times. See *Soprano* and *Voice*. Also a Sax-horn of same pitch, etc., as *Baritone*, but of smaller bore and inferior tone.

Tenor C. The lowest C in the tenor voice; the lowest string of the viola, or tenor violin.

Tenor clef. The C clef, when placed upon the fourth line. See *Clef*.

Tenóre di grázia (It.) (tĕ-*nō*-rĕ di *grä*-tsē-ä.) A delicate and graceful tenor voice.

Tenóre robústo (It.) (tĕ-*nō*-rĕ rō-*boos*-tō.) A strong tenor voice.

Tenor trombone. The B♭ Trombone.

Tenth. An interval measuring ten diatonic degrees, also, an organ-stop tuned a tenth above the diapasons, called, also, decima and double tierce.

Tenúto (It.) (tā-*noo*-tō.) Held on; sustained; or kept down the full time.

Ternary form. The *Rondo*.

Ternary measure. Threefold measure; triple time.

Terzétto (It.) (tāir-*tset*-tō.) A short piece, or trio, for three voices.

Tessitura (It.) (*tĕs*-sē-*too*-rä.) The general position, as to pitch, of the tones of a composition. A work with many high tones is said to have a "high tessitura."

Tetrachord (Gr.) (*tet*-rä-kŏrd.) A perfect fourth.

Theme. 1. A subject, in the development of sonata-form. 2. The *cantus firmus* on which counterpoint is built. 3. The subject of a fugue. 4. A simple tune on which variations are made.

Thesis (Gr.) (thā-sĭs.) Down-beat, the accented part of the bar. See *Arsis*.

Third. An interval measuring three diatonic degrees.

Thirteenth. An interval measuring thirteen diatonic degrees.

Thirty-second note. A demisemiquaver, 𝄰

Thirty-second rest. A rest, or pause, equal to the length of a thirty-second note, 𝄿

Thorough bass. Figured bass; a system of harmony which is indicated by a figured bass. When there is no figure, it is understood that the common chord of such a note is to be used as its harmony. It is a species of musical shorthand much employed in the eighteenth century, when it was often customary to indicate only the bass notes of an accompaniment. To-day it is chiefly used in the study of harmony. The following table will show the manner in which figures are used:

The figure 2 implies a 4th and 6th.
    "   "   3   "   a 5th perfect, or diminished, according to the position of the note in the key.
The figure 4 implies a 5th, or 5th and 8th.
    "   "   5   "   3d and 8th.
    "   "   6   "   3d.
    "   "   7   "   5th and 3d.
    "   "   8   "   3d and 5th.
    "   "   9   "   3d and 5th.

A stroke through a figure directs the raising of the interval by a natural, or sharp, as the case may be. An accidental standing alone implies a corresponding alteration of the 3d of the chord. Horizontal lines direct the continuance of the harmony of the previous chord. If there are no figures under the previous chord, the line or lines direct the continuance of the common chord of the first note under which they were placed.

Thumb-string. Melody-string of the banjo.

Tie. A curved line used to connect or *bind* two notes of the same pitch, the second note being

only a continuation of the first, without separate attack.

Tief (Ger.) (tēf.) Deep, low, profound.

Timbale (Fr.) (tănh-bal.)
Timbállo (It.) (tĕm-bäl-lō.) } A kettle-drum.

Timbre (Fr.) (tănhbr.) *Quality* of tone, or sound.

Time. The measure of sounds in regard to their continuance, or duration. The speed of the rhythm. The rapidity with which the natural accents follow each other. This is the correct meaning of *time*. (See *Tempo*.) Nevertheless, an almost universal custom prevails of using the word *time* to express the *division* of the measure as well as the speed. Such division should properly be called either *rhythm*, or *measure*. For *Time Signature*, see *Signature*. Time is classified as even, triple, and peculiar. Even times are those where the measure divides naturally into halves. When the measure divides naturally into halves or quarters and each of these subdivisions into thirds, the result is compound even time. Triple times occur when the measure divides itself naturally into thirds, and compound triple rhythms are those where the measure divides into thirds, and each of these thirds again subdivides into thirds. Septuple or quintuple times are where the measure divides into fifths, or sevenths.

Timoróso (It.) (tē-mō-rō-zo.) Timorous; with hesitation.

Tímpani (It. pl.) (tĕm-pä-nē.) The kettle-drums.

Toccáta (It.) (tō-kä-tä.) An old form of composition for the organ, or pianoforte, something like our capriccio, or fantasia; a piece requiring brilliant execution, the *toccata* was a technical work (from the word *toccare, to touch*), a study in which some difficulties of execution were always present, and it generally preceded a fugue. In modern times it is still a study, but is more generally founded on the treatment of a single figure.

Toccatina (It.) (tŏk-kä-tē-nä.) A short *toccáta*.

Tocsin. An alarm-bell; ringing of a bell for the purpose of alarm.

Todesgesang (Ger.) (tō-dĕs-ghĕ-*säng*.)
Todeslied (Ger.) (tō-dĕs-lēd.) } A dirge; a funeral song.

Todtenglöckchen (Ger.) (tōd-t'n-*glŏk*-kh'n.) Funeral bell.

Todtenlied (Ger.) (*tōd*-t'n-*lĕd*.) Funeral song, or anthem.

Todten-marsch (Ger.) (*tōd*-t'n-*märsh*.) Funeral march.

Todten-musik (Ger.) (*tōd*-t'n-*mooc*-zĭk.) Funeral music.

Tolling. The act of ringing a church-bell in a slow, measured manner.

Ton (Fr.) (tŏnh.) } Tone, sound, voice, key, mode.
Ton (Ger.) (tōn.) } See *Tone.*

Tonart (Ger.) (*tö*-närt.) Mode, scale, key.

Tone. A given, fixed sound of certain pitch. Sometimes used to signify a certain degree of distance, or interval, between two sounds, as in the major tone and minor tone, whole and semi-tone; also the particular quality of the sound of any voice, or instrument.

Tongue. In the reed-pipe of an organ, a thin elastic slip of metal.

Tonguing. A mode of articulating quick notes, used by flutists and cornetists.

Tonic. The key-note of any scale; the chief, fundamental ground-tone, or first note, of the scale.

Tonic Sol-fa. A method of teaching vocal music, invented by Miss Sarah Ann Glover, of Norwich, England, about 1812 (called by her the *tetrachordal* system), and afterwards perfected by the Rev. John Curwen, who became acquainted with the method in 1841. Its formal basis is the *movable-do* system; the seven usual solmisation syllables are employed, as follows: *doh, ray, me, fah, soh, lah, te*. These syllables with modification for sharping and flatting, are used instead of notes. See "Elson's Music Dictionary."

Ton-leiter (Ger.) (*tōn*-lī-tĕr.) Scale.

Tósto (It.) (tōs-tō.) Quick, swift, rapid.

Touch. Style of striking, or pressing the keys of an organ, pianoforte, or similar instrument; the resistance made to the fingers, by the keys of any instrument, as *hard*, or *heavy; soft*, or *light touch*.

Toujours (Fr.) (too-zhoor.) **Always.**

Tranquíllo (It.) (trän-*queel*-lō.) Tranquillity, calmness, quietness.

149

Transcription. An arrangement for any instrument, of a song or other composition, not originally designed for that instrument; an adaptation.

Transition. Passing suddenly out of one key into another, also a passage leading from one theme to another.

Transposed. Removed, or changed into another key.

Transposer (Fr.) (tranhs-pō-zā.)
Transponiren (Ger.) (*trä is*-pō-*nee*-rĕn.) } Change of key; removing a piece into another key.

Transposing Instruments. The most natural key, the fundamental, harmonically and technically on all instruments, is the *Key of C.* When the note C conceived and played on any instrument actually sounds another note according to standard pitch, the instrument is said to be transposing. For instance, a clarinet that in playing *Middle C* sounds the B♭ below is a transposing instrument standing in B♭, and is known as a B♭ clarinet; C played on an E♭ clarinet would sound E♭, etc. The Contra-Bass and Contra-Bassoon, sounding notes a full octave lower than written, and the Piccolo or Octave Flute sounding them an octave higher than written, are in a way transposing instruments. The definition, however, is chiefly confined to instruments said to be in any other key than C, for instance, clarinets in A, B♭, E♭; trumpets in E, E♭, B♭; horns in D, E♭, F.

Trascinándo (It.) (trä-shi-*nän*-dō.) Dragging the time.

Trattenúto. (It.) (trät-tĕ-*noo*-tŏ.) See *Rattenúto.*

Traurig (Ger.) (*trou*-rĭg.) Heavily, sadly, mournfully.

Tre (It.) (trāy.) Three; *à tre,* for three voices, or instruments.

Treble. The upper part; the highest voice; the soprano.

Treble clef. The clef, the soprano clef.

Tre córde (It.) (trāy kŏr-dĕ.) *Three strings;* in pianoforte music this means that the pedal which moves the keys, or action, the soft pedal, must no longer be pressed down.

Tremándo (It.) (trā-*män*-dō.) \
Tremoládno (It.) (trĕm-ō-*län*-dō.) } *Trembling,* quiv- \
Trémolo (It.) (trā-mō-lō.) ering, a note, or chord, reiterated with great rapidity, producing a tremulous effect.

Tremolant. { An organ or harmonium stop which \
Tremulant. { gives to the tone a waving, trembling, or undulating effect.

Très (Fr.) (trāy.) Very, most.

Triad. Any chord consisting of a root with its third and fifth above.

Triangle. A piece of steel bent into triangle form, yielding a clear ringing sound when struck. It is not treated as an instrument of definite pitch.

Trill (Ger., *Triller;* Fr., *Trille;* It., *Trillo;* in England, *The Shake.*) Two adjacent notes alternating in more or less rapid succession; generally abbreviated as to notation by placing the trill sign *tr.* ⌒⌒⌒ over one of the notes, indicating that this note and the one immediately above are to be alternated to the time value of the given note. The trill may begin on either of the two notes and is generally terminated by a *Turn.* See "Elson's Music Dictionary."

Triller (Ger.) (*trĭl*-lĕr.) } A shake; a trill. \
Trillo (It.) (*tree*-lō.) }

Trio (It.) (*tree*-ō.) A composition for three voices or instruments, or the group of performers. The term *Trio* is also applied to a contrasting movement in compositions like the minuet, march, gavotte, etc.

Triole (Ger.) (*tree*-ō-lĕ.) { A triplet; a group of \
Triolet (Fr.) (*tree*-ō-lā.) } three notes to be played in the time of two.

Trionfále (It.) (trē-ōn-*fä*-lĕ.) Triumphal.

Triplet. A group of three notes played in the usual time of two similar ones.

Tristézza (It.) (trĭs-*tet*-sä.) Sadness, heaviness, pensiveness.

Tritone (Eng.) (trī-tōn.) A superfluous, or augmented fourth, containing three whole steps.

Trochee (Lat.) (trō-kā.) A dissylabic musical foot, containing one long and one short syllable, — ◡

Trómba (It.) (*trōm*-bä.) A trumpet; also an 8-foot reed organ-stop.

Trombone. (Ger., *Posaune*, It. and Fr., *Trombono*.) A wind instrument consisting of a metal tube, bent to convenient length and terminating in a flaring bell. The distinguishing feature is a double slide which can be adjusted in seven "positions" at will. Each "position" yields a fundamental note and its harmonics, the seven "positions" cover a chromatic scale of two and a half octaves with a few good *Pedal* notes.

There is one form of trombone made with valves or pistons, but while easier to play it is generally of faulty intonation and lacks the nobility of tone characteristic of the trombone proper. Trombones are classified as Alto, Tenor, or Bass, according to their pitch. The ordinary trombone of band and orchestra is the Tenor (B♭) with a compass of from *e* below the bass staff to about the 2nd *b♭* above. A mouthpiece similar to that of trumpet is used.

Tronco (It.) (*trōn-kō.*) An indication that sounds are to be cut short.

Tróppo (It.) (*trōp-pō.*) Too much; *nor tróppo*, not too much.

Troubadours (Fr. pl.) (troo-bä-doer.) The bards, and poet-musicians of Provence, and of North France, about the twelfth century. See Rowbotham's "Troubadours and Courts of Love."

Trüb (Ger.) (treeb.) Sad, mournful, gloomy.

Trumpet. A wind instrument consisting primarily of a metal tube bent to convenient length, terminating in a flaring bell. It is played with a cup-shaped mouth-piece and gives the natural harmonics of a fundamental tone. The natural trumpet (without valves) is used only for military purposes at the present time. The trumpet of orchestra and band is equipped with a system of cylindrical or piston valves (see *Valve*) on the Sax system, yielding a chromatic scale. The tone of the trumpet is brilliant, clear and of great carrying power. The ratio between width of bore and length of tube is much more perfect in the trumpet than in the cornet, an instrument of inferior tone, which has been often substituted for it.

The compass of the trumpet is from "*g*" below the treble staff to "*g*" above, sounding as written when played on the C trumpet, and being proportionately transposed as to pitch when played on the trumpets in B♭, G, F (low) D, E♭, F (high), etc.

Tuba (Lat.) (*too*-bä.) The name applied to the deepest Sax-horns. The tuba is made in different pitches, the deepest being called the *contra-bass* (not to be confounded with the string instrument.) The tuba is the natural bass of all brass instruments in orchestra or band. Also the name of a powerful reed-stop in an organ.

Tuba mirabilis (Lat.) (*tū*-bä mē-*rä*-bē-lĭs.) An 8-foot reed-stop, on a high pressure of wind and powerful tone.

Tune. An air; a melody; a succession of measured sounds, agreeable to the ear, and possessing a distinct and striking character.

Tuning-fork. A small steel instrument, having two prongs, which upon being struck gives a certain fixed tone, used for tuning instruments, and for ascertaining or indicating the pitch of tunes. Also the act of raising or lowering the pitch of a string or instrument.

Tuning-hammer. A steel, or iron implement used by pianoforte tuners.

Tuning-slide. A device applied to all brass instruments, to permit of the pitch being adjusted to meet special requirement.

Túrca (It.) (*toor*-kä.) Turkish; *álla Túrca*, in the style of Turkish music.

Turn. An embellishment consisting of a group of rapid notes connecting one principal note with another, also used to terminate the trill. The ordinary turn is written out as follows,

the first and last notes being principal notes. The turn is generally abbreviated in notation by using the turn sign ∼ placed over or after the first principal note. There are many kinds of turns in use. See "Elson's Music Dictionary."

Tútta (It.) (*too*-tä.) ⎫
Tútto (It.) (*too*-tō.) ⎬ All; the whole; entirely; quite.

Tútta fórza (It.) (*too*-tä-*fōr*-tsä.) ⎫
Tútta la fórza (It.) (*too*-tä lä *fōr*-tsä.) ⎬ The whole

power, as loud as possible, with the utmost force and vehemence.

Tútti (It.) (*too-tē.*) All, the entire band, or chorus; in a solo, or concerto, it means that the full orchestra is to resume playing.

Twelfth. An interval measured by twelve diatonic degrees. Also an organ-stop tuned twelve notes above the diapasons.

Tympani (It. pl.) (*tĕm-pä-nē.*) Kettle-drums.

Tyrolienne (Fr.) (*tē-rō-lē-en.*) A song, or dance, peculiar to the Tyrolese.

U

Uebermässig (Ger.) (*ü-bĕr-mās-sĭg.*) Augmented, superfluous.

Uebung (Ger.) (*ü-boong.*) An exercise; a study for the practice of some peculiar difficulty. *Uebungsstück;* an exercise.

Uguále (It.) (*oo-gwä-lĕ.*) Equal, like, similar.

Ugualménte (It.) (*oo-gwäl-men-tĕ.*) Equally, alike.

Umfang (Ger.) (*oom-fäng.*) Compass, extent.

Umore (It.) (*oo-mō-ray.*) Humor, playfulness.

Un (It.) (*oon.*)

Una (It.) (*oo-nä.*) ⎱ A, an, one.

Uno (It.) (*oo-no.*) ⎰

Una córda (It.) (*oo-nä kŏr-dä.*) *One string*, on one string only; in pianoforte-music it means that the soft pedal is to be used. See *Pedal*.

Unison. A unison results when two or more voices or instruments sound precisely the same note; also when two or more voices (theoretically) are written on same degree of staff. A body of singers or instrumentalists may perform an entire phrase or melody in unison. On the piano three strings tuned to the same note are called a unison.

Unter (Ger.) (*oon-tĕr.*) Under, below.

Up bow. The sign ⋁. Used in violin, etc., music.

Ut (Fr.) (*üt.*) The note C; the syllable originally applied by Guido to the note C, or *do*.

V

V. An abbreviation for *Violin, Volti,* (V. S. = volti subito), *Voce* (*m. v. = mezza voce.*) V° or **V**^{cello}, *Violoncello;* V^{la}, *Viola.*

Va (It.) (vä.) Go on.

Vaccilándo (It.) (vät-tshē-*län*-dō.) Wavering; uncertain; irregular in the time.

Vágo (It.) (*vä*-gō.) Vague; rambling; uncertain, as to the time or expression.

Valse (Fr.) (väls.) A waltz.

Valve. A close lid or other contrivance designed to retard or modify the sound of an organ-pipe, or any wind-instrument.

On brass instruments a valve is inserted in the tube, so made that when brought into action the air column is admitted to an additional bit of tubing called a slide.

Three slides of varying length and valves are generally used. The first valve-slide lowering the fundamental and its series of harmonics one step (or a tone), the second a half-step (semitone), and the third a step and a half (tone and a semitone). In combination with the natural harmonics, the three valves produce a chromatic scale. This is the basic principle of the Saxhorn and it is applied with certain modifications of valve (piston or cylinder) to all modern brass instruments.

Vamp. To improvise an accompaniment.

Variations. Repetitions of a theme, or subject, in new and varied aspects, the form or outline of the composition being preserved while the different passages are ornamented and amplified.

Varsovienne. (Fr.) (vär-sō-vē-en.) A dance in moderate tempo, and ¾ time. Named after Warsaw, (Fr.) Varsovie.

Veëménza (It.) (vā-*men*-tsä.) Vehemence, force.

Veláto (It.) (vā-*lä*-tō.) *Veiled;* a voice sounding as if it were covered with a veil.

Vellutáto (It.) (věl-loo-*tä*-tō.) In a velvety manner.

Velóce (It.) (vě-*lō*-tshě.) Swiftly.

Velocíssimo (It.) (vě-lō-*tshēs*-sē-mō.) Very swiftly; with extreme rapidity.

Velocità (It.) (vě-lō-tshē-*tä*.) Swiftness, rapidity.

Ventil (Ger.) (*fěn*-tĭl.) ⎫ Valve.
Ventíle (It.) (věn-*tē*-lě.) ⎭

Verschiebung (Ger.) (fěr-*shēc*-boong.) The soft pedal: *Mit Verschiebung*, with the soft pedal. See *Pedal.*

Verschwindend (Ger.) (fer-*shwind*-ěnt.) Vanishing; dying away

Verse. That portion of an anthem, or service, intended to be sung by one singer to each part.

Vespers. Name of the evening service in the Roman Catholic Church, consisting chiefly of singing.

Vezzóso (It.) (vet-*tsō*-zō.) Graceful, sweet, tender.

Vibráto (It.) (vē-*brä*-tō.) A strong, vibrating, full quality of tone; resonant.

Vibration. The tremulous or undulatory motion of any sonorous body (or of the air) by which the sound is produced, the sound being grave or acute, as the vibrations are fewer or more numerous in a given time.

Viel (Ger.) (feel.) Much; a great deal; *mit vielem tonc,* with much tone.

Vigoróso (It.) (vē-gō-*rō*-zō.) Vigorous, bold, energetic.

Viol. An old instrument somewhat resembling the violin, of which it was the origin; but having six strings and fretted finger-board. It was played with a bow.

Vióla. The tenor-violin; an instrument similar in tone and formation to the violin, but larger in size and having a compass a fifth lower. It is notated in the alto clef, and its four strings are tuned thus:

Its compass in orchestral use is about as follows:

Viol, bass. The violoncello, or small Double-bass. Obsolete term.

Vióla d'amore (It.) (vē-ō-lä dä-*mō*-rĕ.) An instrument a little larger than the *viola,* furnished with frets, and a greater number of strings, seven above the finger-board, and seven below. The name is also given to an organ-stop of similar quality to the *gamba,* or *salcional.*

Violénto (It.) (vē-ō-*len*-tō.) Violent, vehement, boisterous.

Violin. A well-known stringed instrument. It is the most perfect musical instrument known, of brilliant tone and capable of every variety

of expression. The violin has four strings, tuned as follows:

The ordinary orchestral compass of the violin is about

The soloist can play nearly an octave higher. At times the bow of the violin is discarded and the instrument plucked like a guitar; this mode of playing is called *pizzicato*. See Stoeving's "The Violin."

Violinbogen (Ger.) (fee-ō-*leen*-bō-g'n.) A violin-bow.

Violine (Ger.) (fee-ō-*leen*-ĕ.) An organ-stop of 8, 4, or 2-foot tone.

Violoncéllo (It.) (vē-ō-lŏn-*tchel*-lō.) The large or bass violin. The violoncello is as expressive as the violin, but is masculine where the latter is feminine, having a broader, richer tone. It has four strings, tuned as follows,

The compass of the instrument is about

Also an organ stop.

Violóne (It.) (vē-ō-*lō*-nĕ.) The name originally given to the double-bass. The name is also applied to an open wood-stop, on the pedals of an organ.

Virginal. A small keyed instrument, supposed to have been the origin of the spinet, as the latter was of the harpsichord.

Virtuóso (It.) (vēr-too-ō-zō.) A skilful performer upon some instrument.

Vitaménte (It.) (vē-tä-*men*-tĕ.) Quickly, swiftly, briskly, immediately.

Viváce (It.) (vē-*vä*-tshĕ.) } Animated, lively, briskly.
Vívo (It.) (vēe-vō.)

Vocal. Belonging, or relating to the human voice.

Vocalise (Fr.) (vō-kä-leez.) A vocal exercise using vowel sounds.

Vocalize. To practice vocal exercises, using vowel sounds (generally Italian) instead of words, to develop tone and technic.

Vóce (It.) (*vō*-tshĕ.) The voice.

Voice. The sound produced by the vocal organs in singing or speaking. The singing voice is divided into six classes as follows, beginning with the lowest: Bass, Baritone and Tenor (Men's Voices); Alto, Mezzo-Soprano and Soprano (Women's Voices). The so-called *unchanged* voices of young boys also embrace Alto and Soprano. In former times a very high, head voice in men was called Alto. See *Chest-voice* and *Head-voice*. The word is also applied to a "part" in harmonic writing.

Voicing. The adjustment of the parts of an organ-pipe for the purpose of giving it its proper pitch and its peculiar character of sound.

Voix célestes (Fr.) (voo-wä say-lest.) *Celestial voices;* an organ-stop of French invention. Also, a soft stop on the harmonium.

Voláta (It.) (vō-*lä*-tä.) A flight; run; rapid series of notes; a *roulade*, or *division.*

Voll (Ger.) (fŏll.) Full; *mit vollem Werke,* with the full organ.

Volonté (Fr.) (vō-lŏnh-*tä*.) Will, pleasure; *à volontè,* at will.

Vólta (It.) (*vōl*-tä.) Time.

Vólta príma (It.) (*vōl*-tä-*prēe*-mä.) First time.

Voltáre (It.) (vōl-*tä*-rĕ.) To turn; to turn over.

Vólta secónda (It.) (*vōl*-tä sĕ-*kon*-dä.) The second time.

Vólte (It.) (*vōl*-tĕ.) } An obsolete dance in ¾ time,

Volte (Fr.) (vōlt.) { resembling the *galliard,* and with a rising and leaping kind of motion.

Volteggiándo (It.) (vōl-tĕd-jē-*än*-dō.) Crossing the hands on the pianoforte.

Vólti (It.) (*vōl*-tē.) Turn over.

Vólti súbito (It.) (*vōl*-tē soo-bē-tō.) Turn the page over quickly.

Volubilita (It.) (vō-loo-bē-lē-*tä*.) Volubility; freedom of performance.

Volume. The quantity of fullness of the tone of a voice, or instrument.

Voluntary. An introductory performance upon the organ, either extemporaneous, or otherwise.

Von (Ger.) (fōn.) By, of, from, on.

Vorher (Ger.) (fōr-här.) Before; *tempo wie vorher,* the time as before.

Vorschlag (Ger.) (fōr-shläg.) Appoggiatùra, beat.

Vorspiel (Ger.) (fōr-speel.) Prelude, introductory movement.

Vortrag (Ger.) (fōr-träg.) Execution, mode of executing a piece; delivery.

Vox humana (Lat.) (vŏx hu-mä-nä.) *Human voice;* an organ reed-stop of 8-foot tone, intended to imitate the human voice.

W

Wald-flöte (Ger.) (väld-flô-tĕ.) *Forest-flute,* shepherd's-flute; an organ-stop with a full and powerful tone.

Waldhorn (Ger.) (väld-hōrn.) *Forest-horn;* also, the French horn in its natural form, without valves.

Waltz. Originally a round dance in ¾ time. The measure has also been adopted in a form or movement in instrumental or vocal music. The tempo may vary from slow to moderately fast.

Wehmüthig (Ger.) (vä-mü-tĭg.) Sad, sorrowful.

Weich (Ger.) (vīkh.) Soft, gentle.

Well-tempered. A term applied to a satisfactory pitch relationship of sounds.

Wenig (Ger.) (vä-nĭg.) Little; *ein wenig stark,* a little strong; rather loud.

Whole note. A semibreve.

Whole rest. A pause equal in length to a whole note, or to a whole *measure* in every modern rhythm except ½.

Whole step. A major second, sometimes called a *tone.*

Wind chest. An air-tight box under the sound-board of an organ.

Wind instruments. A general name for all instruments, the sounds of which are produced by the breath, or by the wind of bellows.

Wolf. A name applied to an impure fifth, which occurs in pianofortes, or organs, tuned in unequal temperament. Also a discordant sound produced by a faulty string on 'cello, etc.

Wood wind. The orchestral wind-instruments which are made of wood.

Wuchtig (Ger.) (*vooch*-tig.) Weightily, ponderously.

Würdig (Ger.) (*vür*-dig.) Dignified.

Wuth (Ger.) (voot.) Madness, rage.

X

Xylophone. An instrument consisting of a series of graduated wooden bars laid on straw, and struck with a wooden hammer. The scale is generally limited to about two octaves.

Y

Yobel or *Jodel.* The peculiar high warbling of the Swiss and Tyrolean mountaineers, in which falsetto tones are interspersed with chest-tones.

Z

Zart (Ger.) (tsärt.) } Tenderly, softly, deli-
Zärtlich (Ger.) (*tsairt*-likh.) } cately.

Zeffiroso (It.) (zef-fē-rō-zō.) Like a zephyr.

Zélo (It.) (zā-lō.) Zeal, ardor, energy.

Zelóso (It.) (zā-lō-zō.) Zealous, ardent, earnest.

Ziemlich (Ger.) (*tsēem*-likh.) Tolerably, moderately.

Zierlich (Ger.) (*tsēēr*-lich.) Neat, graceful.

Zingarésa (It.) (zin-gä-rā-zä.) In the style of gypsy music.

Zither (Ger.) (*tsit*-ĕr.) An instrument consisting of a shallow wooden sound-box, across which are stretched about thirty strings. A fretted finger-board lies under five of the strings which are used for the melody, while the remainder furnish the accompaniment. The strings are generally plucked with the aid of a thumb ring, although a bow-zither has been invented. The tone is soft and sweet.

Zögernd (Ger.) (*tsô*-ghĕrnd.) A continual retarding of the time; hesitating.

Zu (Ger.) (tsoo.) At, by, in, to, unto.

Zunehmend (Ger.) (tsoo-*nā*-mĕnd.) Increasing.

Zurückhaltung (Ger.) (tsoo-*rük-häl*-toong.) Retardation; keeping back.

Zusammen (Ger.) (tsoo-*zäm*-m'n.) Together.

Zwei (Ger.) (tvsī.) Two.

Zwischen-satz (Ger.) (*tsvē*-shĕn-sätz.) Intermediate theme; episode.

Zwischen-spiel (Ger.) (*tsvē*-shĕn-spēel.) Interlude played between the verses of a hymn. An Intermezzo.

NOTED NAMES IN MUSIC

There has been no attempt to include the many famous singers and artist performers who might be listed under such a heading as above. This list is limited chiefly to composers and authors of works on music.

Abt, Franz. Eilenburg, 1819; Wiesbaden, 1885. Song composer.

Adam, Adolphe-Charles. Paris, 1803-1856. Light operas.

Adams, Stephen. Liverpool, Eng., 1844-1913. (Real name, Michael Maybrick.) Song composer.

Alard, Jean-Delphin. Bayonne, 1815; Paris, 1888. Violinist and composer.

Albeniz, Isaac. Camprodon, Spain, 1861; Cambo les Bains, France, 1909. Pianist and composer.

d'Albert, Eugène. Glasgow, 1864-1932. Pianist and composer.

Alberti, Domenico. Benice, 1707; Formio, 1740. Composer. Invented "Alberti bass."

Albrechtsberger, Johann Georg. nr. Vienna, 1736; Vienna, 1809. Contrapuntist, composer and organist.

Aletter, Wilhelm. Germany, 1867-1934. Composer.

Alkan, Charles-Henri-Valentin. Paris, 1813-1888. Pianist, teacher and composer.

Allitsen, Frances. London, 1849-1912. (Real name, Mary Frances Bumpus.) Composer.

Ambrose, Paul. Hamilton, Ont., Can., 1868- . Composer and organist.

Ambrose, Robert Steele. Chelmsford, Eng., 1824-1908. Composer and organist.

Ambrosio, Alfred d'. Naples, 1871; Nice, 1914. Composer and violinist.

Arcadelt, Jacob. Netherlands, about 1514(?); Paris, 1570-5(?). Flemish composer.

Arditi, Luigi. Crescentino, 1822; nr. Brighton, Eng., 1903. Opera conductor, composer.

Arenski, Anton Stepanovitch. Nijni-Novgorod, 1861; Finland, 1906. Russian pianist and composer.

Arezzo Guido (see Guido).

Armstrong, William Dawson. Alton, Ill., 1868-1936. Composer.

Arne, Dr. Thomas Augustine. London, 1710-1778. Composer.

Artchiboucheff, Nicholas V. Tsarskoe-Sielo, 1858-. Russian pianist, composer.

d'Astorga, Emmanuele, Baron. Palermo, 1681; Prague, 1736. Church composer.

Auber, Daniel-François-Esprit. Caen, 1782; Paris, 1871. Opera composer.

Audran, Edmond. Lyons, 1842; Tierceville, 1901. Composer of light operas.

Aulin, Tor. Stockholm, Sweden, 1866-1914. Violinist and composer.

Aus der Ohe, Adele. Hanover, 1860-1937. Pianist and composer.

Bach family. Noted family of musicians. From 1550 to 1850. (About 400 Bachs are recorded.)

Bach, Karl Philipp Emanuel. Weimar, 1714; Hamburg, 1788. Third son of J. S. Bach. Composer.

Bach, Johann Sebastian. Eisenach, 1685; Leipzig, 1750. Composer.

Backer-Gröndahl, Agatne. Christiania, 1847-1908. Pianist and composer.

Balakirev, Milli A. Nijni-Novgorod, 1836; St. Petersburg, 1910. Russian composer.

Balfe, Michael William. Dublin, 1808; Rowney Abbey, 1870. Opera composer.

Bantock, Granville. London, 1868- . Composer and conductor.

Bargiel, Woldemar. Berlin, 1828-1897. Composer and teacher.

Barnby, Sir Joseph. York, 1838; London, 1896. Organist and composer.

Bartlett, Homer N. Olive, N. Y., 1845; Hoboken, N. J., 1920. Pianist and composer.

Bartlett, James Carroll. Harmony, Maine, 1850-1930. Song composer.

Batiste, Antoine Edouard. Paris, 1820-1876. Organist and composer.

Baumfelder, Friedrich. Dresden, 1836-1916. Composer.

Bax, Arnold. London, 1883- . Composer.

Beach, Mrs. H. H. A. Henniker, N. H., 1867-
Pianist and composer.

Beethoven, Ludwig van. Bonn, 1770; Vienna,
1827. Composer.

Behr, Franz. Lubtheen, 1837; Dresden, 1898.
Salon composer.

Bellini, Vincenzo. Catania, Sicily, 1801; Paris,
1835. Opera composer.

Bemberg, Hermann. Buenos Ayres, 1861- . Opera
and song composer.

Bendel, Franz. Bohemia, 1833; Berlin, 1874.
Pianist and composer.

Benedict, Sir Julius. Stuttgart, 1804; London,
1885. Composer.

Bennett, Sir Wm. Sterndale. Sheffield, 1816; London, 1875. Composer.

Benoît, Pierre-Léonard-Leopold. Harlebeke, Flan-
ders, 1834; Antwerp, 1901. Flemish composer.

Berger, Wilhelm. Boston, 1861; Berlin, 1911. Composer.

Bergh, Arthur. St. Paul, Minn., 1882- . Violinist,
conductor and composer.

Beriot, Charles de. Louvain, 1802; Brussels, 1870.
Violinist and author.

Berlioz, Hector. La Côte St.-André, 1803; Paris,
1869. Composer and critic.

Bertini, Henri. London, 1798; nr. Grenoble, 1876.
Pianist and composer.

Berwald, William. Schwerin, Germany, 1864- .
Composer.

Best, Wm. Thomas. Carlisle, 1826; London, 1897.
Organist and composer.

Bird, Arthur. Cambridge, Mass., 1856; Berlin,
1923. Pianist and composer.

Bischoff, J. W. Chicago, 1850-1909. Blind composer.

Bishop, Sir Henry Rowley. London, 1786-1855.
Composer.

Bizet, Georges. Paris, 1838; Bongival, 1875. Opera
composer.

Bliss, Paul. Chicago, 1872; Owego, N. Y., 1933.
Composer and editor.

Bliss, Peter Paul. Clearfield, Pa. 1838-1876. Hymn
composer.

Bloch, Ernest. Geneva, 1880- . Composer and conductor.

Blumenthal, Jaques. Hamburg, 1829; London, 1908. Song composer.

Boccherini, Luigi. Lucca, 1740; Madrid, 1806. Composer and cellist.

Boëllmann, Léon. Ensisheim, 1862; Paris, 1897. Organist and composer.

Bohm, Carl. Berlin, 1844-1920. Pianist and salon composer.

Boieldiew, François-Adrien. Rouen, 1775; Jarcy, 1834. Opera composer.

Boito, Arrigo. Padua, 1842-1918. Composer and poet.

Bononcini, Giovanni. Modena, 1660; Venice (?), 1750(?). Opera composer.

Bornschein, Franz C. Baltimore, Md., 1879- . Composer.

Borodin, Alexander P. St. Petersburg, 1834-1887. Composer.

Borowski, Felix. Burton, Eng., 1872- . Composer and violinist.

Bortniansky, Dimitri. Gluchov, 1752; St. Petersburg, 1825. Composer.

Bossi, Marco Enrico. Brescia, 1861-1925. Organist and composer.

Braga, Gaetano. Guilianova, Abruzzi, 1829-1907. Cellist and composer.

Brahms, Johannes. Hamburg, 1833; Vienna, 1897. Composer.

Branscombe, Gena. Picton, Ont., Canada ——. Composer.

Brassin, Louis Aix-la-Chapelle, 1840; St. Petersburg, 1884. Pianist and composer.

Bridge, Sir John Frederick. Oldburg, 1844-1924. English organist and church composer.

Brockway, Howard A. Brooklyn, N. Y., 1870- . Pianist and composer.

Brounoff, Platon. Elizabethgrad, Russia, 1869; New York, 1924. Composer.

Browne, J. Lewis. London, 1864; Chicago, 1933. Organist and composer.

Bruch, Max. Cologne, 1838-1920. Composer.

Bruckner, Anton. Ansfelden, 1824; Vienna, 1896. Symphonic composer.

Brüll, Ignaz. Moravia, 1846; Vienna, 1907. Pianist and composer.

Buck, Dudley. Hartford, Conn., 1839; West Orange, N. J., 1909. Organist and composer.

Bull, Dr. John. Somersetshire, 1563; Antwerp, 1628. Organist and composer.

Bullard, Frederic Field. Boston, 1864-1904. Composer.

Bülow, Hans von. Dresden, 1830; Cairo, 1894. Pianist, conductor, composer.

Buonamici, Guiseppe. Florence, 1846 1920. Pianist, conductor and editor.

Burleigh, Cecil. Wyoming, N. Y., 1885- . Composer and violinist.

Burleigh, Harry T. Erie, Pa., 1867- . Negro composer and baritone.

Burmeister, Richard. Hamburg, 1860- . Pianist and composer.

Busch, Carl. Bjerre, Denmark, 1862- . Composer and conductor.

Busoni, Feruccio B. Florence, 1866; Berlin, 1924. Pianist and composer.

Buxtehude, Dietrich. Helsingör, 1639; Lübeck, 1707. Organist and composer.

Byrd, William. London, 1538(?)-1623. Organist and composer.

Caccini, Giulio. Rome, 1558(?); Florence, 1615(?). With Peri, he wrote the first operas.

Cadman, Charles Wakefield. Johnstown, Pa., 1881- . Composer.

Calkin, John Baptiste. London, 1827-1905. Organist and composer.

Cambert, Robert. Paris, 1628(?); London, 1677. First French opera composer.

Campbell-Tipton, Louis. Chicago, 1877-1921. Composer.

Candlyn, T. Frederick H. Davenham, England, 1892- . Composer.

Carissimi, Giacomo. Nr. Rome, 1604; Rome, 1674. Church composer.

Carl, William C. Bloomfield, N. J., 1865-1936. Organist and author.

Carpenter, John Alden. Park Ridge, Ill., 1876- Composer.

Carreño, Teresa. Venezuela, 1853-1917. Pianist and composer.

Chabrier, Alexis Emmanuel. Aubert, 1841; Paris, 1894. Composer.

Chadwick, George Whitfield. Lowell, Mass., 1854-1931. Composer and organist.

Chaminade, Cécile. Paris, 1861- . Composer.

Charpentier, Gustave. Dieuze, Lorraine, 1860- Composer.

Chasins, Abram. New York, 1903- . Composer.

Chausson, Ernest. Paris, 1855; Limaz, 1899. Composer.

Cherubini, Luigi. Florence, 1760; Paris, 1842. Composer.

Chopin, Frédéric. Zelazowa-Wola, Poland, 1809; Paris, 1849. Pianist, composer.

Cimarosa, Domenico. nr. Naples, 1749; Venice, 1801. Composer.

Clarke, Hugh A. Toronto, Can., 1839; Philadelphia, 1927. Composer and author.

Clementi, Muzio. Rome, 1752; London, 1832. Pianist, teacher, publisher and piano-maker.

Clokey, Joseph W. New Albany, Ind., 1890 . Composer.

Clough-Leighter, H. Washington, D. C., 1874- . Composer.

Coerne, Louis Adolf. Newark, N. J., 1870-1922. Composer.

Coleridge-Taylor, Samuel. London, 1875-1912. First eminent composer of African descent.

Concone, Guiseppe. Turin, 1810-1861. Singing master and composer.

Converse, Frederick S. Newton, Mass., 1871- . Composer.

Cooke, James Francis. Bay City, Mich., 1875- . Composer and editor.

Coombs, Charles Whitney. Bucksport, Me., 1859- . Composer.

Copland, Aaron. Brooklyn, 1900- . Composer.

Corelli, Arcangelo. Fusignano, Italy, 1653; Rome, 1713. Violinist and composer.

Cornelius, Peter. Mayence, 1824-1874. Composer.

Costa, Sir Michael. Naples, 1808; Brighton, 1884. Conductor and composer.

Couperin, François. Paris, 1668-1733. Composer.

Couperin, Louis. Paris, 1630-1665. Composer and violinist.

Coverly, Robert. Oporto, Portugal, 1863- . Composer.

Cowen, Frederic Hymen. Kingston, Jamaica, 1852-1935. English composer.

Cramer, Johann Baptist. Mannheim, 1771; London, 1858. Pianist, composer and teacher.

Crist, Bainbridge. Lawrenceburg, Ind., 1883- . Composer.

Cui, César Antonovitch. Vilna, 1835-1918. Russian composer.

Curwen, Rev. John. Heckmondwike, Eng., 1816; nr. Manchester, 1880. Tonic Sol-fa system.

Czerny, Carl. Vienna, 1791-1857. Pianist, teacher and composer.

Dalayrac, Nicholas, Murat, Haute-Garonne, 1753-1809. French dramatic composer.

Dalcroze, Émile Jacques-. Vienna, 1865- . Swiss composer and creator of system of "Eurhythmics."

Damrosch, Walter. Breslau, 1862- . Conductor, composer.

Dancla, Charles. Bagnères-de-Bigorre, 1818; Tunis, 1907. Violinist and composer.

Daquin, Louis-Claude. Paris, 1694-1772. Clavecinist and composer.

Dargomizski, Alexander S. Toula, 1813; St. Petersburg, 1869. Opera composer.

David, Félicien. Cadenet, 1810; St. Germain, 1876. French composer.

David, Ferdinand. Hamburg, 1810; nr. Klosters, 1873. Violinist, teacher, and author.

Davidov, Charles. Goldingen, 1838; Moscow, 1889. Cellist and composer.

Debussy, Achille Claude. St. Germain-en-Laye, 1862-1918. Composer.

Decreus, Camille. Paris, 1876- . Pianist, teacher composer.

DeFalla, Manuel. Cadiz, Spain, 1877- . Composer.

DeKoven, Reginald. Middletown, Conn., 1859-1920. Composer.

DeLeone, Francesco B. Ravenna, Ohio, 1887- Composer.

Delibes, Léo. St. Germain-du-Val, 1836; **Paris,** 1891. Composer.

De l'Isle, Claude Joseph Rouget. France, 1760-1836. Composer of "La Marseillaise."

Delius, Frederick. Bradford, Eng., 1863-1934. Composer.

Dennée, Charles Frederick. Oswego, N. Y., 1863- . Composer.

Densmore, John Hopkins. Somerville, Mass., 1880- . Composer.

Denza, Luigi. Castellmare di Stabbia, 1846-1922. Song composer.

Desprès, Joaquin. Burgundy, 1450(?)-1521. Singer and composer. Regarded as the greatest of his period.

Dett, Robert Nathaniel. Canada, 1882- . Negro composer.

Diabelli, Antonio. Mattsee, 1781; Vienna, 1858. Composer.

Diggle, Roland. London, 1885- . Organist and composer.

Dittersdorf, Karl Ditters von. Vienna, 1739; Rothlhotta, 1799. Composer and violinist.

Döhler, Theodor. Naples, 1814; Florence, 1856. Pianist and composer.

Dohnanyi, Ernest von. Pressburg, 1877- . Hungarian pianist and composer.

Donizetti, Gaetano. Bergamo, 1797(?)-1848. Opera composer.

Dorn, Heinrich Ludwig Egmont. Königsburg, 1804; Berlin, 1892. Prolific composer.

Draeseke, Felix. Coburg, 1835-1913. Composer and teacher.

Drdla, Franz. Moravia, 1868- . Composer and violinist.

Dreyschock, Alexander. Zack, Bohemia, 1818; Venice, 1869. Pianist and composer.

Dubois, Théodore. Rosnay, 1837-1924. Organist and composer.

Dufay, Guillermus. 1400(?)-1474. Singer, organist and composer. Father of the Gallo-Belgic school.

Dukas, Paul. Paris, 1865-1935. Composer.

Durham, Henry Morton. Mass., 1853-1929. Organist and composer.

Dunstable, John. Dunstable (?), 1400(?); Walbrook, 1453. English composer.

Dunn, James Philip. New York, 1884-1936. Organist and composer.

Duparc, Henri. Paris, 1848-1933. Composer.

Dupont, Auguste. Belgium, 1827-1890. Composer.

Dupont, Gabriel. France, 1878-1914. Composer.

Durante, Francesco. Naples, 1684-1755. Composed church music of the Neapolitan School.

Dussek, Johann. Bohemia, 1761; St. Germain-en-Laye, 1812. Pianist and composer.

Dvořák, Antonin. Mühlhausen, 1841; Prague, 1904. Bohemian composer.

Eddy, Clarence. Greenfield, Mass., 1851-1937. Organist and author.

Eggeling, Georg. Germany, 1866- . Composer.

Ehrlich, Alfred Heinrich. Vienna, 1822; Berlin, 1899. Pianist, critic and litterateur.

Eilenberg, Richard. Prussia, 1848-1927. Composer.

Elgar, Sir Edward. Broadheath, 1857-1934. Composer.

Elson, Arthur. Boston, 1873- . Author.

Elson, Louis C. Boston, 1848-1927. Critic and litterateur.

Elvey, Sir George. Canterbury, 1816; Windlesham, 1893. Organist and composer.

Emery, Stephen A. Paris, Me., 1841; Boston, 1891. Theorist and composer.

Enesco, Georges. Roumania, 1881- . Violinist and composer.

Engelmann, Hans. Berlin, 1872; Philadelphia, 1914. Prolific composer

Enna, August. Nakskov, Denmark, 1860; Copenhagen, 1923. Composer.

Ernst, Heinrich Wilhelm. Brunn, 1814; Nice, 1865. Violinist and author.

Ewing, Montague. England, 1890- Composer.

Farjeon, Harry. Hohokus, N. Y., 1878- . Composer.

Farwell, Arthur. St. Paul, Minn., 1872- . Composer.

Faulkes, William. Liverpool, 1863-1933. Organist and composer.

Fauré, Gabriel Urbain. Pamiers, 1845-1924. Composer

Faure, Jean Baptiste. Moulins, 1830-1914. **Baritone** and composer.

Felton, William M. Philadelphia, 1887- . Composer and editor.

Ferrari, Gustave. Geneva, 1872- . Organist and composer.

Ferrata, Giuseppi. Gradoli, Italy, 1865; New Orleans, 1928. Composer.

Fetis, Francois-Joseph. Mons, 1784; Brussels, 1871. Belgian music historian and litterateur.

Fevrier, Henri. Paris, 1875-1932. Composer.

Fibich, Zdenko. Bohemia, 1850; Prague, 1900. Bohemian composer.

Field, John. Dublin, 1782; Moscow, 1837. Pianist, composer. Created the Nocturne.

Fielitz, Alexander von. Leipsic, 1860; Bad Salzungen, 1930. Composer.

Finck, Henry T. Bethel, Mo., 1854; Rumford Falls, Maine, 1926. Critic and litterateur.

Finden, Amy Woodforde-. Valparaiso, Chile (?); London, 1919. Composer.

Fiorillo, Federigo. Brunswick, 1753; Paris(?), 1823(?). Violinist and composer.

Fisher, William Arms. San Francisco, 1861- . Composer and editor.

Flagler, Isaac Van Vleck. Albany, N. Y., 1844-1909. Organist and composer.

Floerscheim, Otto. Aix-la-Chapelle, 1853-1917. Composer and editor.

Flotow, Friedrich von. Mecklenburg, 1812; Darmstadt, 1883. Composer.

Foerster, Adolph Martin. Pittsburgh, Pa., 1854-1927. Composer.

Foote, Arthur Wm. Salem, Mass., 1853-1937. Organist and composer.

Forsyth, Cecil. Greenwich, England, 1870- . Composer.

Foster, Fay. Leavenworth, Kans., ——. Composer.

Foster, Miles Birket. London, 1851-1922. Composer.

Foster, Stephen Collins. Pittsburgh, 1826; New York, 1864. Song composer.

Fourdrain, Felix. Paris, 1880-1923. Composer.

Franchetti, Alberto. Turin, 1860- . Opera composer.

Franck, César-Auguste. Liége, 1822; Paris, 1890. Composer.

Franz, Robert (Knauth). Halle, 1815-1892. Song composer.

Freed, Isador. Russia, 1900- . Composer.

Freer, Eleanor Everest. Philadelphia, 1864- . Composer.

Frescobaldi, Giralamo. Ferrara, 1583; Rome, 1644. Organist and composer.

Friml, Rudolf. Prague, 1881- . Composer.

Fuentes, Eduardo Sanchez de. Havana, 1874- . Composer.

Fumagalli, Luca. Italy, 1837-1908. Composer.

Gabrilowitsch, Ossip S. St. Petersburg, 1878; Detroit, 1936. Pianist, conductor, and composer.

Gade, Niels Wilhelm. Copenhagen, 1817-1890. Composer.

Galloway, Tod Buchanan. Columbus, Ohio, 1863-1935. Composer.

Ganne, Louis-Gaston. Buxieres-les-Mines, 1862-1923. Composer.

Ganz, Rudolph. Zurich, 1877- . Pianist and composer.

Gardner, Samuel. Elizabethgrad, Russia, 1891- . Violinist and composer.

Gatty, Alfred Scott. Ecclesfield, England, 1847; London, 1919. Composer.

Gaul, Alfred Robert. Norwich, Eng., 1837-1913. Composer.

Gaul, Harvey Bartlett. New York, 1881- . Composer and organist.

Gaynor, Jessie Lovel. St. Louis, 1863-1921. Composer and educator.

Geibel, Adam. Neuenheim, Germany, 1855; Philadelphia, 1933. Blind composer.

German, Edward. Whitchurch, Eng., 1862-1936. Composer.

Gershwin, George. Brooklyn, 1898-1937. Composer.

Gevaërt, François-Auguste. Huyse, 1828; Brussels, 1908. Composer, theorist, music historian.

Gibbons, Orlando. Cambridge, 1583; Canterbury, 1625. Composer.

Gigout, Eugène. Nancy, 1844-1926. Organist and composer.

Gilbert, Henry F. Somerville, Mass., 1868; Cambridge, 1928. Composer.

Gilchrist, Wm. Wallace. Jersey City, 1846; Easton, Pa., 1916. Composer.

Gilman, Lawrence. Flushing, N. Y., 1878- . Litterateur.

Giordani, Giuseppe. Naples, 1744; Fermo, 1798. Composer.

Giordano, Umberto. Foggia, 1867- . Opera composer.

Glazounov, Alexander. St. Petersburg, 1865; Paris, 1936. Composer.

Glinka, Michael Ivanovich. Novospaskoï, 1803; Berlin, 1857. Composer.

Gluck, Christoph Willibald Ritter von. Weidenwang, 1714; Vienna, 1787. Composer.

Godard, Benjamin. Paris, 1849; Cannes, 1895. Composer.

Godowsky, Leopold. Wilna, Russ, Poland, 1870-1938. Pianist and composer.

Goetschius, Percy. Paterson, N. J., 1853- . Theorist and author.

Goetz, Hermann. Königsberg, 1840; nr. Zürich, 1876. Composer.

Goldmark, Carl. Hungary, 1830-1915. Composer.

Goldmark, Rubin. New York, 1872-1936. Composer.

Goltermann, Georg Eduard. Hanover, 1824; Frankfort-a-M., 1898. Cellist and composer.

Gomes, Antonio Carlos. Campinas, Brazil, 1839; Para, 1896. Opera composer.

Goodrich, Alfred John. Chilo, Ohio, 1848-1920. Theorist.

Goossens, Eugene. London, 1893- . Composer and conductor.

Goss, Sir John. Fareham, Eng., 1800; London, 1880. Organist and composer.

Gossec, François-Joseph. Vergnies, Belgium, 1734-1829. Composer.

Gottschalk, Louis Moreau. New Orleans, 1829; Rio de Janeiro, 1869. Pianist and composer.

Gounod, Charles. Paris, 1818-1893. Opera composer.

Grainger, Percy. Australia, 1882- . Composer and pianist.

Granados, Enrique Y Campina. Spain, 1867-1916. Composer.

Grant-Schaefer, George Alfred. Williamstown, Ont., 1872- . Composer.

Gretchaninov, Alexander Tichonovitch. Moscow, 1864- Composer.

Grétry, A. E. M. Liége, 1741; Paris, 1813. Opera composer.

Grey, Frank Herbert. Philadelphia, 1883- . Composer.

Grieg, Edvard Hagerup. Bergen, 1843; Christiania, 1907. Norwegian composer.

Griffes, Charles T. Elmira, N. Y., 1884; New York, 1920. Composer.

Grofé, Ferde. New York, 1892- . Composer.

Groton, Frederic. Pongateague, Va., 1880- . Composer.

Grove, Sir George. Clapham, Eng., 1820; London, 1900. Writer on music.

Grovlez, Gabriel. Lille, France, 1879- . Composer.

Grunn, Homer. West Salem, Wisc., 1880- . Composer.

Grützmacher, Friedrich. Dessau, 1832; Dresden, 1903. Composer and cellist.

Guido d'Arezzo. Arezzo, 995(?); Avellano, 1050(?). Reformer of music notation.

Guilmant, Alexandre. Boulogne, 1837-1911. Organist and composer.

Guion, David Wendel. Ballinger, Texas, 1895- . Composer.

Guiraud, Ernest. New Orleans, 1837; Paris, 1892. Composer.

Gurlitt, Cornelius. Germany, 1820-1901. Composer.

Hadley, Henry K. Somerville, Mass., 1871-1937. Composer.

Hageman, Richard. Leenwarden, Holland, 1882- . Composer.

Hahn, Carl. Indianapolis, Ind., 1874-1929. Composer.

Hahn, Reynaldo. Venezuela, 1874- . Composer.

Halévy, J. F. F. E. Paris, 1799; Nice, 1862. Opera composer.

Hall, Robert B. Bowdoinham, Maine, 1859-1907. Composer and band master.

Halvorsen, Johann. Norway, 1864- . Composer and violinist.

Hamblen, Bernard. England, 1877- . Composer.

Hamilton, Clarence Grant. Providence, R. I., 1865-1935. Editor and author.

Hammond, William G. Mellville, L. I., 1874- Song composer.

Handel, George Frideric. Halle, 1685; London, 1759. Composer.

Hanslick, Eduard. Prague, 1825; Vienna, 1904. Music critic and litterateur.

d'Hardelot, Guy (Real name Mrs. W. F. Rhodes). nr. Boulogne sur Mer (?); London, 1936. Song composer.

Harker, F. Flaxington. Aberdeen, Scotland, 1876; Richmond, Va., 1936. Composer.

Harris, Victor. New York, 1869- . Song composer.

Hartmann, Arthur. Hungary, 1881- . Violinist and composer.

Hasse, Johann Adolph. nr. Hamburg, 1699; Venice, 1783. Opera composer.

Hauptmann, Moritz. Dresden, 1792; Leipzig, 1868. Composer and theorist.

Hawkins, Sir John. London, 1719-1789. Music historian.

Hawley, Charles Beach. Brookfield, Conn., 1858; Red Bank, N. J., 1915. Composer.

Haydn, Franz Joseph. Rohrau, 1732; Vienna, 1809. Composer.

Heins, Carl. Tängermunde, 1859-1922. Composer.

Heller, Stephen. Pesth, 1815; Paris, 1888. Pianist and composer.

Henderson, Wm. James. Newark, N. J., 1855; New York, 1937. Music critic and litterateur.

Henschel, Georg. Breslau, 1850; Scotland, 1934. Composer, singer and conductor.

Henselt, Adolf von. Bavaria, 1814; Warmbrunn, Silesia, 1889. Pianist and composer.

Herbert, Victor. Dublin, 1859; New York, 1924. Composer and cellist.

Hérold, Louis J. F. Paris, 1791-1833. Opera composer.

Herz, Henri. Vienna, 1806; Paris, 1888. Pianist and composer.

Hesse, Adolph Friedrich. Breslau, 1809-1863. Organist and composer.

Hildach, Eugene. Mittenberger, 1849; Berlin, 1924. Composer.

Hillemacher, Paul. Paris, 1852; Versailles, 1933. Composer.

Hiller, Ferdinand von. Frankfort, 1811; Cologne, 1885. Composer.

Hiller, Paul. Paris, 1853; Cologne, 1934. Baritone and composer.

Himmel, Friedrich Heinrich. Brandenburg, 1765; Berlin, 1814. Composer.

Hindemith, Paul. Hanou, 1895- . Composer.

Hoffman, Richard. Manchester, Eng., 1831; Mt. Kisco, N. Y., 1909. Pianist and composer.

Hofmann, Heinrich. Berlin, 1842; Gross-Tabarz, 1902. Composer.

Hofmann, Josef. Cracow, 1877- . Pianist and composer.

Hollins, Alfred. Hull, Eng., 1865- . Organist (blind).

Holmes, Augusta Mary Ann. (Irish parents) Paris, 1847-1903. Composer.

Holst, Gustav Theodore. Cheltenham, 1874; London, 1934. Composer.

Homer, Sidney. Boston, 1864- . Composer.

Honegger, Arthur. Le Havre, France, 1892- . Composer.

Hopekirk, Helen. Edinburgh, 1856- . Pianist and composer.

Hopkinson, Francis. Philadelphia, 1737-1791. First American composer.

Horsman, Edward. Brooklyn, 1873-1918. Comp.

Hubay, Jenö. Budapest, 1858-1937. Composer and violinist.

Huber, Hans. nr. Olten, Switz., 1852-1921. Comp.

Huë, Georges A. Versailles, 1858- . Composer.

Huerter, Charles. Brooklyn, 1885- . Composer.

Huhn, Bruno. London, 1871- . Composer.

Hummel, Johann Nepomuk. Pressburg, 1778; Weimar, 1837. Pianist and composer.

Humperdinck, Engelbert. nr. Bonn, 1854-1921. Composer.

Huneker, James Gibbons. Philadelphia, 1860-1921. Litterateur and critic.

Hünten, Franz. Koblenz, 1793-1878. Composer.

Huss, Henry Holden. Newark, N. J., 1862- . Composer.

Hutcheson, Ernest. Melbourne, Australia, 1871- . Pianist and educator.

Hyatt, Nathaniel Irving. Lansingburgh, N. Y., 1865- Composer.

Iljinsky, Alexander. Russia, 1859-1919. Composer.

d'Indy, Vincent. Paris, 1851-1931. Composer.

Ippolitoff-Ivanoff, Michael-Michaelovitch. Gatchina, 1859-1935. Composer.

Ireland, John. Bowdon, England. 1879- . Composer.

Jadassohn, Salomon. Breslau, 1831; Leipzig, 1902. Teacher and composer.

Jaell, Alfred. Trieste, 1832; Paris. 1882. Pianist and composer.

James, Philip. Jersey City, 1890- . Composer.

Jensen, Adolph. Königsberg, 1837; Baden-Baden, 1879. Composer.

Joachim, Joseph. nr. Pressburg, Hungary, 1831; Berlin, 1907. Violinist.

Johns, Clayton. Newcastle, Del., 1857-1932. Pianist and composer.

Johnson, Herbert. Middletown, Conn., 1861: Boston, 1904. Composer.

Johnson, J. Rosamund. Jacksonville, Fla., 1873- . Negro composer.

Jommelli, Nicola. nr. Naples, 1714-1774. Composer.

Jonás, Alberto. Madrid, 1868- . Pianist, teacher and author.

Joseffy, Rafael. Hungary, 1853-1915. Pianist and editor.

Josten, Werner. Elberfeld, Germany, 1888- . Composer.

Juon, Paul. Moscow, 1872- . Composer.

Kalkbrenner, Friedrich Wilhelm. Germany, 1788; nr. Paris, 1849. Pianist and composer.

Karg-Elert, Siegfried. Oberndorf, 1879; Leipzig, 1933. Organist and composer.

Karganov, Genari. Caucasus, 1858-1890. Russian composer.

Kaun, Hugo. Berlin, 1863-1932. Composer.

Kelley, Edgar Stillman. Sparta, Wisconsin, 1857- . Composer.

Kern, Carl Wilhelm. Schlitz, Hesse-Darmstadt, 1874- . Composer.

Key, Francis Scott. Frederick Co., Md., 1780; Washington, D. C., 1843. Wrote the "Star Spangled Banner."

Kiel, Friedrich. Puderbach, 1821; Berlin, 1885. Composer.

Kienzl, Wilhelm. Waizenkirchen, Austria, 1857- . Opera composer.

Kirchner, Theodor. Neukirchen, 1824; Hamburg, 1903. Composer.

Kjerulf, Halfdan. Christiania, 1818-1868. Composer.

Klein, Bruno Oscar. Osnabrück, 1858; New York, 1911. Composer.

Kleinmichel, Richard. Posen, 1846; Charlottenberg, 1901. Pianist and composer.

Klindworth, Karl. Hanover, 1830-1916. Pianist, teacher and editor.

Kneisel, Franz. Roumania, 1865-1926. Violinist and editor.

Kocian, Jaroslav. Bohemia, 1884- . Violinist and composer.

Koelling, Karl W. P. Hamburg, 1831; Chicago, 1914. Composer.

Köhler Louis. Brunswick, 1820; Königsberg, 1886. Pianist and composer.

Kontski, Antoine de. Cracow, 1817; Ivanitchi, 1899. Pianist and composer.

Kopylow, Alexander. Petrograd, 1854-1911. Composer.

Korngold, Erich Wolfgang. Moravia, 1897- . Composer.

Koschat, Thomas. Austria, 1845; Vienna, 1914. Composer.

Kotzschmar, Hermann. Finsterwald, Germany, 1829; Portland, Maine, 1909. Composer.

Kramer, A. Walter. New York, 1890- . Composer and editor.

Krehbiel, Henry Edward. Ann Arbor, 1854; New York, 1923. Critic and litterateur.

Kreisler, Fritz. Vienna, 1875- . Violinist and composer. (Now a citizen of France.)

Krenek, Ernst. Vienna, 1900- . Composer.

Kreutzer, Conradin. Mosskirch, Baden, 1780; Riga, 1849. Opera composer.

Kreutzer, Rodolphe. Versailles, 1766; Geneva, 1831. Violinist and author.

Kriens, Christiaan. Amsterdam, 1881; Hartford, Conn., 1934. Composer.

Kroeger, Ernest R. St. Louis, 1862-1934. Pianist and composer.

Kubelik, Jan. nr. Prague, 1880- . Violinist and editor.

Kücken, Friedrich Wilhelm. Bleckede, Hanover, 1810; Schwerin, 1882. Song composer.

Kuhe, Wilhelm. Prague, 1823; London, 1912. Composer.

Kuhlau, Friedrich. Hanover, 1786; Copenhagen, 1832. Composer.

Kuhnau, Johann. Saxony, 1660; Leipzig, 1722. Composer.

Kullak, Theodor. Posen, 1818; Berlin, 1882. Pianist, teacher and author.

Kunkel, Charles. Sippersfield, Germany, 1840; St. Louis, 1923. Composer and publisher.

Kürsteiner, Jean Paul. Catskill, N. Y., 1864- . Composer.

Labitzky, Joseph. Czechoslovakia, 1802; Karlsbad, 1881. Composer.

Lachner, Franz. Rain, Bavaria, 1804; Munich, 1890. Composer.

Lack, Theodore. Quimper, France, 1846-1921. Composer.

LaForge, Frank. Rockford, Ill., 1879- . Composer, accompanist and teacher.

Lalo, Edouard. Lille, 1823; Paris, 1892. Composer.

Lambert, Alexander. Warsaw, 1862-1929. Pianist and author.

Lang, Benjamin Johnson. Salem, Mass., 1837; Boston, 1909. Pianist and conductor.

Lang, Henry Albert. New Orleans, 1854; Philadelphia, 1930. Composer.

Lange, Gustav. Schwerstedt, 1830; Wernigerode, 1889. Pianist and composer.

Lanner, Joseph. Austria, 1801-1843. Waltz composer.

Lansing, Abram Winne. Cohoes, N. Y., 1861-1928. Composer.

Lassen, Eduard. Copenhagen, 1830-1904. Composer.

Lasso, Orlando di. Mons, Belgium, 1520(?); Munich, 1594(?). Composer.

Lavalée, Calixa. Verchères, Canada, 1842; Boston, 1891. Composer.

Lavignac, Albert. Paris, 1846-1916. Composer and author.

Lebert, Sigmund. Ludwigeburg, Germany, 1822; Stuttgart, 1884. Composer and author.

Lecocq, Charies. Paris, 1832; Guernsey, England, 1911. Operetta composer.

LeCouppey, Felix. Paris, 1811-1887. Composer.

Lefébure-Wely, Louis J. A. Paris, 1817-1869. Composer.

Lehar, Franz. Komorn, Hungary, 1870- . Composer of light operas.

Lehman, Evangeline. Detroit, Mich.- . Composer.

Lehmann, Liza (Mrs. Bedford). London, 1862-1918. Song composer.

Lemont, Cedric W. Fredericton, N. B., Canada, 1879- . Composer.

Lekeu, Guillaume. Belgium, 1870; Angers, 1894. Composer.

Lemare, Edwin H. Isle of Wight, 1865; London, 1934. Organist and composer.

Léonard, Hubert. nr. Liége, 1819; Paris, 1890. Violinist and teacher.

Leoncavallo, Ruggiero. Naples, 1858-1919. Opera composer.

Leroux, Xavier. Velletri (Papal States), 1863; Paris, 1919. Composer.

Leschetizky, Theodor. Austrian Poland, 1830-1915. Pianist. teacher and author.

Liadov, Anatol. St. Petersburg, 1855-1914. Composer.

Lichner, Heinrich. Harpersdorf, 1829; Breslau, 1898. Composer.

Liebling, Emil. Pless, Silesia, 1851; Chicago. 1914. Pianist and composer.

Lieurance, Thurlow. Oskaloosa, Iowa, 1878- . Composer.

Lincke, Paul. Berlin, 1866- . Composer.

Liszt, Franz. Raiding, Hungary, 1811; Bayreuth, 1886. Pianist and composer.

Litolff, Henry Charles. London, 1818; Paris, 1891. Pianist, composer and publisher.

Locatelli, Pietro. Bergamo, Italy, 1693; Amsterdam, 1764. Composer.

Loeffler, Charles Martin. Muhlhausen, Alsatia, 1861; Medfield, Mass., 1935. Violinist and composer.

Loeschhorn, Albert. Berlin, 1819-1905. Pianist, composer and author.

Loewe, Carl. nr. Halle, 1796; Kiel, 1869. Song and ballad composer.

Loomis, Harvey Worthington. Brooklyn, 1865; Boston, 1930. Composer.

Lortzing, Albert. Berlin, 1803-1851. Opera composer.

Lotti, Antonio. Hanover(?), 1667; Venice, 1740. Organist and composer.

Löw, Joseph. Prague, 1834-1886. Composer.

Lully, Jean-Baptiste. Florence, 1633; Paris, 1687. Opera composer.

Lynes, Frank. Cambridge, Mass., 1858-1914. Composer.

Lvoff, Alexis von. Reval, Russia, 1799; Kovno, 1870. Violinist and composer. Wrote "Russian Hymn."

MacDowell, Edward Alexander. New York, 1861-1908. Pianist and composer.

MacFadyen, Alexander. Milwaukee, Wis., 1879- . Composer.

MacFarlane, William Charles. London, 1870- . Composer and organist.

Macfarren, Sir George Alexander. London, 1813-1887. Composer.

Mackenzie, Sir Alex. Campbell. Edinburgh, 1847; London, 1935. Scotch composer.

Mahler, Gustav. Kalescht, Bohemia, 1860; Vienna, 1911. Conductor and composer.

Maier, Guy. Buffalo, N. Y. Pianist and editor.

Mailly, Alphonse. Brussels, 1833-1918. Organist and composer.

Maitland, Rollo. Williamsport, Pa., 1884- . Composer and organist.

Malipiero, G. Francesco. Venice, 1882- . Composer.

Mana-Zucca. b. N. Y.; res. Florida. Composer.

Manney, Charles Fonteyn. Brooklyn, N. Y., 1872- . Composer.

Mansfield, Orlando Augustine. England, 1863-1936. Composer and organist.

Marchesi, Mathilde. Frankfort-a.-M., 1826; London, 1913. Singing teacher and author.

Marks, James Christopher. Cork, Ireland, 1863- . Composer.

Marschner, Heinrich. Zittau, Saxony, 1795; Hanover, 1861. Opera composer.

Marteau, Henri. Rheims, 1874; Lichtenberg, 1934. Violinist and composer.

Martini, Giovanni B. (Padre Martini). Bologna, 1706-1784. Composer.

Martucci, Giuseppe. Capua, 1856; Naples, 1909. Composer.

Marzo, Eduardo. Naples, 1852; New York, 1929. Composer.

Mascagni, Pietro. Leghorn, 1863- . Opera composer.

Mason, Daniel Gregory. Brookline, Mass., 1873- . Litterateur and composer.

Mason, Lowell. Medfield, Mass., 1794; Orange, N. J., 1872. Pioneer in American music.

Mason, William. Boston, 1829; New York, 1908. Pianist and composer.

Massenet, Jules. Monteaux, 1842; Paris, 1912. Opera composer.

Mathews, W. S. B. New London, N. H., 1837; Denver, 1912. Litterateur and educator.

Matthews, Harry Alexander. Cheltenham, England, 1879- . Composer.

McDonald, Harl. Boulder, Colo., 1899- . Composer.

Medtner, Nikolai. Moscow, 1879- . Composer.

Méhul, Etienne-Nicolas. Givet, 1763; Paris, 1817. Opera composer.

Mendelssohn (-Bartholdy), Felix. Hamburg, 1809; Leipzig, 1847. Composer.

Mercadante, Saverio. Altamura, 1795; Naples, 1870. Opera composer.

Merkel, Gustav. Saxony, 1827; Dresden, 1885. Organist and composer.

Messager, André. France, 1853-1929. Composer.

Meyerbeer, Giacomo (Jacob Liebmann Beer). Berlin, 1791; Paris, 1864. Opera composer.

Meyer-Helmund, Erik. St. Petersburg, 1861; Berlin, 1932. Composer.

Meyer-Olbersleben, Max. Weimar, 1850-1927. Composer.

Milhaud, Darius. France, 1892- . Composer.

Mills, Sebastian Bach. England, 1838; Wiesbaden, 1898. Pianist and composer.

Millöcker, Karl. Vienna, 1842; Baden, 1899. Operetta composer.

Mlynarski, Emil. Kibarty, Poland, 1870; Warsaw, 1935. Composer.

Mokrejs, John. Cedar Rapids, Iowa(?) ——. Composer.

Molique, Wilhelm Bernhard. Nuremberg, 1802; Kannstadt, 1869. Violinist and composer.

Montani, Nicola A. Utica, N. Y., 1880- . Composer and authority on Gregorian music.

Montemezzi, Italo. Verona, Italy, 1875- . Opera composer.

Monteverde, Claudio. Cremona, 1567; Venice, 1643. Composer.

Morley, Thomas. England, 1557(?); London, 1604. Composer and contrapuntist.

Morrison, Charles Sumner. Senacaville, Ohio, 1860; Grand Haven, Mich., 1933. Composer.

Moscheles, Ignaz. Prague, 1794; Leipzig, 1870. Pianist, teacher and author.

Moszkowski, Moritz. Breslau, 1854; Paris, 1925. Pianist and composer.

Moussorgski, Modest Petrovitch. Toropetz, 1839; St. Petersburg, 1881. Composer.

Mozart, Wolfgang Amadeus. Salzburg, 1756; Vienna, 1791. Composer.

Musin, Ovide. Nandrin, Belgium, 1854; Brooklyn, 1929. Composer and violinist.

Nachez, Tivadar. Budapest, 1859; Lucerne, 1930. Composer and violinist.

Napravnik, Edward Frantsovitch. Bohemia, 1839-1915. Composer.

Nardini, Pietro. Tuscany, 1729-1793. Composer and violinist.

Navrátil, Karl. Prague, 1867- . Composer.

Neidlinger, William Harold. Brooklyn, 1863; Orange, N. J., 1924. Composer.

Nessler, Victor E. Baldenheim, 1841; Strassburg, 1890. Opera composer.

Nevin, Arthur Finley. Edgeworth, Pa., 1871- . Composer.

Nevin, Ethelbert. nr. Pittsburgh, 1862; New Haven, 1901. Composer.

Nevin, George B. Shippensburg, Pa., 1859; Easton, 1933. Composer.

Nevin, Gordon Balch. Easton, Pa., 1892- . Composer and organist.

Newman, Ernest. Liverpool, 1869- . Author and editor.

Newmarch, Rosa Harriet. England, 1857- . Author.

Nicholls, Heller. England, 1874- . Composer.

Nicodé, Jean-Louis. nr. Posen, 1853; Dresden, 1919. Pianist and composer.

Nicolai, Otto. Königsberg, 1810; Berlin, 1849. Opera composer.

Niemann, Walter. Hamburg, 1876 . Composer.

Nin, Joaquin. Havana, 1883- . Composer.

Noble, Thomas Tertius. Bath, 1867. English-American composer and organist.

Nordoff, Paul. Philadelphia, 1909- . Composer.

Nordraak, Rikard. Christiania, 1842; Berlin, 1876. Composer.

Novello, Vincent. London, 1781; Nice, 1861. Composer and publisher.

Offenbach, Jacques. Cologne, 1819; Paris, 1880. Creator of Opéra Bouffe.

O'Hara, Geoffrey Chatham, Ont., Canada, (?). Composer.

Orem, Preston Ware. Philadelphia, 1864-1938. Composer, editor and author.

Ornstein, Leo. Krementchug, Russia, 1895- . Comp.

Orth, John. Annweiler, 1850; Boston, 1932. Comp.

Pachulski, Heinrich. Russia, 1859- . Composer.

Paderewski, Ignaz Jan. Podolia, Poland, 1859- . Pianist and composer.

Paganini, Niccolo. Genoa, 1782; Nice, 1840. Violinist and composer.

Page, N. Clifford. San Francisco, 1866- . Composer and editor.

Paine, John Knowles. Portland, Me., 1839; Boston, 1906. Composer and teacher.

Paisiello, Giovanni. Taranto, 1741; Naples, 1816. Opera composer.

Paladilhe, Émile. Montpelier, France, 1844; Paris, 1926. Composer.

Palestrina, Giovanni Perluigi da. Palestrina, 1515(?); Rome, 1594. Composer.

Palmgren, Selim. Björeborg, Finland, 1878- . Composer.

Panofka, Heinrich. Breslau, 1807; Florence, 1887. Violinist, singing master and author.

Panseron, Auguste-Mathieu. Paris, 1796-1859. Singing master and author.

Parker, Horatio W. Auburndale, Mass., 1863; Cedarhurst, N. Y., 1919. Organist and composer.

Parry, Sir Charles Hubert H. Bournemouth, Eng., 1848; Knightscroft, 1918. Composer.

Peery, Rob Roy. Saga, Japan, 1900- . Composer and editor.

Perabo, Ernst. Wiesbaden, 1845; Boston, 1920. Pianist and composer.

Pergolesi, Giovanni Battista. Jesi, 1710; nr. Naples, 1736. Composer.

Peri, Jacopo. Rome (?), 1561; Florence, 1633. The first opera composer.

Perosi, Don Lorenzo. Tortona, 1872- . Composer.

Perry, Edward Baxter. Haverhill, Mass., 1855; Camden, Maine, 1924. Lecturer, pianist and author.

Pessard, Émile L. F. Montmartre, 1843-1917. Composer.

Philipp, Isidor. Pesth, 1863- . Composer.

Piccinni, Nicola. Bari, 1728; nr. Paris, 1800. Opera composer.

Pierné, Gabriel. Metz, 1863-1937. Composer.

Pinsuti, Ciro. Florence, 1829-1888. Composer and singing teacher.

Plaidy, Louis. Hubertsburg, 1810; Grimma, 1874. Piano teacher and author.

Planquette, Robert. Paris, 1850-1903. Operetta composer.

Pleyel, Ignaz-Joseph. nr. Vienna, 1757; nr. Paris, 1831. Composer and piano maker.

Poldini, Eduard. Pest. 1869- . Composer.

Ponce, Manuel M. Mexico, 1886- . Composer.

Ponchielli, Amilcare. nr. Cremona, 1834; Milan, 1886. Opera composer.

Popper, David. Prague, 1843; Baden Baden, 1913. Cellist and composer.

Porpora, Nicolo. Naples, 1686-1766(?). Singing master.

Poulenc, Francis. France, 1889- . Composer.

Powell, John. Richmond, Va., 1882- . Composer.

Praetorius, Michael. Thuringia, 1571-1621. Composer.

Pratt, Waldo S. Philadelphia, 1857- . Litterateur.

Prokofieff, Sergei. S. Russia, 1891- . Composer.

Protheroe, Daniel. So. Wales, 1866; Chicago, 1934. Composer.

Prout, Dr. Ebenezer. Northamptonshire, Eng., 1835; London, 1909. Theorist and composer.

Puccini, Giacomo. Lucca, 1858; Brussels, 1924. Opera composer.

Pugnani, Gaetano. Turin, 1731-1798. Composer and violinist.

Purcell, Henry. London, 1658-1717(?). Composer.

Quilter, Roger. Brighton, England, 1877- . Composer.

Raabe, Peter. Frankfort am Oder, 1872- . Composer.

Rachmaninoff, Sergei V. Novgorod, 1873- . Pianist and composer.

Radecke, Robert. Dittmansdorf, 1830; Wernigerode, 1911. Composer.

Raff, Joachim. Lachen, Switz., 1822; Frankfort, 1882. Composer.

Rameau, Jean-Philippe. Dijon, 1683; Paris, 1764. Opera composer and theorist.

Randegger, Alberto. Trieste, 1832; London, 1911. Composer and singing master.

Rasbach, Oscar. Dayton, Ky., 1888- . Composer.

Ravel, Maurice. Pyrénées, 1875-1937. Composer.

Ravina, Jean-Henri. Bordeaux, 1818; Paris, 1906. Composer.

Rebikoff, Vladimir Ivanovitch. Siberia, 1866-1920. Composer.

Reger, Max. Brand, Bavaria, 1873; Leipzig, 1916. Composer.

Reinecke, Carl. Altona, 1824; Leipzig, 1910. Composer, pianist and teacher.

Respighi, Ottorino. Bologna, 1879; Rome, 1936. Composer.

Rheinberger, Joseph. Vaduz, 1837; Munich, 1901. Organist and composer.

Rhené-Baton. Calvados, 1879- . Composer.

Richter, Ernst Friedrich. Gross-Schonau, 1808; Leipzig, 1879. Theorist and composer.

Richter, Hans. Raab, Hungary, 1843: Bayreuth, 1916. Conductor.

Riemann, Hugo. nr. Sondershausen, 1849; Leipzig, 1919. Theorist.

Ries, Franz. Berlin, 1846; Naumberg, 1932. Composer and publisher.

Rimski-Korsakov, Nicolai. Tikhvin, Novgorod, 1844-1908. Composer and conductor.

Rinck, Johann. Elgersburg, 1770; Darmstadt, 1846. Organist and composer.

Ringuet, Leon. Louiseville, P. Q., Canada, 1858; Montreal, 1932. Composer.

Roberts, John Varley. Stanningley, England, 1841; Oxford, 1920. Composer and organist.

Rode, Pierre. Bordeaux, 1774; nr. Damazon, 1830. Violinist.

Rogers, James H. Fair Haven, Conn., 1857- . Organist and composer.

Rolfe, Walter. Rumford, Maine, 1880- . Composer.

Romberg, Sigmund. Hungary, 1887- . Composer of light operas.

Ronald, Landon. (Real name L. Russell.) London, 1873-1938. Composer.

Root, Frederic Woodman. Boston, 1846; Chicago, 1916. Composer.

Root, George Frederick. Sheffield, Mass., 1820; Bailey's Island, Maine, 1895. Composer.

Ropartz, J. Guy. Guingamp, France, 1864-1935. Composer.

Rosenthal, Moriz. Lemberg, 1862- . Pianist and author.

Rossini, Gioacchino Antonio. Pesaro, 1792; Paris, 1868. Opera composer.

Rotoli, Augusto. Rome, 1847; Boston, 1904. Composer.

Rousseau, Samuel Alexandre. Aisne, 1853; Paris, 1904. Composer and organist.

Rubinstein, Anton. Wechwotynecz, 1830; St. Petersburg, 1894. Composer and pianist.

Russell, Louis Arthur. Newark, N. J., 1854-1925. Composer and author.

Ryder, Thomas Philander. Cohasset, Mass., 1836; Somerville, Mass., 1887. Composer.

Saar, Louis Victor. Rotterdam, 1868; St. Louis, 1937. Composer.

Sacchini, Antonio M. G. nr. Naples, 1734; Paris, 1786. Opera composer.

Saenger, Gustav. New York, 1865-1935. Composer and editor.

Safonoff, Vassily Ilyitch. Caucasus, 1852-1918. Composer and conductor.

Saint-Saëns, Camille. Paris, 1835-1921. Organist, pianist and composer.

Salieri, Antonio. Legnago, 1750; Vienna, 1825. Composer. Teacher of Beethoven.

Salter, Mary Turner. Peoria, Ill., 1856-1938. Composer.

Salter, Sumner. Burlington, Iowa, 1856- . Composer.

Sammartini, Giovanni Battista. Milan, 1700-1775. Composer.

Sapelnikoff, Vassily. Odessa, 1868- . Composer.

Sarasate, Pablo de. Pamplona, Spain, 1844; Biarritz, 1908. Violinist and composer.

Sartorio, Arnoldo. Frankfort am Main, 1853-1936. Prolific composer.

Satie, Erik. Honfleur, France, 1866-1925. Composer.

Sauer, Emil. Hamburg, 1862- . Pianist and composer.

Sauret, Émile. Dun-Le-Roi, 1852; London, 1920. Violinist and composer.

Sawyer, Henry S. New York, 1864- . Composer and editor.

Scarlatti, Alessandro. Sicily, 1659; Naples, 1725. Founder of Neapolitan School of Opera.

Scarlatti, Domenico. Naples, 1685-1757. Composer.

Scharwenka, Philipp. Posen, 1847; Bad Nauheim, 1917. Pianist and composer.

Scharwenka, Xaver. Posen, 1850; Berlin, 1924. Pianist and composer.

Schelling, Ernest. Belvedere, N. J., 1876- . Composer and pianist.

Schillings, Max. Düren, 1868; Berlin, 1933. Composer.

Schindler, Kurt. Berlin, 1882; New York, 1935. Composer and editor.

Schmitt, Florent. France, 1870- . Composer.

Schönberg, Arnold. Vienna, 1874- . Composer.

Schradieck, Henry. Hamburg, 1846; Brooklyn, 1918. Violinist and author.

Schubert, Franz. nr. Vienna, 1797; Vienna, 1828. Composer.

Schuett, Eduard. St. Petersburg, 1856; Meran, Italy, 1933. Composer and pianist.

Schulhoff, Julius. Prague, 1825; Berlin, 1898. Composer.

Schumann, Clara. Leipzig, 1819; Frankfort-a.-M., 1896. Pianist and composer. (Wife of Robert S.)

Schumann, Georg Alfred. Saxony, 1866- . Composer.

Schumann, Robert. Zwickau, 1810; nr. Bonn, 1856. Composer.

Schütz, Heinrich. Köstritz, 1585; Dresden, 1672. "Father of German Music."

Schytte, Ludwig. Aarhus, Denmark, 1850; Berlin, 1909. Pianist and composer.

Scott, Cyril Meir. Oxton, Cheshire, England, 1879- . Composer.

Scott, John Prindle. Norwich, N. Y., 1877; Syracuse, 1932. Composer.

Scriabine, Alexander. Moscow, 1872-1915. Pianist and composer.

Seeboeck, William Charles Ernst. Vienna, 1859; Chicago, 1907. Composer.

Seiss, Isidor. Dresden, 1840; Cologne, 1905. Pianist and composer.

Selmer, Joban. Christiania, Norway, 1844; Venice, 1910. Composer.

Sevčik, Otakar. Horaždowitz, Bohemia, 1852; Pisek, Bohemia, 1934. Violinist and teacher.

Sgambati, Giovanni. Rome, 1843-1914. Pianist and composer.

Shakespeare, William. Croydon, England, 1849; London, 1931. Author of works on voice.

Sharp, Cecil James. London, 1859-1924. Composer and author.

Shelley, Harry Rowe. New Haven, 1858- . Composer.

Sherwood, Wm. Hall. Lyons, N. Y., 1854; Chicago, 1911. Pianist and composer.

Shostakovitch, Dmitri. Leningrad, Russia, 1906- . Composer.

Sibelius, Jan. Finland, 1865- .. Composer.

Sieber, Ferdinand. Vienna, 1822; Berlin, 1895. Singing master and author of vocal methods.

Sieveking, Martinus. Amsterdam, 1867- . Composer.

Siloti, Alexander. Charkov, 1863- . Pianist and composer.

Simonetti, Achille. Tuoni, 1857; London, 1928. Composer and violinist.

Sinding, Christian. Kongsberg, Norway, 1856- . Composer.

Sitt, Hans. Prague, 1850; Leipzig, 1922. Violinist and composer.

Sivori, Ernesto Camillo. Genoa, 1815-1894. Violinist and composer.

Sjögren, Emil. Stockholm, 1853-1918. Composer.

Smart, Henry. London, 1813-1879. Organist and composer.

Smetana, Friedrich. Bohemia, 1824; Prague, 1884. Composer.

Smith, John Stafford. Gloucester, 1750; London, 1836. Composer of "Anacreon in Heaven" (Star Spangled Banner).

Smith, Sydney. Dorchester, England, 1839; London, 1889. Composer and arranger.

Smith, Wilson G. Elyria, O., 1855; Cleveland, 1929. Composer and pianist.

Smyth, Ethel Mary. London, 1858- . Composer.

Söchting, Emil. Saxony, 1858- . Composer.

Södermann, August Johan. Stockholm, 1832-1876. Composer.

Somervell, Arthur. Windermere, England, 1863; London, 1937. Composer.

Sousa, John Philip. Washington, D. C., 1856; Reading, Pa., 1932. Bandmaster and composer.

Sowerby, Leo. Grand Rapids, Mich., 1895- . Composer.

Spalding, Walter Raymond. Northampton, Mass., 1865- . Musicologist.

Spaulding, George L. Newburgh, N. Y., 1864; Roselle Park, N. J., 1921. Prolific composer.

Speaks, Oley. Canal Winchester, Ohio, 1876- . Composer.

Spendiarov, Alexander. Russia, 1871-1928. Composer.

Spindler, Fritz. Würzbach, 1817; nr. Dresden, 1905. Pianist and composer.

Spohr, Louis. Brunswick, 1784; Cassel, 1859. Violinist and composer.

Spontini, Gasparo. Majolati, 1774-1851. Opera composer.

Spross, Charles Gilbert. Poughkeepsie, N. Y., 1874- . Composer and pianist.

Stainer, Sir John. London, 1840-1901. Organist and composer.

Stcherbatcheff, Nicolai de. Russia, 1853- . Composer.

Steibelt, Daniel. Berlin, 1765; Petrograd, 1823. Composer.

Sternberg, Constantin von. St. Petersburg, 1852; Philadelphia, 1924. Pianist and composer.

Stewart, Humphrey John. London, 1856; San Diego, Calif., 1932. Composer and organist.

Still, William Grant. Woodville, Miss., 1895- . Negro composer.

Stojowski, Sigismund. Poland, 1870- . Composer and pianist.

Stokowski, Leopold. London, 1882- . Conductor.

Stradella, Alessandro. Naples, 1645(?); Genoa, 1681(?). Composer.

Strauss, Johann (Sr.). Vienna, 1804-1849. "Father of the Waltz."

Strauss, Johann. Vienna, 1825-1899. "Waltz King" and operetta composer.

Strauss, Oscar. Vienna, 1870- . Composer of light opera.

Strauss, Richard. Munich, 1864- . Composer.

Stravinsky, Igor Fedorovitch. Russia, 1882- . Composer.

Streabbog, L. S. (Jean-Louis Gobbaerts). Antwerp, 1835; Brussels, 1886. Prolific composer.

Strickland, Lily. Anderson, S. C., (?)—. Composer.

Strube, Gustav. Ballenstedt, 1867- . Violinist and composer.

Stults, Robert Morrison. Hightstown, N. J., 1861; Ridley Park, Pa., 1933. Composer.

Suk, Josef. Krecovic, Bohemia, 1874; Prague, 1935. Violinist and composer.

Sullivan, Sir Arthur. London, 1842-1900. Operetta composer.

Suppé, Franz von. Dalmatia, 1820; Vienna, 1895. Operetta composer.

Svendsen, Johan S. Christiania, 1840; London, 1888. Composer and violinist.

Taneieff, Sergei. Russia, 1856-1918. Composer.

Tansman, Alexander. Lodz, Poland, 1897- . Composer.

Tartini, Guiseppe. Istria, 1692; Padua, 1770. Violinist and composer.

Tausig, Carl. Warsaw, 1841; Leipzig, 1871. Pianist and composer.

Taylor, Deems. New York, 1885- . Composer and critic.

Tcherepnin, Alexander. St. Petersburg, 1899- . Composer.

Tcherepnin, Nikolai. St. Petersburg, 1873- . Composer.

Temple, Hope (Mme. André Messager). Dublin (?); London, 1938. Song composer.

Tenaglia, Raffaelo. Orsogna, Italy, 1884- . Composer.

Terry, Robert Huntington. Hudson, N. Y., 1877- . Composer.

Thalberg, Sigismund. Geneva, 1812; Naples, 1871. Pianist and composer.

Thomas, Ambroise. Metz, 1811; Paris, 1896. Opera composer.

Thomas, Arthur Goring. Sussex, 1850; London, 1892. Composer.

Thomé, Francis. Port Louis, Mauritius, 1850; Paris, 1909. Composer.

Titl, Anton Emil. Moravia, 1809-1882. Composer.

Tombelle, Fernand de la. Paris, 1854-1928. Composer.

Toscanini, Arturo. Parma, 1867- . Conductor.

Topliff, Robert. London, 1793-1868. Blind organist and composer.

Tosti, F. Paolo. Ortona, 1846; Rome, 1916. Song composer.

Tours, Berthold. Rotterdam, 1838; London, 1897. Editor and author.

Tozer, John Ferris. Exeter, 1857- . Composer.

Trotère, H. (Real name Henry Trotter.) London, 1855-1912. Composer.

Truette, Everett E. Rockland, Mass., 1861-1933. Composer and organist.

Tschaikovsky, Peter Iljitch. Votinsk, 1840; St. Petersburg, 1893. Composer.

Upton, George P. Boston, 1835; Chicago, 1919. Critic and litterateur.

Vaccai, Niccolò. Tolentino, 1790; Pesaro, 1848. Singing master and author of vocal method.

Van der Stucken, Frank. Fredericksburg, Texas, 1858; Hamburg, 1929. Conductor and composer.

Veracini, Francesco Maria. Florence, 1685; Pisa, 1750. Violinist and composer.

Verdi, Giuseppe. Roncole, 1813; Milan, 1901. Opera composer.

Vieuxtemps, Henri. Verviers, Belg., 1820; Algiers, 1881. Violinist and composer.

Vilbac, Alphonse Charles Renaud de. Montpellier, 1829; Brussels, 1884. Composer.

Viotti, Giovanni Battista. Fontaneto de Po, 1753; London, 1824. Violinist and composer.

Vivaldi, Antonio. Venice, 1680-1743. Composer.

Vogrich, Max. Hermannstadt, 1852; New York, 1916. Composer.

Volkmann, Robert. Saxony, 1815; Pesth, 1883. Composer.

Voss, Charles. Pomerania, 1815; Verona, 1882. Composer.

Wachs, Paul. Paris, 1851-1915. Composer.

Wagner, Richard. Leipzig, 1813; Venice, 1883. Dramatic composer.

Waldteufel, Emil. Strassburg, 1837; Paris, 1915, Composer.

Wallace, Wm. Vincent. Waterford, Ireland, 1814; France, 1865. Composer.

Warren, Samuel Prowse. Montreal, 1841; New York, 1915. Organist and composer.

Watts, Winter. Cincinnati, Ohio, 1886- . Composer.

Weber, Carl Maria von. Eutin, 1786; London, 1826. Opera composer.

Weckerlin, Jean Baptiste Théodore. Alsatia, 1821; Trottberg, 1910. Composer and author.

Weelkes, Thomas. England, 1578-1623. Composer.

Weingartner, Felix. Dalmatia, 1863- . Conductor and composer.

Whiting, Geo. E. Holliston, Mass., 1842; Cambridge, Mass., 1923. Organist and composer.

Widor, Charles Marie. Lyons, 1845; Paris, 1937. Composer and organist.

Wieniawski, Henri. Poland, 1835; Moscow, 1880. Violinist and composer.

Wihtol, Joseph. Russia, 1863- . Composer.

Wilhelm, Carl. Schmalkalden, 1815-1873. Composer of "Die Wacht am Rhein."

Wilhelmj, August. Nassau, 1845; London, 1908. Violinist and composer.

Willeby, Charles. Paris, 1865- . Composer.

Wilm, Nicolai von. Riga, 1834; Wiesbaden, 1911. Composer.

Wilson, Grenville Dean. Plymouth, Conn., 1833; Nyack, N. Y., 1897. Composer.

Wohlfahrt, Heinrich. Germany, 1797-1883. Composer and author.

Wolf, Hugo. Windischgratz, 1860; Vienna, 1903. Composer.

Wolf-Ferrari, Ermanno. Venice, 1876- . Composer.

Wollenhaupt, Heinrich Adolf. nr. Leipzig, 1827; New York, 1863. Pianist and composer.

Wolstenholme, Wm. Blackburn, Eng., 1865-1931. Organist and composer (blind).

Wood, Sir Henry J. London, 1870- . Conductor and composer.

Woodman, Raymond Huntington. Brooklyn, 1861- . Composer.

Woodward, Herbert Hall. England, 1847-1900. Composer.

Work, Henry Clay. Middletown, Conn., 1832; Hartford, 1884. Composer.

Wrangell, Wassili Georgevitch. St. Petersburg, 1862-1901. Composer.

Wyman, Addison P. Cornish, N. H., 1832; Washington, Pa., 1872. Composer.

Yradier, Sebastian. Spain, 1809-1885. Composer.

Ysaÿe, Eugène. Liége, 1858-1931. Violinist and composer.

Zarlino, Gioseffo. Chioggia, 1517; Venice, 1590. Theorist.

Zichy, Geza. Sztára, Hungary, 1849-1924. Left-hand pianist. Composer.